Lean Transformations

When and How to Use Lean Tools
and Climb the Four Steps of Lean Maturity

Thijs Panneman

MudaMasters

Copyright © 2019 Thijs Panneman
All rights reserved.

Published by MudaMasters, Dublin, Ireland
Visit: **www.mudamasters.com**

First edition, August 2017
Second edition, October 2019

ISBN 13: 9781696198868

# Introduction     5

## PART 1: THE ROLE OF THE LEAN TRANSFORMATION LEADER     8

### Chapter 1: Leading Change     9
### Chapter 2: Teaching Tools and Skills     16
     2.1   Preparing a Training Element     18
     2.2   Plan for Repetition     22
### Chapter 3: Coaching Your Colleagues     25
     3.1   The Mentor-Mentee Relationship     27

## PART 2: UNDERSTANDING THE LEAN PHILOSOPHY     31

### Chapter 4: Implementing flow     32
     4.1   How lead time became the number one KPI     33
     4.2   Improving Flow to Reduce Lead Time     37
### Chapter 5: While Reducing Waste, Overburden, and Imbalance     40
     5.1   The Eight Traditional Wastes     42
     5.2   Waste in an Office Environment     50
     5.3   Overburden     54
     5.4   Imbalance     59
### Chapter 6: Encouraging the Fourteen Lean Management Principles     65

## PART 3: THE FOUR LEVELS OF LEAN MATURITY     73

### Chapter 7: Level One: Setting Standards     79
     7.1   Setting the Standard with 5S     80
     7.2   Setting the Standard with Standard Work     94
### Chapter 8: Level Two: Checking the Standard     111
     8.1   Checking the Standard with Kamishibai     112
     8.2   Checking the Standard with Team Boards     120
### Chapter 9: Level Three: Improving the Standard     141
     9.1   Improving the Standard with Kaizen     142
     9.2   Improving the Standard with A3 Problem-Solving     154
     9.3   Improving the Standard with D2MAIC Projects     160

**Chapter 10:  Level Four: Linking Improvement to Company Goals        172**
    10.1 The Daily Management System        173
    10.2 Hoshin Kanri        180

# PART 4:   PROCESS REDESIGN TO IMPROVE FLOW............184

    **Chapter 11:  Introduction to Value Stream Mapping        185**
        11.1 Takt, Cycle, Process, Waiting, and Lead Times        188
        11.2 Pull Production: Three Strategies        194
        11.3 The Value Stream Mapping Event        198
    **Chapter 12:  Mapping the Current State        201**
    **Chapter 13:  Mapping the Future State        216**
    **Chapter 14:  Tools useful While Creating the Future State VSM        230**
        14.1 Line balancing with a Yamazumi chart        230
        14.2 Improving the Production Schedule with Load Levelling        240
    **Chapter 15:  Value Stream Mapping in the Office        249**
        15.1 Project VSM        251
        15.2 Office VSM        256
        15.3 Critical Question Analysis        260

# PART 5:   LEAN TOOLS EXPLAINED ........................................262

    **Chapter 16:  Autonomous Maintenance        263**
        16.1 How to Implement Autonomous Maintenance        265
    **Chapter 17:  Single Minute Exchange of Die (SMED)        268**
        17.1 Eight SMED techniques        269
        17.2 How to Implement SMED        271
    **Chapter 18:  Kanban        273**
    **Chapter 19:  E-mail and Phone Optimization        277**

# Conclusions................................................................................282
# Acknowledgments ....................................................................286
# References.................................................................................288

# Introduction

Lean is a name given to the philosophy that Toyota used to become one of the world's most successful auto manufacturer and I have been interested in lean and the practices used within this philosophy since I was a student. Lean tools were always a small part of the many different subjects within the courses I have followed.

It was only after I started my first full-time job at a glass tube factory in the Netherlands that I learned that lean was not just about the tools. Lean could be so much more than one person leading a project that improves flow. Real value for the company is created when everybody in the organization continuously improves his or her processes—long after the lean transformation leader has left. Therefore, my job changed, and I became not only a lean project manager but also a lean trainer and coach.

A lot of training material was available within the company, but I wanted to understand the lean philosophy even more, so I started reading management books. I read books about Toyota, about lean, about leadership, and about change management. I loved reading management books because I could use whatever interesting thing I read in the books in my workshops and in the trainings that I offered.

There was only one issue. I was reading so many books that it was impossible to implement all the ideas that I got from reading them. So, I started to write about them on www.mudamasters.com. I did it at first for myself, so I could capture within a thousand words what I learned from each book I read. Later, I also started writing about my practical experience with the different lean tools and principles.

This way the organization where I worked could pull ideas from me when needed. I would no longer push all the ideas I had on the organization, but I would store all my knowledge on my blog so that I could find it quickly whenever somebody asked for my help on a specific topic.

Five years have gone by since I started publishing my notes, and I've read and absorbed more than a hundred management books while practicing what I've learned within my job.

The larger my blog became, the more often this question arose: How does it all fit together? I found that this question was often missing in other books. Organizations go with the trend of implementing a tool but fail to understand how it can help them improve their performance and therefore the tool was not used to its full potential. This is where the idea for this book started. This book is for everybody who would like to understand the lean philosophy and how to use lean tools to improve their business. It is a summary of everything I have learned in the past ten years on how to transform your organization into a lean organization, where each tool helps to improve performance. It is a combination of the theory I have learned from the many books I've read and the many workshops and training sessions where participants told me about their own experiences with the different lean tools and how they helped them in specific situations.

I managed to group most of what I learned into five categories, each of which is represented in one part of this book. The first part is about the role of the lean transformation leader. The chapters in this part include what I learned about leadership (chapter 1), about teaching (chapter 2), and about mentoring (chapter 3).

The second part of this book is an introduction to the lean philosophy. It discusses the *why* and the *what* of the term *flow* (chapter 4), the three enemies of lean— imbalance, overburden and waste (chapter 5)—and the fourteen management principles that describe lean behavior, first described by Liker (2004) (chapter 6).

The third part of this book describes the foundation for bottom-up improvement in what I coined: the four levels of lean maturity. In these four levels of lean maturity, I describe different tools that can help you change your company into a true lean organization. The levels of maturity are setting the standards (chapter 7), checking the standards (chapter 8), improving the standards (chapter 9), and linking improvements to your organizational goals (chapter 10). In each chapter, I will describe what tools to use and how to implement them, to climb to the next level of lean maturity.

The fourth part of this book is about the top-down improvements that can be implemented in projects and during workshops next to the bottom-up improvements described in part 3. This part is about redesigning processes to improve flow. It starts with an introduction to value stream mapping as a tool to improve the process flow (chapter 11). We then move into current state value stream mapping (chapter 12) and how to create the future state VSM (chapter 13).
After that, the two tools that play a major role in value stream mapping are described in more detail: one for line balancing and one for load leveling (chapter 14). Part four concludes with a chapter on how value stream mapping can be used in the office environment (chapter 15).

Finally, where part 4 mainly focuses on tools that help improve the flow between process steps, part 5 discusses a couple of lean tools that one can use to improve the process steps themselves. We start with Autonomous maintenance to improve the uptime of machines (chapter 16), followed by the changeover reduction tool called Single Minute Exchange of Die (SMED) (chapter 17), thoughts about e-mail (chapter 18), and the visual card system for which the Japanese word is *kanban* (chapter 19).

I hope you will find many new ideas in this book about how to start or continue your own lean journey, and I hope you enjoy reading it.

Thijs Panneman

# PART 1:

# THE ROLE OF THE LEAN TRANSFORMATION LEADER

To kick-off this book, I want to start with my favorite definition of what a lean organization is. A lean organization is an organization in which all employees continually use a variety of tools to visualize problems and solve them in such a way that those problems never occur again (Ballé and Ballé 2012). The transformation toward a lean organization is therefore all about changing the culture of the organization into a **culture of continuous improvement**, which includes all its members, from shop-floor operators to higher management.

In order to create a different culture, you need people to set the example and help and encourage other people to do the same. Within the context of creating a culture of continuous improvement based on the lean philosophy, I call these people lean transformation leaders.

The lean transformation leader has the role of a change agent, helping the organization and its leaders embed the principles of continuous improvement into organizational values to make sure everybody in the organization starts improving his or her processes.

This part of the book contains chapters that can equip you to think about how you want to change your organizational culture. It is split into three chapters. Chapter 1 describes what kind of leader the transformation leader (and preferably all other leaders in the organization) should be, and it includes five elements of change management that you need to consider when managing change. Chapter 2 describes the importance of being able to teach, how to design a training element in seven steps, and the power of repetition. We finish this part with chapter 3, which describes the importance of coaching and the four phases of a coaching relationship.

# Chapter 1:
# Leading Change

> *It is not necessary to change.*
> *Survival is not mandatory.*
> —W. Edwards Deming

If you would like to change an organizational culture, you cannot simply command people to do things differently than how they did before. Commanding might work on the very short term but as soon as you leave the room, people will go back to their own old way of working.
To really change a culture, the people in the organization must want to change their behavior themselves, which is why leadership in the twenty-first century is all about inspiring people to continuously improve the processes in which they work (Scholtes 1998). Only when people are inspired to improve processes will they continue to do so when you are not around.

So how do you convince others to improve their processes? How do you lead the change? To help us define the role of the lean transformation leader, this section describes two theories that can help you: John Maxwell's theory on the five levels of leadership (Maxwell 2011) and Mary Lippitt's five elements of successful change (Lippitt 1987).

In his book, *the five levels of Leadership* (Maxwell 2011), John Maxwell describes five levels of leadership maturity, from leadership based on position (level 1) to becoming a leader by developing other leaders (level 5). Interesting to note beforehand is, that the levels on which you act can differ depending on the person you work with. You can, for example, be a level 3 leader with one colleague, and a level 4 with another.

At the first level of leadership, a leader leads based on **POSITION**. People do what you ask them to do based on your hierarchical position. The first major downside of this level of leadership in terms of changing organizational culture is that the leader is not influencing his or her team. The leader uses hierarchical power alone to get things done.

A second major downside of this type of leadership is that nothing happens when you are not around to tell people what to do. This means you as a leader must spend a lot of time thinking about what other people should do, tell everyone all the time, and continuously check-up on whether they have done what you've said.

Another downside is that, if people don't really believe in what you are asking them to do, they will only do exactly what you've asked them to do and nothing more (Daniels 2000). If you cannot explain why a certain task is important and you must pull rank to get it done, your subordinates will do only what is just enough to avoid drawing your attention.

At the second level of leadership, a leader leads based on **PERMISSION**. At this level, you form relationships with your team members, and they are willing to follow you and the directions you're giving, based on those relationships.

Note, that this is a level of leadership that any person in the organization can achieve, even a person who does not have a position with authority.

One downside of this type of leadership is that building the required relationships takes time, especially when a leader is new to the group. It could also result into to people wanting to please others to such an extent that the main organizational targets are not considered anymore.

At the third level of leadership, position and permission are combined into **PRODUCTION**. At this level, you are influencing the way people are working based on relationships, and you are influencing bottom-line results while you do it. At this level of leadership, the leader puts in many hours working with the team to generate results.

But, even though results are achieved in the short term, they are not enough for the long term, because even if team members like the leader and are influenced by that leader, if the leader switches to another job or function, the team might stop performing because the leader is such an important part of the routine that the team developed to work successfully.

This is where the next level comes in. The fourth level of leadership is about

**PEOPLE DEVELOPMENT**. This is an even higher level for reaching results. At this level, you as a leader don't necessarily focus on getting the results yourself. Instead, you spend about 80 percent of your time coaching and empowering others to be productive, so that they can achieve the results that you aim for.

When translating this to creating a culture of continuous improvement, the leader can develop a team and coach them how to use lean management principles (described in chapter 6) to increase performance. And when the team achieves a certain level of maturity, the leader can focus on developing people in other teams.

The fifth and highest form of leadership is even better: the **PINNACLE**. This is the level of leadership in which leaders have built other leaders who build leaders. The only thing better than a good leader, is a good leader who is good at developing other leaders. It is this multiplier effect that can generate major results for the organization as a whole. That is, when all teams are focused on reaching the same targets.

If our goal is to change the culture of an entire organization by changing the way people think and act, I believe the lean transformation leader should at least act at leadership level four, developing people in a way that they are motivated to improve their processes on a continual basis.

Having a level-five leader is even better, as he or she has an even larger effect on the organization due to the multiplier effect.
We will see in chapter 6 that Toyota have defined the principle of leaders building leaders internally as one of its fourteen management principles that have led to its success (J. K. Liker 2004).

The implication is that the lean transformation leader is more than a project leader who implements the lean process as part of his or her job. Changing the culture of your organization requires not only the implementation of tools to make your processes more effective but also requires a mindset change of all the people working in that process.
Everybody needs to reflect on his or her way of working, and this might change from senior management to operator. In most companies, it's a full-time job.

Developing yourself as a highly effective leader by going through the five different stages of leadership is not easy, and it takes a lot of time. In every new environment in which a leader acts, he or she must start back at level one, investing in relationships while generating short-term results and developing more leaders at the same time.

Every company that wants to go on a lean journey should have a dedicated person to facilitate the change full-time. If you cannot assign the resources to this extent, *lean* will only be seen as a project, and you will achieve only a margin of the many advantages the lean philosophy has to offer.

The lean transformation leader is part of the leadership team or at least takes part in leadership team discussions. It is there where strategic decisions are made, and the lean process can help in achieving that strategy.

An external consultant can bring in a lot of knowledge and help train people on specific tools and skills. Because of the usually short time frame, he or she can only do that based on level-one leadership. In the end, to make the transformation sustainable, it is the internal lean transformation leader who must lead the cultural change together with the management team.

A second helpful theory in leading the change is that of Mary Lippitt (Lippitt 1987). She developed a model for leading complex change with the following five key elements of change: vision, commitment (incentives), resources, skills, and plan.

The first step for successful change is having a **VISION**. If you do not know where you want to go and how far, how can you define the right improvement steps to get there? Authors like Rother (2010), Liker (2004), and Suzaki (1993) all describe the importance of defining the vision as the first step toward cultural change. This might seem self-evident, but I once had the pleasure of meeting a management team that came to us because its members had problems "implementing lean." When I asked what the team's definition of lean was and what the members wanted to achieve with lean (in other words, their vision), they all gave different answers. If no consensus exists on what lean is supposed to bring you as an organization, how can you know if it is a success or a failure?

A clear vision is also the foundation for proper goals setting, in which goals are cascaded into the whole organization. When we focus on implementing a culture of continuous improvement, it is important that everybody improves with the same intentions and end goals in mind (which we will discuss in the fourth level of lean maturity, chapter 10). The first step in this case is that the management team agrees on what the company goals are. The vision needs to be catchy and motivating to all in the organization. It needs to be specific and something that all employees can relate to. It must motivate them to give the organization their best.

No one ever changed the world with a battle cry of "maximize shareholder value."

The second element for successful change is **COMMITMENT**, which is the result of creating the right incentives. When a company decides to use a certain philosophy to guide cultural change, such as lean, it is important to act on that decision and make it more than just empty words. Committing to something means more than just being involved.

Being committed to do something means being willing to put a tattoo on your arm instead of wearing a T-shirt for the occasion. Commitment also means setting the right example, to "walk the talk." No matter what you say and how often you say it, everybody in your environment will always judge you (mostly unconsciously) on how you act (Kouzes and Posner 2012). If you want others to act in a certain way, do it yourself first.

As we go through a variety of lean tools in the following chapters, we will see that a lot of them are most valuable only when management participates in continuously improving processes by using the daily management structure, preventive problem-solving, daily coaching, and mini-audit checks.
Only when management acts on the vision of continuous improvement can real cultural change happen. Every leader in the organization needs to be a role model for the new culture. It is the job of the lean transformation leader to support the management team in reaching that realization and to coach the team members through the process of their personal development journeys.

When you know where you want to go and are committed to doing so, you need **RESOURCES**, the third element for successful change, to get there. Resources can be described in different ways.

First, **time** is needed. If you think you can create a cultural change with one person spending two days a week on this task, forget it! In my first position as a lean deployment manager in a factory with two hundred people, we spent three years of coaching and facilitating with two people fully available for the lean transformation—and we were still not close to being finished with improving our processes and encouraging our colleagues to focus on improving their own processes.

Next to the time it takes for a culture to change, it also takes time to think about improvements and to implement these. Lean has everything to do with bottom-up improvement, which means that every employee should have the time to focus on improving his or her working routines. In each department where we implemented the first set of lean tools (which part 3 describes), we organized monthly workshops in which representatives of each shift were available to work on improvements that whole day instead of working in regular production. Another example is the time that engineering and technical staff needs to implement improvement suggestions that production employees make without being able to implement those suggestions by themselves. Not every improvement will result directly in bottom-line business improvements, but when people learn how to implement changes; their tenth improvement might just be a breakthrough idea! In this way, the cultural change requires investments up-front. The implementation of many small changes today will lead to breakthrough improvements in the future.

In addition to the resource of time, **financial resources** are necessary to implement improvements. Nothing is more frustrating for employees than hearing that their ideas will not be implemented because they are too expensive. Unfortunately, a budget usually has a limit, and there will always be the need for determining priorities to decide which improvements will be implemented and in what sequence. One way of dealing with this is allocating a budget to a team and having the members decide which improvements to spend resources on based on the vision and goal hierarchy mentioned in the vision paragraph. The key is to communicate the priorities of the organization and to explain why an idea does not fit that priority when it is rejected.

The fourth element for successful change is **SKILLS**. Especially in the lean philosophy, there are numerous lean tools that can help you make your department work more efficiently. Without the skills to use these tools properly, fear and insecurity will exist among the people who are supposed to use the tools to improve their processes. The lean tools used at Toyota only worked successfully because the employees knew how to use them properly (Rother 2010). Every time you want to use a lean tool, you must make sure you provide the proper training for the people who are going to be using it.

As Kotter (Kotter 1996) describes in his eight-step model for change, you should focus on generating measurable results as quickly as possible to show people that the new strategy (and vision) is the right one. For that, you need skilled people to choose the right tools for the specific situation and to teach colleagues how to use the tools to their advantage.

Finally, a **PLAN**, the fifth element for successful change, is needed to determine what actions are chosen to reach the vision (or the yearly targets that were derived from that vision) and what tools are needed to optimize a specific value stream. Choose the right metrics (or key performance indicators, KPIs) based on leading indicators (also see chapter 8) to measure whether people are spending their time optimally and to measure a few lagging-results-based indicators to check if the plan leads to the improvements that are defined in the vision (Webers 2010).

Facilitating cultural change is one of the hardest things there is; human behavior does not easily change. By focusing on the five elements described above (vision, commitment, resources, skills, and plan), you can avoid a few of the most common mistakes and make the change smoother.

On a leadership level, it is necessary to continually build a new generation of leaders to make sure change is sustainable and people keep on improving their work. The world needs more level-five leaders. You need more level-five leaders.

**Key Points:**
- *There are five levels of leadership.*
- *If you want to lead a cultural change, you must be at least at level four: developing people.*
- *When you lead the change, keep the five elements of change in mind: vision, commitment, resources, skills, and plan.*

# Chapter 2:
# Teaching Tools and Skills

> *The one exclusive sign of thorough knowledge is the power of teaching.*
> —Aristotle

If you want to develop other people, and develop more leaders, being able to teach others is one important aspect of your job. Facilitating internal training programs is quite useful for more than just sharing knowledge, because teaching your colleagues gives you the opportunity to build a relationship with the people in that training. Therefore, training with internal trainers is my preference over hiring external trainers.

In one of the companies where I worked, my favorite part of the job was to teach a two-week advanced lean leadership training. In that course, theory was combined with lots of teamwork. It was a tough training course, and the training was set up in a way that most participants go through a change curve to finally embrace the fourteen management principles at the end of it (see chapter 6).

Spending two whole weeks with a group of colleagues is a privilege. As a trainer, you get to know your colleagues better, and they get to know you better personally and what you stand for in terms of lean behaviors. Next to that, it is an excellent opportunity to serve as a role model demonstrating the lean behaviors as well.

As a trainer, you therefore benefit just as much from these training sessions as the participants, if not more. That's because if you do the sessions right, building these relationships brings you up to level-two leadership with the participants (Maxwell 2011).

As both you and the participants go back to your daily jobs, these relationships help all of you to achieve the organizational vision, when you can coach the participants in improving their processes and even in developing their lean leadership skills.

Aside from the relationships that are developed, these training courses can benefit your knowledge as well. This is because discussing the lean tools with so many individuals and listening to their personal experiences with that tool will increase your own knowledge on the topic. By sharing and linking the theory to practical experiences, you increase the knowledge of the organization (Aslander and Witteveen 2010).

In teaching lean tools, the main thing with which I like to start every theory block is the reason we are doing all this, the why. I like asking the why-question because it sets everything in perspective (Sinek 2009). With the company goal in mind, people can use the different lean tools in a way that means then can directly affect the company's profitability. Focusing on the why helps the trainees understand the importance and purpose of the different tools and enables them to use the tools in the proper context.

The next few pages will describe how to design a training element that helps to include the *why*.

**Key Points:**
- *To develop others, you need to be able to train them.*
- *Training gives you the opportunity to share knowledge with the group and build your relationships with the participants*
- *Always include the* why *of whatever it is that you are teaching*

## 2.1 Preparing a Training Element

*Every movie contains a hook: the first ten minutes
that makes everybody in the audience wanting to see the other eighty.*
- Patrick Lencioni

There are multiple ways of teaching in a classroom setting. I use as few presentation slides as possible—or even no slides at all. Instead, I ask questions in combination with the use of storytelling. This approach is based on the idea that you must engage your audience before you present a solution to a problem.

Patrick Lencioni describes *the hook* in the movie business as the first ten minutes of the movie which grabs the audience and makes them want to watch the remaining eighty minutes. A training session should have that same hook (Lencioni 2004). You should make your audience members curious in the beginning so that they pay more attention later.

If you are a trainer and must teach people about a certain tool, the following **seven steps** based on a book by Dutch training specialist Karin de Galan (2008) might help building storytelling in your training.

The first three steps are what she describes as "the slide." With it, you make your participants curious about what you are about to share with them because they have made a connection between the problem you want to solve and their working environment (the *why*). The slide acts as the hook.
This means, that when you combine a story to hook you audience with asking the right questions to the group to get to the *why*, you have slid down Galan's slide within a few minutes.

Steps four through seven are called "the stairs." These steps describe how to prevent a problem or effect from occurring or reoccurring by evoking different behaviors in certain situations (the what).
In this case, a tool can be used to help you behave in a certain way. One example is having an agenda for a meeting. The agenda helps you remember what topics to address. When the agenda also includes time slots, it can help you keep your meeting within a planned time frame.

Again, storytelling and asking questions can help you to connect with your audience. The story you tell could be a personal anecdote from a horrible meeting you once attended. When you then ask the group for improvement ideas, I am pretty sure that having a clear agenda with dedicated time slots will be mentioned.

Let's now look at the 7 steps for designing a training element in more detail. According to Galan, each training session of about twenty minutes should include the following:

1. Explain the **effect** you want to achieve—the change that people should experience at work. You can do this by showing a short video and/or asking the group questions. Let's look at a sample topic: the team board. The team board is a physical board. A team meets in front of it to discuss the team's performance, problems, and improvement. The board itself shows the agenda of the meeting, which makes the meeting more efficient. As an introduction to the topic of a team board meeting, you show a video of a bad example of a meeting. After that, you ask the group to tell you what was wrong with the meeting shown in the video. The participants can then list all the things they saw—for instance, not following an agenda, not keeping notes, people arriving late, etc.
2. People always experience effects in certain **situations**. The second step therefore is to ask the group members if they can name a situation in which they experienced the effect described in step one. In this case, you ask the group members if they recognize what they saw in the video. Have they been in similar situations? This helps encourage participation and help you interact with the participants in making the training content as relevant as possible for them.
3. **Behavior** influences situations. What behavior leads to certain situations? How can we minimize negative effects? This step is about having the group list the behavior that leads to the situation and the effects.
In the example of the bad team board meeting from step one, this could be not having an agenda, not having clear key performance indicators (KPIs), not starting on time, people coming late, etc.
4. Now it is time to **present the tool or theory** that will help us change the negative behavior of step three. The scene is set, and your participants will be eager to learn how to improve the situations they brought up in the first minutes of the training session. This is the moment when you as the trainer can present the theory of the tool. How does this tool help us behave in a

way that prevents the negative effects from occurring?
5. **Explain how the tool will help** the group in changing behavior and therefore certain effects. This is the first and only part of the training session for which you might use slides. However, do not focus on the details of the tool, but explain how you and the group will conduct certain steps. Chapter 8 will describe in more detail the *how* and the *what* of the team board.
6. Practice the theory with **a question or a small assignment** to check if the group members have understood what the tool is all about. People will understand the tool better when they have had to think about it in a creative way. One of my favorite questions to ask a group is about the Pareto principle, also known as the 80/20 rule. This principle states, that 80% of a company revenue is achieved with about 20% of its products, that 80% of your time are spend on 20% of your clients, or, as Mr. Pareto found originally: that 80% of the wealth of a country is in the hands of 20% of the population. Many people have heard about this principle but seem to believe that the sum of the two numbers, 80 and 20, must add up to 100. Which is, when you think about it, not necessary at all. 80% of problems could occur in 10% of your products for instance, and you could spend 90% of your time on 20% of your customers. So, the question I ask the group after explaining what the 80/20 rule means is: "could it also be an 80/30 ratio in a particular situation? Most people in the group must think about it for a minute that in fact, it can be. But after that, they will never forget it!
7. Hand out **an assignment** for the participants or teams to practice what they've just learned. Let them report their results, provide feedback on how to improve the result even further, and reflect on how the tool was useful in solving the assignment.

A second way of connecting with your audience is **TELLING A PERSONAL STORY** that guides you through the parts of the topic you want to explain. Aristotle wrote that true persuasion only takes place when you can connect with *ethos* (ethics), *logos* (logic), and *pathos* (emotion). The presentations that people rate the highest and remember the most are the ones that include at least **65 percent pathos**, which you can achieve by storytelling (Gallo 2014).

My experience tells me that storytelling really works. For instance, one of the stories that is remembered most after our trainings is the story about the basement of my colleague and friend, Gunnar. His girlfriend wants to move in and brings a lot of boxes with her. It is time for Gunnar to clear out his basement and 5S (the workplace organization tool that uses five Japanese words starting with "S," as described in chapter 5.1) is the lean tool to use.

Then there's my story about a Dutch guy who moves to Germany and wants to uphold the German tradition of barbecuing in the city park. (In conjunction with that story, we practice the use of tools for mapping the process.) These stories are the most memorable parts of our training. Participants talk about these stories years after they have completed the training.

It does not really matter what you use as an example. Think of a story that you can tell with personal emotion, and your audience will buy into it.

**Key Points:**
- *Presenting a certain tool in a training session is just one out of seven parts of a training block. You must engage the audience first by presenting it with a problem the members relate to.*
- *Use personal stories to illustrate your topic.*
- *Ask questions to encourage participants to tell their stories.*

## 2.2 Plan for Repetition

*Unless you build in some form of repetition, 80 percent of your one-hour presentation will be forgotten within twenty-four hours.*
- Tony Buzan

Repetition is important for long-term learning (Buzan 1979). If you don't build in repetition to your training sessions, the participants will have forgotten 80% of the content of the training within 24 hours. You have multiple ways as a trainer to help your audience remember what you have said. You can tell a personal story, associate with other stories and examples, and use the power of repetition. Ideally, the repetition takes place after twenty-four hours, in time frames of one week, one month, and six months (Buzan 1979).

Always keep in mind that you, as the lean transformation leader, are busy with the topics of your training every day, but for your participants, a particular training session might be the first time they are hearing about the topics. When you teach 10 different technical tools in one full day of training spending 30 minutes on each of them, how do you make sure they remember all 10 of them?

Listed below are some ideas of how to repeat the topics in classroom training. You can use them at the beginning of the day, after a break, or even between two training sessions. Asking participants to repeat parts of the theory is better than repeating the theory by yourself, but the use of other techniques, such as games, is even better. For instance, you might participants think about the meaning of a word, theory, or tool and how to present it.

**The question game**. All participants stand up, and the trainer asks questions. When a participant answers a question correctly, he or she can sit down. To make this game challenging, you can ask open questions that require the participant to think about the topic.
Let the participants for instance think of an example of one of types of waste (see chapter 5.1) in his or her working environment. Or, have them think about examples where they have seen somebody living by one of the fourteen lean principles (see chapter 6). A third idea is to ask for examples of how 5S (chapter 7.1) could prove beneficial in the working environment. Finally, you could ask

participants to explain the *why* a lean certain tool, which in the end should always be about finding the next area of improvement.

**The depiction game**. Since lean has a lot to do with visual management, depiction exercises are not only fun to do but also directly related to lean. In these games, individuals have to explain tools, processes, or principles using only hand-drawn pictures.
You´d be surprised how creative people are when you hand out this assignment. In the end, participants must explain everything using drawings only. The participants can take this experience back to their working environments and start practicing depicting element of lean there.

**The storytelling game**. Why should you as a trainer do all the storytelling? You can ask the group or a participant to explain a certain topic using a one-minute story. The story can be fictional or based on real-life experience.

**Charades** is another useful game. In it, a person or team acts out a word or phrase without using words. With a preparation time of only ten minutes, I´ve seen perfect examples of teams mimicking six of the management principles without using a word.

To get repetition of the ideas during the time frame that falls outside the training session (Buzan 1979), you can organize a **reunion meeting** each month for six months after the training. Participants can tell one another how the newly taught theory has impacted their working life and what they have planned for the near future.

Another way to help people remember different aspects of lean is using the system the mini-audit tool ***kamishibai*** (described in chapter 8.1). With a regular kamishibai check, one can ask colleagues to explain a word, tool, or list.

Sending **newsletters** that cover topics from the training provides another opportunity for participants to remember and reflect again on what they have learned.

Also, in all the workshops you are facilitating, you should repeat theories and explain the tools again, their meanings, and their purpose. Applying them directly after your introduction as a team will make the learning even more effective. Do not assume that the participants of a training session will remember. You will see happy faces when you repeat elements of the training prior to the participants applying those elements in real life.

And finally, when your training is a repetitive event, you can **invite previous participants** to visit the end of future trainings. Doing this would assume that you have scheduled an informal final hour of a training session that would probably last multiple days. This way, the newly trained and previously trained will share experiences with one another, and the previously trained will remember their own training.

**Key Points:**
- *Repeat training material often and in different ways to help the participants remember it better.*
- *The best way to encourage retention of the material is to have participants repeat the material for you.*

# Chapter 3:
# Coaching Your Colleagues

*Except for love, there is no greater gift one can give another than the gift of growth.*

Official training events are, unfortunately, not enough by themselves to change an organizational culture. They do, however, provide the opportunity to teach and practice skills and behaviors in an environment outside our normal work. If you want to change daily behaviors, you have to be on top of them within the training and within every individual's daily job after the training. This is where coaching comes into play as an important skill for a lean transformation leader. Having coaches facilitating repetition of the new way of working helps people internalize it so they can conform to it (Deutschman 2007).
It is only after enough people have internalized and conformed to the new behavior that it has a change on being part of the culture.

One way in which managers and supporting personnel can take on the coaching role is during **gemba walks**. These are time slots in which you walk the gemba (Japanese term for "place where it happens") without having an agenda and just talk to the people who work there. These are the times to get to know your colleagues (and build on your relationships), learn about the processes in your team or organization, and find possibilities for individual coaching and/or the next improvement for a process.

There are two aspects of a gemba walk. The first one is learning and understanding a process that you are investigating by interviewing colleagues who are involved in that process every day. Second, you can coach colleagues in improving their process by supporting the problem-solving activities they're working on.

Bottom-up improvements are the foundation of every lean initiative, so it is important to **ask your colleagues about their continuous improvement activities** during gemba walks. Rother (2010) describes five coaching questions you can ask during a gemba, which is directly related to finding the next area of improvement. These questions are as follows:

- How are you doing? To use a few management buzz words: people are a company's most valuable asset. Showing an interest in them is the first step in making people feel valued at work.
- How is the process you are working in going today? This question helps you to learn more about what is happening at this workstation.
- Are you currently involved in improvement activities?
  What is the improvement goal of this department? You are now focusing the conversation on improving the work.
- What is holding you back at this workstation in terms of morale or effectiveness? If the previous question did not lead to constructive ideas, this one might.
- How can I help you improve this? This final question encourages initiative but also let's others know that you are willing to support them with improving their work.

As a lean transformation leader, your job can involve more coaching than simply engaging in gemba walks. It can contain more intensive coaching. Bell (1996) wrote a book, *Managers as Mentors*, about managers who want to transform their management style into a coaching style (Bell 1996). In the next paragraph, we'll discuss the five phases of a coaching relationship.

**Key Points:**
- *The best way to offer support to someone is to visit that person at his or her workplace.*
- *Ask questions to find out what that person is working on and how you can support that person when necessary.*

## 3.1 The Mentor-Mentee Relationship

*If you are successful, it is because somewhere, sometime, someone gave you a life or an idea that started you in the right direction.*
—Melinda Gates

Being a mentor is about being the person who Melinda Gates talks about in the above quote. You need to be there for your colleagues and help them start off in the right direction.

The foundation to coaching or mentoring is the relationship between the mentor and mentee. This is a voluntary relationship that has **nothing to do with power** (Bell 1996). Good mentors are like friends or family, which means the relationship should create a safe environment in which the mentor shows patience and acceptance for the mentee to make the mentee feel comfortable enough to be open and honest. Do you remember the 5 levels of leadership from chapter 1? A level 1 leader might already get in trouble here.

When the mentor should be seen as **a supporting partner who** encourages the mentee in achieving his or her goals. The mentee is responsible for the progress (which usually means doing something with the feedback and tips that he or she is receiving), and the mentor is responsible for offering enough support (being available to meet the mentee on a regular basis). The best mentoring relationships are the ones in which both the mentor and mentee learn from each other.

There are four phases of an evolving coaching relationship: surrendering, accepting, giving, and extending. Understanding these phases can help any mentor to be more effective (Bell 1996).

The first phase of the coaching relationship is **SURRENDERING**. What can you do as a mentor to form a supporting relationship? Bell describes the following steps: The first step describes the **creation of fellowship ("I am like you")**. It is important that the mentee knows that the two of you are on the same level. To help create that sense of fellowship, you can make friendly gestures like offering a cup of coffee, and you can relate to his or her emotions to let the mentee know you can empathize, having experienced similar situations. Showing a positive attitude and actively listening to what the mentee has to say also positively influences the relationship. Needless to say, you cannot fake interest to a person. As a mentor or coach, you need to have certain personality traits that include a preference for working with people and being able to deal with feelings and emotions. This is not for everyone.

When the foundation for the relationship is established, it is important to **discuss goals and take advantage of the moments when** you're supposed to give feedback. For instance, if a team leader would like to receive coaching on leading a team board meeting, you should join the meetings once a week and give personal feedback afterward.

Another way of keeping your relationships pure is to think about **the way you ask questions**. The best questions are those that require the mentee to use what Bell calls *higher-level thinking*. They are evaluative questions (What would you do differently next time?) or comparison questions (How does this situation differ from that one?). Try not using the word *why* as a starting word of the question because that can lead to the mentee feeling judged and negatively influence openness (Bell 1996). I'm pretty sure Bell is referring to the "why did you do that?" kind of why questions, not the "why should you use this great lean tool?" kind of questions.

The second phase of the coaching relationship is **ACCEPTING**. In this phase, the mentor's focus is on understanding the mentee's situation and setting aside bias and prejudice. It is important in this phase of the relationship for the mentee to know that the mentor has understood the mentee's needs and fears, which are connected, without judgment.

There are **four main types of needs** that can be identified, each with its own fear: the need for performance with a fear of failure, the need for recognition with a fear of rejection, the need for power with a fear of showing weakness, and the need for control with a fear of making mistakes. It is your job as mentor to treat these fears as rational things.
Whenever you want to show your mentee that you have really listened, you can summarize what you've heard.

Bell describes **four ways of summarizing,** the power of which lies in using different words than the mentee has used. That means restating the same story in your own words, making a general statement a specific one, making a specific statement a general one, or rephrasing the statement by using opposite terms.

After listening to the mentee and understanding where he or she is coming from, it is time for the **GIVING** phase. The most important thing to keep in mind is not to come across as a know-it-all or too bossy. It is not you who should come up with the improvement ideas; you should rather guide the mentee to develop new approaches themselves.

Bell describes the following **five tips not to be too pedantic**. Tip one: remove words like "I want you to" and "you should" from your vocabulary. That sounds too much like a boss and less like a friend. Tip two: record and listen to yourself; ask yourself whether you sound like a boss or a friend. Tip three: remove things from the environment that might suggest that you are not equal, like a desk or even clothing style. Tip four: use perspectives of others to create a newer, more effective perspective on things. Tip five: take learning seriously, but yourself—not too much.

**Take enough time for coaching.** By taking the time for your mentee, you show that his or her efforts and performance are important to you. Do not look at your watch during your talks. That is a sign of a lack of interest because it suggests that you are anxious to go somewhere else. When you do have a smaller period available, choose to do a part of the coaching topics in a good way instead of covering bits and pieces of all the topics.
Use your passion to inspire. Passion is honest, authentic, and contagious, so it is advisable to show it when you have it.

A final tip in giving advice is to **split positive and negative feedback**. When you use both in the same sentence or talk, the two compensate for each other and the message gets lost in the middle. Therefore, you should banish words like 'but' from your vocabulary and stop using the hamburger approach in which you try to cover up corrective feedback between two compliments. It will only cause confusion with the mentee when you do (Daniels, 2000).

Finally, in the **EXTENDING** phase, focus on inviting the trainee to take over the thinking process. This means the mentor will less and less explain the details of what he or she thinks needs to be done. You will focus on asking questions so that the mentee alone finds out the answers. This way **the mentee does now do both the thinking and the doing**.

For the mentee to be able to solve problems, the mentor does need to **provide the right information**, including background information such as the organizational vision and the goals for the department. The mentor explains the big picture, and the mentee defines next steps to be taken and the details to flesh out the picture.

Teaching people how to do their own thinking is an important preparation for abnormal situations, so make sure you ask the mentee for the reasoning behind any actions. That improves thinking and reflection.

**Key Points:**
- *Coaching requires a supportive relationship that is not based on power.*
- *Before you can advise your mentee, you really must understand the mentee and work on the relationship.*

# PART 2:

# UNDERSTANDING THE LEAN PHILOSOPHY

Part 1 described the importance of leadership for any (lean) transformation initiative and the need for the lean transformation leader to be a trainer and a coach to be able to facilitate this cultural change.

Part 2 will describe what the term *lean* means. In these chapters, we will create a common understanding of what lean is, where it is from, and why it is so important. It will describe what is it that the lean transformation leader will probably to be teaching and coaching to gain an understanding about this philosophy that helps you built a culture of continuous improvement.

The following chapters each describe part of the what I believe to be the three most important principles of the lean philosophy.
Chapter 4 will describe what *flow* means in more detail, and how it is linked to the number one KPI in lean initiatives: lead time.
Chapter 5 introduces the three enemies of lean, *muda, muri and mura*, or in English terms: waste, overburden and imbalance. The main idea is that you remove these three enemies from your process to improve the flow and thereby lead time.
Chapter 6 will then describe the cultural aspect of the Toyota system. The 14 management principles from Likers Toyota way (Liker, 2004). Only by living by these management principles, you will be able to continuously keep on reducing the three enemies of lean, and therefore continuously keep on improving the process flow.

# Chapter 4:

# Implementing flow

> *Lean is actually common sense.*
> *— participants from many of my lean trainings*

There are many definitions of what lean is, most of them having to do with "eliminating waste" and "doing what is right for the customer." The idea behind this is that customers are paying for our product or service, therefore we should always focus on serving them best. Everything that does not add value to customers is called waste, or non-value-adding activities. This is why we always try to reduce the time and money we spend on these wastes.

Wastes have a sense of worthlessness in them, so the parts of your job that you do not like or that even annoy you are possibly waste because you feel they are worthless. In this sense, lean is common sense.

Before we go into detail about how we would like the lean philosophy to reduce waste, let us look at where the term *lean* comes from.
The first time the word *lean* was used was in an article in the *MIT Sloan Management Review* written by John Krafcik (Krafcik 1988). He wrote an article about the findings of research on different automobile factories in the world and found that Japanese manufacturers were quite different from the North American and the European ones.

## 4.1 How lead time became the number one KPI

*Lead time is the only metric that improves quality,
delivery and costs at the same time.*

Krafcik's research found that Japanese plants were able to reach both high levels of quality and productivity at the same time, whereas other factories scored only high on one of the two on average (Krafcik 1988). Krafcik found that Japanese automobile plants and the automobile plants of Europe and North America differed in three respects: the level at which the workforce is trained, the way that products are designed, and how the production system is organized.

It was regarding the production system that Krafcik first mentioned the difference between a just-in-time (JIT) lean production model (with only 0.2 days of inventory in the production line) and a just-in-case buffered production system (with an average of 2.0 days of inventory in Europe and 2.9 days of inventory in North America).

More research followed, and in 1990, Womack, Jones, and Roos published a book offering more insight into the differences among automobile plants, as shown below in figure 1.

The number of hours needed to assemble a car in Japan was about half of that in North America and one-third of that in Europe (seventeen, twenty-five, and thirty-six hours, respectively); defects per hundred cars were almost one-fourth fewer than in North America and 40 percent fewer than in Europe (sixty, eighty-two, and ninety-seven defects, respectively).

This means Toyota had found a method to break through the iron triangle of quality, cost, and delivery, a triangle in which the improvement of one element usually leads to the diminishment of the other two (Gort 2015).

Since Toyota was able to reduce costs, improve quality, and improve delivery all at the same time, it is no wonder producers in North America and Europe were interested in Toyota´s way of working.

|  | Japan | North America | Europe |
|---|---|---|---|
| **Output** | | | |
| Productivity (hours per car) | 17 | 25 | 36 |
| Quality (defects per 100 cars) | 60 | 82 | 97 |
| **Layout** | | | |
| Sq. Ft./car/yr. | 5.7 | 7.8 | 7.8 |
| Rework space (%) | 4.1 | 13 | 14 |
| Material buffers (days) | 0.2 | 2.9 | 2.0 |
| **Employees** | | | |
| Employees in teams (%) | 69 | 17 | 0,6 |
| Job rotation (1–4, 4 is most) | 3 | 0.9 | 1.9 |
| Suggestions per employee per year | 62 | 0.4 | 0.4 |
| Functional groups (number) | 12 | 67 | 15 |
| Training new employees (hours / year) | 380 | 46 | 173 |
| Absenteeism (%) | 5 | 12 | 12 |

*Figure 1: 1989 benchmark of assembly plants of high-volume producers (Womack, Jones, and Roos 1990)*

After the benchmark study, Womack and Jones wrote a book on the lean production system called *Lean Thinking* (1996). In it, the secret of the great results of Toyota were linked to a short lead time, the time it takes to produce a car from start to finish. Note that the production system was only one of the three aspects Krafcik identified in 1988; the other two, product design and flexible workforce, are less highlighted in their book.

Womack and Jones identified five steps as a starting point for organizations that want to implement a lean production system:

The first step is to identify what **the value** is that the process creates for the customer.

The second step is to map **the value stream**, the set of activities that are necessary to perform the three main management activities: product design, production order intake and planning, and the actual production.

Step three is about **implementing flow**, a state of no disruption in the value stream, which leads to a reduction of lead time. In this method, all activities that directly contribute to the forming of the product are called value adding activities. All activities that do not directly contribute to the product are called non-value adding activities. Non-value adding activities can be used as a synonym for the earlier described *waste*.

Step four is **implementing pull** as much as possible, which means producing only what the customer actually demands. Here and throughout the book, I use the word customer in a broader sense. It can be the end-customer who buys the product, but also the internal customer, the department or colleague working on the product after you.

And finally, step five is **striving for perfection**, which means that we believe we can continuously improve our process, and therefore we never stop improving.

Part 4 gives more information about these five steps and describes the improvement of the value stream in general.

Jeffrey Liker (2004) wrote a second famous lean book, The Toyota Way, which includes many lessons for organizations that would like to use the lean philosophy to improve performance. One of the lessons was that simply removing waste whenever you encounter it is not a good idea. There is a reason why the waste is there. Waste is the result of overburden and imbalance. Improvement activities should therefore not just be about removing waste but about understanding where the waste is coming from, why it is there, and how we can improve the process in a sustainable way that removes the root cause of the waste. Together imbalance, overburden and waste are referred to as *the three enemies of lean*.

A second lesson from Liker's book is that Toyota´s success was not only about value stream optimization but also about behaviors. Toyota´s cultural success can be described in fourteen management principles, which can guide us in understanding how the lean tools are used.

Part 3 of this book is dedicated to describing the maturity of lean culture, in which a combination of lean tools is used on a daily basis to improve all process steps within a value stream. Each of the tools are linked to the three enemies of lean, and they are also linked to the fourteen management principles.

Before we go into the details of lean maturity and value stream improvement, we'll discuss the importance of flow (chapter 4), the three enemies of lean (chapter 5), and the fourteen Toyota principles (chapter 6) in more detail.

**Key Points:**
- *The word lean was used for the first time in 1988 in an article that compared auto manufacturers around the world.*
- *Because Japanese companies reached high levels of quality and delivery at low costs, more studies followed.*
- *Toyota differentiated itself from other carmakers in part by focusing on lead time.*
- *To be able to improve lead time, a theory about value-adding activities and non-value-adding activities was born.*

## 4.2 Improving Flow to Reduce Lead Time

*A process should be like a river, where your product or service is the water that is continuously in motion.*

The word *flow* has two metaphors. With respect to production processes, you can refer to the metaphor of a river, where water flows without stopping from one place to another so that we can deliver to the customer as soon as possible. This means that ideally, a product in a factory should be in constant transformation, without any interruptions.

For indirect labor or office work, you can refer to the state of mind in which people like to work the most: working in flow (Womack and Jones 1996). In this sense, the term *flow* is the label for work that is highly satisfying (Csikszentmihalyi 1990). Elements of work that improve satisfaction are having a clear objective, working on a task that requires all your attention, experiencing a sense of challenge, the perception that your skills are adequately used, and working where there are no interruptions (Csikszentmihalyi 1990).

To prevent interruptions, a good plan A should have a plan B that is at least as good. Teams should be able to solve their own problems as much as possible to prevent management from feeling the need to intervene in the process. This principle can be called self-healing flow (Duggan 2012). It's self-healing because the people immediately involved in the problem know how to fix the flow when it is broken and don't have to depend on other functions and departments.

Within lean, the measure for efficiency of all processes, the speed of the flow, has an impact on the **lead time.** We can define lead time as the total time it takes for a product or service to go through the entire process. The shorter the lead time, the better for the manufacturer, because the lead time directly influences the time the customer must wait before receiving the product. It also makes the organization more flexible in responding to changes in the market.

On top of that, we remember from the previous paragraph that lead time is the only measure that positively influences all three elements of the iron triangle: costs, delivery, and quality (Gort 2015). The shorter the lead time, the fewer inventory is kept in the process, which means less bound capital. With a shorter lead time, the organization can respond better to changes in customer demand and therefore deliver what's needed more easily. Finally, the quality improves because a shorter lead time leads to a faster feedback loop whenever there is a problem. The shorter the time between producing the error and receiving feedback about it, the fewer items can possibly be affected by it.

In an ideal process, there are no waiting times, which means value is being added to the product or service all the time. In this sense, the product is always in transformation. It flows through the process without having to wait for somebody or something to continue building the product.

In addition to the lead time, a couple of other time measurements help in the analysis of the efficiency of the flow: process time, the time a product is being worked on at a workstation; and cycle time, the rate at which products come out of the workstation or production line. We can compare the cycle time for a complete production line (or value stream) with the takt time; the interval in which the customer is buying your product or service, to calculate whether the processes can fulfill customer demand. Chapter 11 describes each of these times in more detail.

All processes have lead times, and unfortunately in traditional processes, most of that lead time is waiting time. **Waiting time** means the product or service is waiting for someone or something to continue working on it. Waiting products mean more inventories, and inventory holds up capital, increases the risk of obsolescence and defects, and most importantly, slows down the speed at which we can fulfill customer demand—so flow and the reduction of waiting time are important (Womack and Jones 1996).

An ideal process has no waiting time and therefore no inventory. In an ideal process, the products flow from one workstation to another without interruption.

Within the lean philosophy, we seek to improve the flow of all processes, not just the production processes. This book focuses on two different categories of flow: the flow of materials and information (Rother and Shook 1999) and the flow of problems (Ballé and Ballé 2012).

Part 4 discusses **the flow of materials and information**, where value stream mapping and several supporting lean tools are described to reduce the lead time for products and services sold to the customer. These processes include production processes, but you can use the same tools to improve indirect processes, such as quality handling, project management, and research and development projects.

**Improving the flow of problems** is an area where the cultural aspect of lean plays a vital role. We will learn in part 3 that a true lean organization solves problems by identifying the root cause, which leads to lots of small countermeasures that improve performance. The daily management meetings, described in chapter 8, discuss and track these problems. Several tools are described, and they facilitate all employees being able to solve problems to improve the flow of materials and information.

**Key Points:**
- *Among other things, lean is about improving the flow.*
- *Improving flow means reducing lead time.*
- *There are two types of process flows that lean helps improve: the flow of material and information and the flow of problems.*

# Chapter 5:

# While Reducing Waste, Overburden, and Imbalance

*If you don't take the time to reflect on how you´ve spent your time, how do you make sure you are adding value to the customer?*

So how can we improve flow? Toyota has developed its production system around eliminating three enemies: **waste** (*muda*), **overburden** (*muri*), and **imbalance** (*mura*).

Waste is the direct obstacle to flow. There are eight distinctive types (described in 5.1 and 5.2), and all lead to waiting times and therefore longer lead times in a process. Simply taking out the waste does not work. Usually there is a reason the waste is there, and this reason often has to do with the other two enemies: overburden (which 5.3 describes) and imbalance (described in 5.4). This means the three enemies of lean are **interrelated** and should therefore be considered simultaneously.

You will find the three enemies of lean in both production and office processes. I even dare to say that you can find more evidence of those enemies in office processes than in production processes. One reason for this is that production processes are visible. Everybody who walks through a factory can see the inventory waiting to be worked on. In the office environment, however, processes are often hidden in mailboxes, and in information technology systems. Inventories can hide in those for a long time before somebody notices them.

Though it is the goal of lean to reduce all three enemies of lean, it might not be possible to remove all of them completely.
In terms of waste, unless your factory is placed next to your customer, there will always be some sort of transportation necessary to get the product to your customer. We should focus on reducing the transportation time and costs as

much as we can, but 100 percent reduction is not realistic.

The same holds true for overburden. There may always be a time when machines or people must give that little extra effort or time to make sure customer demand is fulfilled. There is nothing wrong with this if you can thereby get a huge order of extra products or win over a new client. The problem exists when you are expecting this from your machines or people all the time to a point where a colleague or machine burns out.

Finally, even imbalance cannot always be reduced 100 percent. When you are producing different products, they are bound to require different materials, different ways of working, or even different process times. This is even more true in project work, where every project is different, or in the financial world, where you need to deliver a financial report at the end of each month.

In the next four paragraphs, each of the enemies of lean is described in more detail. Chapter 5.1 describes the eight traditional types of waste and how to find them. Chapter 5.2 describes alternative types of waste for the office environment. Chapter 5.3 is all about overburden, and Chapter 5.4 explains imbalance.

**Key Points:**
- *The three enemies of lean are imbalance, overburden, and waste.*
- *These three are interrelated and affect one another.*
- *When reducing one of them, take the other two into account.*

## 5.1 The Eight Traditional Wastes

*Can we talk about the word queue? How many of those letters are really necessary? I count one.*

Muda is the Japanese word for waste and includes non-value-adding activities that prevent flow and lead to longer lead times. We consider all activities as non-value-adding if a customer would not be willing to pay for those activities if given the chance to decide. Originally, Ohno (Ohno 1988) defined seven types of waste, all of which are interrelated. A little later, an eighth waste was added to the Toyota handbook (J. K. Liker 2004).

This section describes the eight different wastes, each with an example of that waste in production and in the office environment and lean tools that help find them and eliminate them. As a mnemonic device, the first letters of the eight wastes form the acronym **DOWNTIME**.

**DEFECTS** are products or services that are moved to the next process step that do not conform to customer specifications. In a production environment, a defect could be a product or part that does not function properly or a product that is incomplete when it arrives to the customer.

A defect in an office environment could be a typo in an IT system that prevents the process from continuing, or it could even be the sending of a wrong attachment in an e-mail.

Defects usually lead to rework and/or extra work to make sure the customer receives the products or services ordered. Because this process includes a feedback loop from the customer to the workstation and extra time spent to fix the problem, defects have a negative influence on the lead time and therefore on the flow of the process.

You can use at least two tools to prevent defects from happening: poka-yoke and standard work. **Poka-yoke** is the Japanese method of eliminating the possibilities of building defective products. One example is the oxygen and vacuum tubes in an operating room. These are designed in such a way that it is impossible to connect the tube to the wrong machine, as shown in figure 2.

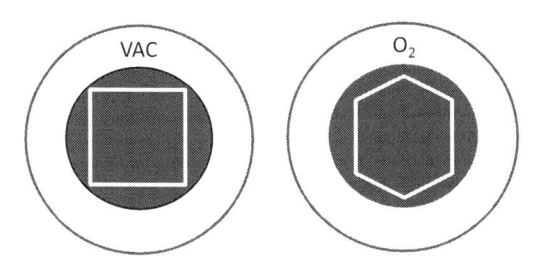

*Figure 2: VAC and O2 connectors in a hospital*

There are two different types of poka-yoke systems: a warning system, which sends a signal when there is a deviation from the standard; and a control system, through which a machine automatically stops whenever there is a deviation from the standard (Shingo 1989).

**Standard work** means each task is described in detail in the so-called *standard operating procedures* (SOPs). When tasks are performed in a standard order, the chances of mistakes are reduced. Imbalance, due to different operators performing the same tasks, is also reduced. In a lean production system, everybody should have some form of standard work, even if the nature of the job only makes it possible to define only a certain percentage of tasks as standard tasks (Mann 2005).

**OVERPRODUCTION** means producing more than the customer needs. This is a waste because resources are already invested in products or services that will not be worked on after the current process step.
One example in production is producing components that are needed further downstream of the workstation, but it is unknown when they are needed exactly. I personally have encountered products in warehouses that have been sitting there for multiple years waiting to be processed.
In the office environment, the input of electronic tickets for change requests for IT or engineering can be considered overproduction when the resources of the receiving department are restricted, and it is uncertain whether the department personnel have the capacity to work on the request. The people who need the IT changes simply push the next number of requests into the system, hoping they will be implemented, spending time following procedures and filling out forms.

Overproduction is sometimes referred to as "the mother of all wastes." It leads to all other kinds of waste because the product or service moves through the entire process with both value-adding activities and non-value-adding activities.

You can reduce this type of waste using tools like SMED and kanban. **SMED** is an abbreviation of Single Minute Exchange of Die, which basically means "quick changeover." When changeovers are short, you can produce in smaller batches—and therefore reducing the time that a customer order is waiting to be allocated to an production order—which directly reduces the production lead time of the process. SMED at a high level consists of two steps and is described in more detail in chapter 17:

- Do as many tasks as possible when the machine is still running on the current batch.
- Reduce the amount of time needed to do tasks with the machine offline, using the parallelization of tasks and implementing small machine changes and the design of tools needed to perform the changeover (Shingo 1989). This can be done by eliminating tasks or doing some tasks in parallel.

The second tool you can use to reduce overproduction is **kanban**. Kanban is a Japanese term for a self-managing production system in which the material moves down the value stream while the information about what to produce moves upstream (Geiger, Hering and Kummer 2011).
With kanban, signals (visual cards) are sent from the end of the process, the final inventory from which the customer has taken products. The signals say exactly how much of a product has been used up downstream, which means that it then needs to be replenished. Every workstation receives its own signal (usually an actual plastic or cardboard card) from its downstream workstation, which informs the upstream station about what product to produce and how many items to produce. Chapter 19 will describe Kanban in more detail.

In the office environment, every task that needs to be done can be shown on Post-it notes on a board containing three columns: to do tasks, in progress tasks, and finished tasks. You can define the maximum number of tasks in progress, which means a new task can only be started when another one is finished. In this case, only when a team member has finished a task can he or she request the next one.

**WAITING** is the third waste and includes parts, e-mails, and transactions in the Enterprise Resource Planning systems that are waiting to be completed on the shop floor, that are in somebody´s mailbox. And what about all the people who are waiting for one person at the start of a meeting? These are all non-value-adding times in the process, directly increasing the lead time and obstructing flow.

Waiting time is directly linked to inventory. Whenever products are sitting in inventory, they are technically waiting to be processed. The same holds for e-mails waiting to be read or answered. We therefore measure inventories on the value stream map in waiting time.

Tools that help find waiting time in a process are takt time, and line balancing.

**Takt time** is the interval in which the customer buys the product—the amount of product demanded by customers for a certain amount of time. For instance, when customer demand is 365 products a year, takt time is one day.

This means the factory should ideally produce one product a day to stay flexible for changes in customer demand. When production is faster than takt, products must wait in the warehouse until they can be shipped to the customer. When production is slower than takt, it's even worse—the customer has to wait for his order. (see chapter 11.1 to learn more about takt time).

The third tool to reduce waiting times in a process is **line balancing**. This tool is used to balance a line in a way that all sequential workstations have equal cycle times (Duggan 2002). When the cycle time of station two is longer than that of station one, every product that comes from station one has to wait, or station one has to wait until station two has finished its cycle. A visual to which helps balancing a production line is *yamazumi,* which chapter 14 will describe.

**NONUSED TALENT** includes employee knowledge and skills not being used to their full potential. For instance, a high-skilled worker might have to do work that is relatively easy. Or that worker might be firefighting (addressing unexpected problems) all the time instead of focusing on continuously improving in the long run. Firefighting by itself is a waste (excess processing) when the problem is not really solved. We will come back to this topic in chapter 9.

Another example is not inviting the expert of a workstation to the value stream mapping events and thereby failing to use his or her input to identify the problems within that value stream. This could lead to an entire management team focusing on the wrong problems and later having to evaluate and solve the problems all over again.

The tool to reduce this non-used talent is **training.** As we saw in figure 1 in chapter 2.1, in 1989 Toyota invested six times as many training hours (380) in new employees as North American assembly plants (with 46 training hours per employee per year) and more than twice as many as European assembly plants (with 173 training hours per employee per year) (Womack, Jones and Roos 1990). Everyone in the organization should be trained to use tools like 5S, standard work, team boards, and continuously improve their own processes. This is where the Japanese term *kaizen* comes in, a small improvement for the good. The link between these four tools is as follows: the improvement loop supports small improvements done by the operators, which can be shared using the team boards and are documented and sustained in standard work and the 5S standards. We will come back to these tools in part 3 of this book.

In addition to learning these tools, employees should be trained in practical problem-solving using **5x Why** (The technique where the person asks why as many times as necessary to get to the root cause of a problem) to get to the root cause of a problem instead of fixing symptoms. Chapter 9 describes more details of different problem-solving techniques at different problem complexities, and the role of each employee in using them.

**TRANSPORT**, the fifth waste, includes all movements of products between workstations, paperwork between departments, or digital processes between multiple individuals. The product moves around without actually being altered. The lead time and even staff hours are increased when a physical product is being transported without adding value to the customer.
One way to reduce transport of products within the process is to change the lay-out of it to a production line or a work cells set-up (see chapter 11.1). To minimize transport of tools by people that are necessary to work on the products, 5S can be implemented.

With **spaghetti diagrams,** you can draw all movements of people, products and tools with a pen on a plant map. Decide on a person, product, part or file to follow, and observe every movement. Draw each movement on the map and analyze the results. Are there some frequent distances that you can reduce with the help of 5S?
One way to reduce the amount of transport in production is by changing the

layout of the plant into **production lines** in which a product flows through the same workstations in the same order. A second option is the use of **work cells**, where small production lines are built in a U shape. Input and output of each workstation should all be on the same side to reduce distance between cells. A product can flow through the cells needed for that particular product.

For paper processes in which lots of signatures are necessary—such as quality issues or project charters—having a fixed moment in the day where the majority of people meet to work on those charters in one go (in a work cell fashion) is a possibility. Doing this prevents one person from walking around the entire site searching for people to sign the document.

Finally, using **5S** (a tool for workplace organization) can reduce the transport of tools by operators. When every workstation has a standard location to keep all the tools needed at that workstation the operator does not need to walk around to look for a tool that is needed. One example is the use of the shadow board, which is a board on the wall where life size pictures of the tools that are meant to hang are posted. This helps to immediately visualize when a tool is missing and what tool it is.

**INVENTORIES** are the products or services that are waiting at a workstation, in an e-mail account, or in the ERP system to be completed. The more parts that are waiting for the same operation, the longer one particular part has to wait its turn, hence the longer the waiting time is.

Waiting times directly increase the lead time of a product or service and therefore make the organization slower in responding to customer demand. In addition to that, physical inventory costs money in the form of physical space costs, management costs, insurance costs, and the costs of obsolescence. Depending on the product, these costs together could add up to about 18–35 percent of total material costs on a yearly basis (Dominick und Lunney 2012), depending on what industry you are in.

Tools that can help reduce the amount of inventory in production are **work cells** and **kanban**, which were both described earlier.

Even better than reducing inventory is to eliminate it all together, which would mean creating a one-piece flow line. With **one-piece flow**, production batches are reduced to one item at a time. This means you immediately reduce the amount of work in process (WIP) to a factor of the size of the current batch size. One-piece flow is described in more detail in chapter 11.

**MOTION**, waste number 7, describes the movement of people and machines that are not actually working on the product or service. For instance, such movement might be looking for the right screwdriver to tighten a screw or searching for a document for ten minutes on a computer drive to send as an attachment of an e-mail.
In addition to the time it takes to reach that part or click through multiple folders on your computer, motion has a clear link with overburden.
Motion is one of the wastes that should not always be reduced to zero. Taking out the most difficult motions of a person's work cycle might be an improvement in terms of ergonomics but taking out all movement might have a negative effect on health, which can lead to a lot of other problems, with long absences as a possible result.

Tools that help you reduce the waste of moving include **standard work**, **5S**, and **spaghetti diagrams**, all introduced earlier in this chapter.

The eighth and final waste is **EXCESS PROCESSING**, and it means doing extra things that the customer is not asking for (or would not be willing to pay for if you were to ask them). This could include building in product features or adding more accessories than the customer needs; it also includes the rework that is necessary to repair defects. Adding packaging materials for internal transport (between floors, departments, or even sites) that are then removed again are also examples of excess processing.

In the office environment, excess processing could mean adding more pages or text to a document than necessary or spending time in making an extra-fancy layout for a presentation for your manager.

The first tip in reducing this type of waste is by simply asking your customer whether he or she really needs those e-mails, reports, and bells and whistles on the product or slide layout.

A **process map** is a tool that you can use to systematically find non-value-adding activities. This is a kind of flow chart with six types of symbols: process step, delay, inventory, decision, measurement, and transport. The best way to create a process map is by observation to make sure you draw all the hidden wastes in the process that are not stated in the "official" way of working.

Observation is not only important for creating a process map. The best way of finding waste in any process is to observe them (Ballé and Ballé 2005). Taiichi Ohno was famous for his standing-in-the-circle exercise. Managers had to stand in one spot in the factory and simply observe what wastes they could see (Liker 2004).
The same would work in an office environment. Simply taking the time to really see what is going on in a process can be the input for a long list of wastes.

The examples of each of the above types of waste are just a small sample of possibilities. It is important to understand that a lot of waste is designed into the system to buffer problems and prevent one problem from leading to more problems at downstream workstations. One example is the use of inventories between two machines to prevent the second machine from starving when the first machine is broken down. Simply taking away the inventory does reduce the lead time on paper, but it definitely does not solve the problem that the inventory was hiding—in this case, the reliability issues of the first machine.

Usually waste derives from one or both of the other two enemies of lean: overburden and imbalance. We will discuss these after we have taken a look into the wastes, or non-value-adding activities, in an office environment.

**Key Points:**
- *The Toyota handbook describes eight categories of waste, which can be remembered by the acronym DOWNTIME.*
- *For each type of waste, there are multiple tools that you can use to show the waste and the goal to eliminate it.*

## 5.2 Waste in an Office Environment

*In production, the non-value-adding activities add up to 90–95 percent of the total work. In an office environment, this percentage is probably higher.*

Even though it is possible to find examples for each of the eight wastes in an office environment, my experience in training tells me people still find it difficult to define improvements in their indirect processes. To help drive improvement in an office environment, Lareau (2003) and Webers (2010) both describe a long list of potential office wastes. This chapter lists the twelve most powerful ones, in four categories: human waste, process waste, information waste, and problem-solving waste.

**HUMAN WASTE** includes wastes that prevent people from using their full potential (Lareau 2003). This category includes goal-alignment waste, task waste, and waiting.

**Goal-alignment waste** is the productivity that is lost due to people working on different goals that collide with one another. In the worst-case scenario, different teams even cancel out one another's improvements because they have different targets. We will learn in the chapter on the daily management system (chapter 10) how to make sure all department KPIs are aligned with one another.

**Task waste** is the waste of productivity due to time spent on tasks that are unnecessary or misplaced, leading to a team not meeting its targets. It is very generous of a person in a certain function to help another department when he or she has knowledge from previous experience to help a colleague. It can, however, result in having this nice person performing the task time and time again, having to leave his or her work to get the other department's work done. In this situation, it is important for the helper to teach the colleague her or she is helping how to perform the task.

**Waiting** (actually one of the original eight wastes (Ohno 1988)) is the third type of human waste and includes waiting for colleagues in meetings, waiting for information from another person or department, or waiting for software to process information on your computer. Reducing the time you have to wait is one form of taking action, and it might be through addressing the topic with the person who is late or reluctant to send you information. This requires however that the people can reflect on their own behavior, which is a nice opportunity to discuss the theory which describes people as either victims, or players.

A victim always talks about external factors that influence the situation (Kofman 2006). I am late this this meeting because "I got stuck in traffic" or because "the previous meeting took longer than planned." A player, on the other hand, looks for internal factors that have led to the problem (Kofman 2006). A player thinks things like, "I chose to stay in the meeting because…" and "I chose not to send you that information because…" To be able to reduce waiting time, or many other wastes for that matter, we need people who are willing to take responsibility for the situation. We need more players!

**PROCESS WASTES** include wastes that arise due to the mistakes in the process design or the fact that people are not sticking to the standard processes (Lareau 2003).

**Waste of control** is the first type of waste in this category. For example, managers check up on their team members to see if they still follow the process without actually contributing to improvement activities of that process. This and other micromanagement processes not only waste the time of the manager but also keep team members from solving real problems and doing real work. Leader standard work (chapter 7.2), in which the main tasks of every manager indirect role are described, can help reduce this waste.

**Standardization waste** exists when extra resources are consumed because not everybody is working according to the documented standard. To prevent this waste, you need to document and share among team members the current, most-efficient way of working.

**Work-around waste** is the waste that exists when processes are designed so poorly that employees spend their time firefighting problems that occur due to the poor design.

If the problems are not solved preventively, this behavior leads to people following unofficial processes in addition to the official process just to get their jobs done. In this case, it is important not to blame the people for leaving the standard; you must understand why they are doing it. The system triggers all behavior, including behavior outside the official system (Morieux and Tollman

2014).

**INFORMATION WASTE** includes all time that is wasted due to people searching for, checking, and correcting information.

**Missing-information waste** exists when people have to call or write other colleagues to ask for information and wait for the others to respond with the information that is needed.

**Irrelevant-information waste** exists when people spend their time collecting and documenting information that is not adding value for the customer.

**Inaccurate-information waste** exists when people have to spend time correcting information (which corresponds to the traditional waste *defects*) that was created in the previous process steps (which corresponds to *rework*).

In addition to these nine wastes from Lareau (2003), Webers (2010) adds a view of other nontraditional types of waste. From his list of the three types of **PROBLEM-SOLVING WASTE,** I add to Lareau's nine wastes the following: comfort waste, engagement waste, and solving waste.

**Comfort waste** exists when targets aren't stretching. In a working environment, people in general are not really motivated to improve anything unless someone asks them.
Setting measurable targets helps them to visualize this task, and it challenges people to upgrade their performance (Webers 2010).

**Engagement waste** is the result of asking people to take responsibility for events or results that they cannot influence themselves and have no control over. How can you expect people to use tools like the team board if those tools do not help them do their daily work? And how does it make you feel if a Key Performance Indicator (KPI) is red on your board, but you have no way of influencing it?

**Solving waste** is the incapacity to solve problems due to people working on problems without focusing on the real root cause. When people do not address the root cause in the problem-solving process, the problem will possibly reoccur and require attention a second time.

**Key Points:**
- *Everything that the customer does not prefer to pay for is waste, and we can use different categories that can help us identify different types of waste.*
- *Human waste prevents people from using their full potential.*
- *Process waste is made up of the mistakes in the process that make it possible for people to make mistakes.*
- *Information waste is the time that is wasted due to people searching, checking, and correcting information.*
- *Problem-solving waste arises when the opportunities for problem-solving are not used.*

## 5.3 Overburden

*A plant in which everyone is working all the time is very inefficient.*
—E. Goldratt

The Japanese word for the second enemy of lean is *muri*, which means overburden. Overburden means that operators or machines are pushed to their natural limits, which potentially leads to problems (Liker 2004). The quality of the output suffers because of the state of the machine or person performing, which means overburden leads to waste (Hines, Found and Griffiths 2011). Another way of describing overburden is to say that the machines are over-utilized, where more work is done on the machine than it is capable of doing.

One example is the battery of an old car overheating, which can eventually lead to a defective battery followed by a breakdown of the car. Another example is the use of memory-intensive software on a personal computer that has insufficient memory power to complete calculations quickly, which leads to waiting time.

In terms of human overburden, being stressed can lead to you wanting to do something really quickly, which usually leads to more defects. Even worse is if you get overburdened and cannot work at all for a while, which is what we now usually describe as people experiencing a *burn-out*.

Not only does overburden lead to defects—it also leads to longer waiting times (Gort 2015). Queuing theory shows us that the lead time of a process increases exponentially when the utilization degree increases (Hopp and Spearman 2000). The lead time doubles when the utilization of a process increases from 80 to 90 percent, and it doubles again when it increases from 90 to 95 percent (Gort 2015).

Remember that lead time is the one measure that reduces all three aspects of the iron triangle—cost, delivery, and quality—so it is wise to prevent the utilization degree of your processes, machines, and people from exceeding 80 percent (Suri 2010).

In a **MACHINE ENVIRONMENT**, overburden depends on machine performance, which can best be measured by the overall equipment effectiveness (OEE) of the machine (King 2009).
The OEE includes measures for availability, performance, and quality—with the goal of preventing the machine from breaking down.

You can minimize machine-related overburden by maintaining all machines as effectively and efficiently as possible. To improve the OEE of a machine and prevent overburden, you can use both preventive and autonomous maintenance (Tajiri and Gotoh 1992). The main idea of both these programs or tools is that it is better to spend more planned time maintaining the machine, than it is to spend unplanned time fixing it.

**Preventive maintenance** means keeping a machine in operating condition by means of inspection, detection, and prevention of failures (Wireman 1992). By maintaining the machine, you can prevent breakdowns that would otherwise lead to defects or—even worse—accidents. The underlying thought is that preventive maintenance is cheaper than waiting for the machine to break down and having to fix it. Preventive maintenance does not only reduce machine overburden, it also reduces variation for the technical staff. The number of unplanned jobs they receive decreases, while the number of planned maintenance jobs increases.

One example of preventive maintenance is getting your car checked at a garage regularly to prevent you from having breakdowns while on the road. I personally would much rather be having my tires changed before they are completely worn out, than to risk them exploding on the highway.

**Autonomous maintenance** is the next step after preventive maintenance, and it means that operators routinely perform key maintenance tasks on a machine, which is traditionally done only by the best few individuals (Floyd 2010). The rationale is that operators work with the machines all day, so they notice abnormalities instantly. In addition, they reduce the workload of technical staff by performing these small maintenance tasks.

Our car checkup might be too complicated for most of us, but to keep a bike chain lubricated and the tires inflated is not so difficult. Doing so is an example of autonomous maintenance by which the owner prevents future breakdowns.

Implementing autonomous maintenance is described in seven steps (Tajiri and Gotoh 1992):

1. Initial cleaning
2. Contamination prevention
3. Creating cleaning standards
4. Introducing total machine inspection
5. Creating a standard interval for total machine inspections and cleaning
6. Preventing defects from reaching other workstations
7. Focusing on improvement activities to increase OEE

A detailed description of autonomous maintenance can be found in chapter 16.

You can calculate whether it is cost-efficient to have a preventive (or autonomous) maintenance program on a machine by comparing the costs of breakdowns (calculate the average cost per repair plus the average cost of lot production and multiply that sum to the number of breakdowns per year) with the costs of inspection (cost of activity times the number of inspections per year) (Wireman 1992).

In the **HUMAN ENVIRONMENT**, the lagging indicator of **employee absenteeism** can indicate overburden. In the twenty-first century, more and more people end up at home with a burn-out, which means they are literally overburdened up to a point where they cannot work for a period of up to six months or even longer (Westendorp and van Bodegom 2015).

Apart from absenteeism, Yerkes and Dodson (1908) found that for complex tasks, performance as a result of level of arousal is like a parabola in which performance increases when the arousal rises, but only up to a certain point. After that, more arousal (then perceived as stress) leads to lower performance (Yerkes and Dodson 1908).

Tools that can help reduce people-related overburden are the team board, 5S, standard work, and using jidoka (automatic line stop) principles, that are described next.

You can partly prevent absenteeism caused by overburden through using a **team board** (discussed in chapter 8.2), which includes metrics—such as the amount of overtime, stress levels of individuals, or even team members' moods—that make these topics part of the daily communication within the team. Obviously, only showing data is not enough to reduce the overtime hours and improve people's moods. You need to discuss situations when people are constantly overburdened with work and act before the situation gets out of hand.

**5S**, which leads to an organized workstation, prevents people from having to search for materials or tools. It reduces time for searching, but it also reduces stress (Asefeso 2014). Most of us feel more relaxed when our desks are free of clutter and unnecessary items.

**Standard work** describes the safest and most efficient method of performing a task. Having clear standard operating procedures prevents people from performing unsafe actions to get the job done, using a machine the wrong way, or moving by hand products that are too heavy.

**Jidoka** describes the possibility of stopping the production line whenever there is a problem (Gorecki and Pautsch 2010). At Toyota, this translates into the so-called *andon*, a cord hanging above the production line. Whenever an employee pulls the cord, all employees are notified by visual and sound signals that tell them where the problem occurred. The team leader can help try to solve the problem and when the problem cannot be solved within the takt time, production is stopped across the entire line. With the line stopped, people can completely focus on solving the problem at hand. Stopping the line also prevents the error from infecting multiple products or batches and therefore prevents more defects.

The jidoka principle is described in four steps:
1. Find a deviation
2. Stop production
3. Fix the problem for the short term
4. Analyze the root cause of the problem to prevent it from happening again

The link between imbalance and waste goes both ways. When machines or people are overloaded, more mistakes are made that could lead to defects. But overburden can also result from removing too much waste from the process. Say you remove a buffer of inventory without changing the actual reason the inventory is there in the first place. Chances are that inventory is there to buffer for imbalance to prevent overburden. Simply removing the buffer will increase overburden again (Hopp and Spearman 2000), which will in turn lead to more waste.

Even though the tools above influence overburden, the most important factor that influences it has not been mentioned yet. It is imbalance (Hopp and Spearman 2000), the third enemy of lean. This is what the next chapter is all about.

> **Key Points:**
> - *Overburden leads to waste when people or machines are over-utilized; they produce more defects, leading to more rework and the lead time of the process increasing exponentially.*
> - *You can use different tools to measure overburden for both people and machines.*
> - *Better than measuring overburden and fighting it after it occurs is preventing overburden by reducing imbalance.*

## 5.4 Imbalance

*The easiest way to overburden your people? Squeeze in extra work at the end of the reporting period as you try to make your numbers.*

The Japanese word *mura* (imbalance or variability) is the last of the three enemies of lean and is often the reason the other two enemies exist (J. K. Liker 2004).

We discussed the exponential relationship between utilization and lead time in the previous chapter. What we have not discussed yet is the steepness of the curve, which shows how much the imbalance of a process influences lead time. This is where variability comes into play. Figure 3 shows the difference between two processes with different variabilities (Howell, Ballard and Hall 2001). From this figure we can read that the higher the variability, the steeper the curve and therefore the more impact utilization has on the production lead time.

This is because it is not only the process time itself that can vary between products. Longer process times on one product lead to longer waiting times of all the other products that are now having to wait their turn to be worked on, so the more the process time of individual products vary, the more the waiting times vary as well.

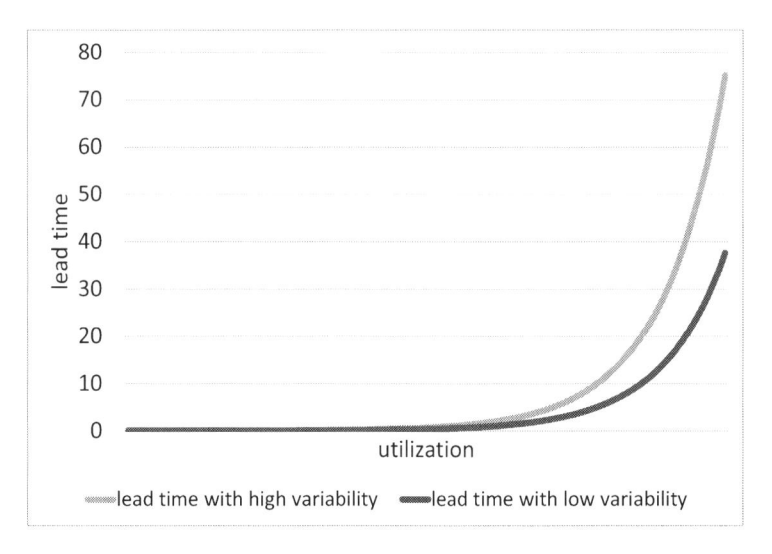

*Figure 3: Influence of imbalance on lead time*

You can calculate the impact of utilization on the lead time of a process via the magnifying effect: M = u / (1-u), in which M is the magnifying effect that tells you to what factor your waiting times will blow up, and u is the utilization of the person or machine (Suri 2010). Using this formula, a utilization rate of 75 percent results in a magnifying factor of three, whereas a utilization rate of 90 percent results in a magnifying factor of nine. This tells us that by increasing the utilization of a machine by 15 percent in this case, the waiting time triples (Suri 2010).

There are two types of variability in each system: daily variability and special-cause variability. Most of the variability exists in the first category, and you can solve it by taking a closer look at processes that are used daily (Scholtes 1998). Therefore, lean tools like value stream mapping and process mapping are important. They help in gaining an understanding of how our processes work and where the daily variability takes shape. This is also where six sigma practices can support you, in which you can discover and validate the causes of variation with the help of statistical calculations.

So where does this variability or imbalance come from? Some comes from the customer side, some has to do with how we have designed our internal processes, and some has to do with human behavior.

First, there is the fluctuation in **CUSTOMER DEMAND**, which leads to fluctuation in the amount of work for employees. In a production environment, this could mean a team is supposed to build five products in one day and fifteen in the next. In an office environment, accounting is a great example of this. During the first three weeks of the month, the financial department has time for lots of different things, but during the fourth week, its members are totally focused in working on financial reports that they need to deliver for month-end closing.

The extent to which variation of customer demand influences our internal processes has to do with **cooperation in a supply chain**. The reason Toyota was able to implement flow in its processes in combination with a high variety of parts is that it built a local network of adaptable suppliers (Krafcik 1988).

When organizations in a supply chain do not share information about customer demand or inventory levels, the **bullwhip effect** emerges whenever customer demand fluctuates. This effect describes how a small change in customer demand from the end of the supply chain is amplified as it moves up to the beginning of the supply chain (Hopp and Spearman 2000). This situation, in turn, leads to large inventories in the overall supply chain. Each link (provider) in the supply chain will have the tendency to order "extra" when it cannot meet an order due to an unexpected shift in customer demand, especially when a backlog exists. The longer the total lead time in the supply chain (delivery times between the links), the higher the bullwhip effect. Also, the higher the number of links in the chain, the greater the bullwhip effect will be. In this sense, each link in the chain is a customer of the link upstream in the chain.

The following are recommendations to reduce the variation of customer demand and thereby reduce the bullwhip effect:

**Reduce the number of links in a supply chain** with, for instance, insourcing. Becoming a lean organization will free up capacity. Why not use that capacity to insource parts of a process to reduce the complexity and, with that, variation? This way you kill two birds with one stone, eliminate waste (freeing up time), and use that time to eliminate variation, which indirectly reduces even more waste.

**Reduce the number of suppliers** to reduce the number of relations that have to be managed. Toyota and Nissan have 75 percent fewer suppliers than do the big three—GM, Ford, and Chrysler (Hines 2009). This also makes it easier to form long-term relationships with your suppliers (Gort 2015).

**Reduce delivery times** between links by looking for local suppliers. Offshoring across the world? The possible six weeks of transport time has a huge effect on inventories and lead times within the supply chain, which decreases the speed with which you can respond to changes in customer demand.
Compared to American auto producers, Toyota has a relatively large group of local suppliers in its network (Lyer, Seshadrei and Vasher 2009). Because the suppliers are local, deliveries of parts can be smaller and faster compared to suppliers that have to send parts over across the world.

**Create transparency between links in the supply chain** when it comes to order portfolios. This will reduce the tendency to increase the order size at every link. The relationship between the organization and supplier should be about long-term partnerships (J. K. Liker 2004) in which the two parties work together to improve the value chain.

**Plan your marketing campaigns** in a way that ensures different regions do not have the same product available through the same special offer at the same time (Lyer, Seshadrei and Vasher 2009). Instead of having one major peak in demand, you now have several smaller ones.

**Combine related product options into packages** (Lyer, Seshadrei and Vasher 2009). Analyze what combination of product options are sold together and use the Pareto principle to define packages of most-used options. Eliminate the individual options to reduce imbalance.

**Limit product offerings per region**. Related to the previous statement, you might find that certain regions hardly request a certain product option. Eliminating these options will reduce imbalance (Lyer, Seshadrei and Vasher 2009).

Second, **IMBALANCE IN PROCESS AND CYCLE TIMES** per product or service at one workstation can occur, which also can lead to imbalance in workload per person.

Let's use the production of customer-specific wooden tables as an example. The number of tables I have in my order book does not necessarily say something about my workload. The workload depends on the specifications of every single table.

In a project environment—for instance in engineering—one change request for a machine can take up way more time than a second change. The number of changes an engineer can implement per week cannot be defined without detailed analysis of every specific change request.

Then you must consider the cycle times. When the intervals in which products are produced on two sequential workstations differ, either waiting times are built into the system or a buffer of material between the two workstations is used to prevent the second machine from idling. This is where lean terms *flow* and *pull* from chapter 4 are important. Flow is the ideal condition of the process in which there is no imbalance or variability, which can lead to overburden and waste. How to implement flow will be addressed in part 4.

Different methods exist to reduce variance in the processes. The variation in product mix has relatively low impact on a production process when the processing times are balanced for different products. There are at least four methods to reduce this form of variance: modular product design at the design level, production leveling in production planning, building flow at the production level, and implementing standard work and 5S at the workstation level.

At the level of **product design**, you can reduce the variation between products by using simpler designs. Remember from chapter 4.1 that simple product design was one of the three reasons why Toyota was so successful (Krafcik 1988). Using standard modules will reduce the number of possible material routings in the factory and therefore reduce the amount of inventory. It will also reduce the management complexity for managers and indirect functions, such as procurement and engineering. One example of modular design is a series of wardrobes at furniture company IKEA where a choice among a number of drawers, doors, and handles leads to a relatively large number of combinations for customers to buy.

A method used to reduce the impact of customer variance in the production planning is the lean tool **heijunka** (production leveling). With heijunka, you define a fixed interval in which all product types can be produced in a fixed sequence (Floyd 2010). The shorter the intervals, the more often a product is produced and the shorter the lead time of each product will be. Because the lead time is reduced, the uncertainty tied to customer demand also drops.

When yearly customer demand is cut into smaller pieces, changes in customer demand can be smoothed out between the different production runs. To implement heijunka, you should minimize changeover times to minimize their cost. A tool that can be used for reducing changeover times is SMED (Single Minute Exchange of Die), which chapter 21 describes. Chapter 14.2 will describe heijunka in more detail.

Next to optimizing product design and production planning, the way products move through the plant should also be optimized. In chapter 4 we learned that ideally products **flow** through the plant; products never have to wait to be worked on as they move between the necessary workstations. When the processing time of workstation two is longer than workstation one, either every product coming from workstation one has to wait before workstation two can work on it, or workstation one has to wait for free capacity at workstation two. Chapter 14.1 describes a graphical way of demonstrating the line balance in a tool called *yamazumi*.

At the workstation level, we can **document how a job should be done,** up to a certain extent. All repetitive handling should be optimized to minimize production variation. **Standardizing procedures and layout** prevent different work cycles for different operators performing the same task, and they prevent employees from searching for materials or tools they need. Standard work describes the safest and most efficient method to perform a certain sequence of tasks, while 5S describes the safest and most efficient layout for a workstation. Reducing variation is one of the reasons these two tools form the basis of every lean implementation, which is why they are the foundation of the lean maturity model described in part 3.

Finally, we can use **six sigma projects** to reduce variability. These are the types of projects that focus on reducing the variation between the different moments in time you produce the same product, and the number of defects a process produces. (The name six sigma refers to a capability of a process in which there are only 3.4 defects per million products).
One example is a sugar packaging line where we pack bags of 1kg of sugar. When we measure the weight of the bags, their weight could vary between 990 and 1010 grams. In this example, a six-sigma project could be defined to reduce this variation and bring it back to a hypothetical 997-1003 grams per bag.

Because variability is directly linked to imbalance, six-sigma projects play a big role in continuous improvement, and therefore also in Lean manufacturing.
Six sigma projects usually follow a five-phase approach: Define, Measure, Analyze, Improve and Control, DMAIC for short, and we will discuss a variety of this approach called D2MAIC, where a discovery phase is added to the DMAIC, in chapter 9.3.

**Key Points:**
- *The best way to improve flow is to reduce waste from the process.*
- *The best way to reduce waste is to reduce overburden.*
- *The best way to reduce overburden is to reduce imbalance.*

# Chapter 6:
# Encouraging the Fourteen Lean Management Principles

*Using tools to optimize processes is only one small aspect of
Toyota´s success. The real value can be found
in its cultural values and principles.*

All lean tools that are developed at Toyota are developed with only one goal: helping find the next problem to solve (Rother 2010). The tools are there to support certain behavior, in this case making problems visible so they can be solved (principles seven and five).

If you want your organization to stay competitive, improvement is not just a one-time thing; your organization needs to become a learning organization (Ballé and Ballé 2012) (J. K. Liker 2004) (Senge 1990). In his book *The Toyota Way*, Liker (2004) describes fourteen lean principles, which when combined give more of an insight into creating a culture of continuous improvement than merely providing a description of the tools that are used to eliminate imbalance, overburden and waste from all processes.

**One: Base your decisions on a long-term philosophy.**
This principle is the foundation of all other principles and is incorporated into Toyota's mission: TO DO THE RIGHT THING FOR THE COMPANY, ITS EMPLOYEES, THE CUSTOMER, AND SOCIETY AS A WHOLE. Assigning extra tasks to get a nice number in a monthly report or at the end of the year is *not* long-term. Neither is using the productivity gains to reduce head count. Long-term has to do with a vision of what the organization should look like in a year or even five years, as described in chapter 1.

Many people underestimate the complexity of this principle. Most managers are so busy with trying to survive the day that there is no time left to think about tomorrow. Yet the need to think about long-term strategy is especially vital when there are many problems during a regular workday. Reflecting on who your customers are and what your vision of the future for the company is can help you break through the cycle of continuous firefighting.

The idea is to focus all activities in the organization on the same long-term organizational goals that are derived from the vision. How the vision can be cascaded to team goals is described in chapter 10.

**Two: Create continuous flow.**
As mentioned in chapter 4, creating flow means reducing the lead time as close to the process time as possible, by eliminating as much waiting time as possible.

Flow is the result of eliminating waste from the process. However, implementing flow is also a tactic that can help you reflect on what wastes exist in the process that you need to eliminate to create flow (Ohno 1988). This is what this principle is about. Try to implement flow in a process and see what problems come up. You should focus on diminishing these problems.

**Three: Use pull systems to avoid overproduction.**
Unfortunately, not every part of the process can be designed in a one-piece flow setting in which products and parts move through the process one by one. For example, it would be inefficient for a supplier to deliver every single bolt in a separate delivery. It would, however, also be inefficient to fill the truck with as many bolts as possible at every delivery. That scenario would lead to high inventories of the individual bolts at the production site.

The lean term to deal with this problematic situation is called *pull*, which is the principle to minimize the waiting times of parts when flow is not possible. The philosophy of pull is that material or information is only produced when it is needed downstream. You can implement this by using either first in, first out (FIFO) lanes or a supermarket between process steps. More information on these different pull strategies can be found in chapter 11.2.

**Four: Level out the workload.**
We already learned that imbalance leads to overburden and waste. This principle is about leveling the workload to prevent people from overburdening themselves. As with the fable about the tortoise and the hare, "slow and steady wins the

race."

The tool to use here is *heijunk*a. With heijunka, the orders that are released into production are sorted in a way that the sorting levels out both the high and the low peaks of the workload. A certain interval is determined in which all types of products are produced. The shorter the interval, the better balanced the work for both people and machines and the smoother the demand to upstream processes and suppliers will be (Liker 2004). Chapter 14.2 discusses heijunka in more detail.

**Five: Stop and fix the problem.**
This describes the principle of solving the problems that multiple lean tools demonstrate. Within Toyota, first the workstation and possibly the entire line will be stopped when there is a problem that cannot be fixed within takt time (Gorecki and Pautsch 2010). The lean tool describing a system that automatically detects defects and stops production is the earlier described jidoka.

It is better to stop production and fix the problem at the root cause, than to continue production at the risk of creating further defects. Second, it is better to solve the problem preventively by improving the standard—thus preventing it from happening again (Ballé and Ballé 2012)—than to tackle the symptoms of the problem in isolation of the cause. The latter is also known as "firefighting," which carries the risk of dealing with the same problem more than once. Chapter 9 will discuss solving problems in a preventive way.

**Six: Work with standards.**
Remember that standard work describes the current best way of performing a certain task. This could consist of the required cycle time, a work sequence, an explanation on how to perform the task, and a standard amount of stock at hand.

Standards are also the foundation for continuous improvement. When there is no standard, there is no stable process, and when there is no stable process you cannot make improvements (Ohno 1988).

Standards are also necessary for sustaining improvements (Imai 1986), training purposes (Ballé and Ballé 2012), and reducing the chance of waste, overburden, and imbalance within a workstation by making sure all operators have the same safe way of working; they will create the product or service in the most effective way currently known to deliver good-quality output.

Standards come in different forms and should be defined for all roles in the organization, from production to indirect functions to managers (Daniels 2000). Chapter 7.2 further explains how.

**Seven: Make problems visual.**
The goal of all lean tools is finding the next problem to solve (Rother 2010), and one aspect of that is to make the problems visual. Lean is about continuously improving performance by solving problems. The different lean tools help you find and demonstrate these problems (Ballé and Ballé 2012).

You can see the 5S system, for instance, as a continual process of improving the working environment as well as a just-in-time system for information flow. The Ss in the 5S system stand for sort, straighten, shine, standardize, and sustain. By visualizing where a certain tool needs to be, you immediately see when it is missing; you can act before you actually need the tool. Chapter 7.1 describes 5S in more detail.

The team board and the daily management structure are two other examples of visual management tools. You can use them to show and list the problems a team has in terms of performance. Here, metrics are used to be able to compare the current status and the goal status so that problems become visible before they get out of hand. Think of this as the speedometer in a car and the road signs that tell you the maximum speed you should drive through a curve on the highway. No accidents have happened yet, but with both your current speed and target speed values, you have the opportunity to adjust your speed. Chapter 8.2 describes the team boards.

Value stream mapping is another tool that visually demonstrates problems, in this case the problems of wastes. You use this tool to design or redesign processes. Part 4 of this book is dedicated to this tool.

**Eight: Use only reliable, tested technology.**
The idea that automation is always the most efficient way to do things is outdated. People tend to go with the latest technology fad, implementing it in the middle of a process, hoping that it will solve all the experienced problems. What people tend to forget is the difficulty inherent in attempting to customize the new technology for your specific environment. Only after the new technology is implemented do many problems come up, leading to extra work. Haste is

waste in this sense and making decisions slowly (principle thirteen) is important when considering a new technology.

Liker (2004) describes the importance of the technology being helpful for people. It should take over complex parts of the job routine, so it is possible for the person to focus on more value-adding, process-enhancing activities.

**Nine: Grow your leaders internally.**
One difference between Toyota and many other companies is that Toyota hires far fewer external managers for available management positions. Why would you try to hire somebody from outside and have this person learn the way things are done when you already have a pool of people available within your organization who process in depth knowledge of the company and its products?
To be able to utilize this potential, a company must invest in the next generation of leaders to make sure they embrace the same philosophy and leadership traits that the company values. Within Toyota, this means that people are continually trained to be able to coach others in problem-solving (Liker and Convis 2102). As we learned from chapter 1 and 3, coaching is an important part of level 4 leadership, which includes a long-term coaching relationship. An organization could implement this via a sort of apprentice system in which all leaders train their successors to prevent radical changes and variation in leadership style after the new manager has taken over.

**Ten: Develop exceptional people and teams.**
Within a lean organization, everybody participates in continually improving his or her work. Everybody uses standards, and everybody is part of a daily team board meeting where people discuss the team performance and problems. In 1989, Toyota invested more than twice the number of hours in training as its European competition and more than eight times the North American competition (Womack, Jones and Roos 1990). This degree of training is necessary because it is impossible to produce products or services that are both high quality and cheap without using skilled workers (Ford 1988). The better you train your people, the easier it will become to grow the next generation of leaders internally.

One of the challenges is to promote teamwork and make sure that teams do things instead of talking about things. Within Toyota, every five to seven employees answer to a team leader. Within these small teams, a team leader can coach their team members in using the standard system for continuous improvement (5S, standard work, team boards, kaizen, and kamishibai) and be a facilitator of their team. Because all team members participate in continuous improvements, the standard work does not dissatisfy operators but supports growth toward self-actualization.

**Eleven: Respect your network partners.**
If you wish your organization to perform well in the long term, you need to work together with your partners by focusing on long-term partnerships and growing common goals together. Liker (2004) describes the supply-chain-need hierarchy where you first need a stable relationship with your partners before you can become a learning organization. One cannot optimize the supply chain if the business relationships are unfair or unreliable or when expectations are unclear. By working together in the supply chain, you can achieve more benefits (for instance, in terms of lead time) than when every link in the chain optimizes itself (Harris, Harris and Streeter 2011).

Remember that having good partnerships with a flexible supplier network is one of the three main reasons Toyota is more successful than European and North American auto manufacturers (Krafcik 1988). The difference between a true supplier-customer partnership and a short-term relationship is like the difference between a marriage and a fling. Having a fling with a supplier means that you only work together until something better (cheaper?) comes along. Only marriage describes a true long-term partnership in which two parties help each other grow (Gort 2015).

**Twelve: Go see for yourself.**
Seeing for yourself is a behavior concerning data-gathering for problem-solving. Never base decisions on data from your screen; always go to the gemba (shop floor) to see the problem for yourself. Talk with the operators who encounter the problem and support them in fixing it. Data from a computer screen can be false, incomplete, or even outdated. By going to the gemba, you do not depend solely on data; you can use all your senses to get a better grasp of what is going on. When a picture is worth more than a thousand words, how much is going to the gemba worth?

When you go to the gemba, do not make assumptions about what happened. Instead, make use of your people skills by asking those on the shop floor what has happened.

As a true lean leader, never miss an opportunity to go to the gemba and solve a problem. A call from the shop floor is more important than a call from top management, as your main job as manager is to support your team in problem-solving (J. K. Liker 2004).

**Thirteen: Make decisions slowly, by consensus, and implement them rapidly.**
"Haste makes waste" is a saying that fits well for this principle. Not taking the time to think thoroughly about improvements or solutions can lead to multiple problems, including extra work, defects, or even angry and disappointed colleagues. Whenever a problem occurs, take the time to find the real root cause of the problem before implementing any countermeasures. In terms of problem-solving, the A3 form and 5x Why (both described in 9.2) are key tools you can use (Shook 2008) and discuss within team board meetings to generate consensus on complex decisions (Suzaki 1993).

**Fourteen: Use hansei (reflection) and continuous improvement (kaizen) to become a learning organization.**
One definition of *reflection* is honestly to judge both your successes and failures in your actions (Kotter 1996). On a problem-solving level, reflection means to think about the following questions: What improvement did you implement? What was the impact? Was the impact exactly what was expected? What can you do better next time?

On a change-management level, people should reflect on their actions in another way: Was my behavior a good example today? Did I contribute in changing the organizational culture into a culture of continuous improvement (Suzaki 1993)?

This reflection needs to focus on the process and the standards, not on the people who worked in the process (J. K. Liker 2004). As I like to put it: If you are looking to find a root cause of a problem to be able to find a countermeasure, we should to do a 5x *why*, not a 5x *who*.

Even though Liker describes this management principle last, to me it is number one in importance. Reflection is not only important at work but also at home.

Reflecting on how you spend your time and comparing that with what you find important in life helps you increase happiness (Miedaner 2000) (S. Covey 1989). In addition to this, self-reflection leads to internal motivation, which helps people perform better in their jobs (Pink 2010).

Growth is only possible when you take the time to reflect on performance, which means performing a proper root-cause analysis on process-oriented problems (5x Why) and implementing proper countermeasures to prevent the problem from reoccurring.

At management and leadership levels, use leader standard work (chapter 7.2) to reflect on how you spend your time and how that decision influences the extent to which you are contributing to both your personal goals and organizational goals.

The fourteen principles help you grasp an understanding of the way that Toyota is organized. A nice way of reflecting on these principles is to ask people if they can give personal examples of demonstrating one of these behaviors in the past week. You will see that even though they look easy on paper, they are actually relatively difficult to live by.

In the following parts of the book, a variety of lean tools will be described to improve flow and reduce the three enemies of lean. For every individual tool, I will also describe how it can contribute to showing the lean behavior that is linked to the fourteen principles described in this chapter.

> **Key Points:**
> - *The fourteen principles describe behaviors that facilitate becoming a true learning organization.*
> - *A learning organization is an organization that is continually solving problems.*
> - *Lean tools are designed to identify the next problem to solve.*

# PART 3:

# THE FOUR LEVELS OF LEAN MATURITY

*A culture of continuous improvement is about setting, checking, and improving standards while linking the improvements to your company goals.*

In part 2 we discussed the importance of flow, the three enemies of lean that prevent flow in a process, and the fourteen behavioral principles that guide us in improving flow.

The previous chapters have already mentioned many lean tools. This part, which encompasses chapters 7 to 10, will provide a structure in which you can use the different tools and link them to a level of lean maturity. In my **LEAN MATURITY MODEL**, I distinguish four levels, as shown in figure 4. In addition to the tools that you can use to attain the different levels of maturity, you will also notice a change in the role you play as the transformation leader.

**Level one is about setting standards**. This is where tools such as 5S and standard work are used to define the current way of performing the job in the most effective and efficient way. Both will be discussed in chapter 7.

5S is a tool used to organize a workplace by creating standards. Most organizations start their lean journey with a 5S event in which all employees clean out their desks and workstations and define the best workstation setup to be able to work efficiently. This is also the first opportunity to do a waste analysis and improve productivity.

Standard operating procedures (SOP), as mentioned above, describe when to do a task, how to do it, and how long it should take. Documenting how a job should be done, especially noting the tricks that experienced workers have, is important to make sure knowledge is kept within the organization and does not leave the organization when an employee does. The standards also help train new employees at new roles. They are also the foundations on which improvements are built

This level of maturity, in which standards are defined, is also required for quality audits and international standards like ISO.
Level-one lean organizations are stressed when an external party (or internal higher management for that matter) announces an audit because they are not sure everything is documented properly, let alone that all standards are adhered to. Over the weeks before the audit, management does as many quick fixes as possible to prevent the auditor from finding inconsistencies, after which the organization moves back into its old habits until the next audit is announced.

The role of the transformation leader in a level-one organization is like a project leader who has to push all activities into the organization. You are the one who has to explain to employees that they should do 5S, and you are held responsible for implementing it, which could even lead to you putting down the markers on the floor yourself just to achieve the target.

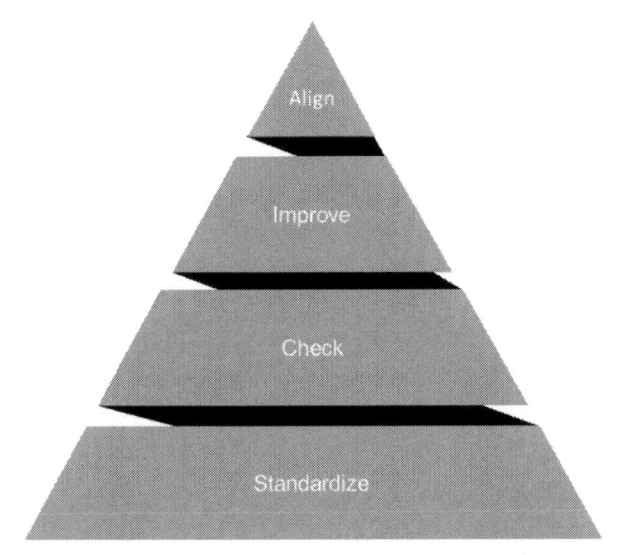

*Figure 4: The four levels of lean maturity*

The problem with these organizations is that they start the lean journey with an event like 5S, but they have no system capable of sustaining the standards, which means that whatever cleaning has been done in the original 5S event, the cleanliness is not sustained of time. This is where the next level of lean maturity comes in.

**Level-two organizations regularly check if standards are adhered to**. After standards are defined, the next step in becoming lean mature is using the standards to check whether you are performing as was defined at the first level.

Does the 5S standard still suffice? Are people working according to their SOP? Are we delivering our product or service as planned in terms of time and quality? And is this way of working still compliant with the ever-changing environment? This is the level in which tools such as kamishibai (mini-audit) and a team board are used to check and show the deviations from the standard.

The small kamishibai audits, as we will see in chapter 8.1, can contain small standards to be checked—for instance, 5S standards—but also any SOP that is important for delivering quality in a timely manner.

The team board, which is discussed further in chapter 8.2, is a visual management tool that continually tracks whether a team is performing as planned and encourages the team to talk about improvement.

A level-two lean organization is an organization in which people discuss performance regularly, but nothing happens with the information they gather. One possibility is that targets are met every time, and the daily performance meeting does not change anything in the way that the team works in the future.

Another possibility is that the team board shows problems when a KPI is not met (and therefore shows a lot of red), but nobody takes the time to solve the problems in a preventive way. When this happens, the KPI's on the board will continue to stay red over time.

At this level of maturity, both kamishibai and the team board are used on a push basis. For instance, a worker might say, "The boss says we should have a stand-up meeting, so now we have one." Or a reaction might be, "My lean manager says I should do kamishibai checks, so now I do them." This means the *why* is not fully understood. Even though the structure of lean tools is in place, it is not used to its full potential, namely finding the next improvement opportunity, which brings us to level three.

**Level-three organizations continuously improve their standards.** This level of lean maturity describes an organization in which the deviations from the standard are used to improve the standards on a continual basis. In this case, visual management tools like 5S, team boards, and kamishibai lead to discussions about why the deviation was really there (the root cause) and about defining actions to solve the problem in such a way that it will not reoccur. For improving standards, you can use tools such as kaizen, A3 reports and D2MAIC projects.

Kaizen is a Japanese word that means "change for the good." As we will see in chapter 9.1, it implies many small incremental daily improvements by all teams. A true lean culture exists when everybody improves their own process a little bit every day.

A3 is the tool used for personal coaching in which the A3 form contains all information needed to lead a discussion between a team member and his or her mentor (which preferably is the manager). The goal is to solve a problem or implement an improvement based on a root-cause analysis. Chapter 9.2 describes this tool in more detail.

The third type of problem-solving tool are D2MAIC projects. This tool is used for problems that cannot be solved with a simple root-cause analysis. The problem is so complex, that a special team needs to be set up to deal with this problem: the project team. D2MAIC refers to the different phases of a project, and they are all described in chapter 9.3.

The organization is starting to pull for support from the lean transformation leader at this point. Even though a transformation leader has to explain what kaizen is and coach the organization into proper problem-solving and documentation of the improvements, the innovators and early adaptors, who will be about 16 percent of the population (Rogers 1995), will start improving their work and hand in suggestions for improvement without you asking for it.

Level-three organizations have team boards and a kaizen suggestion system in place and people are starting to work on improvements themselves, but they have difficulties measuring the impact of these improvements on organizational goals. This is the power of level-four organizations.

**Level four is the highest level of maturity, in which improvements are linked to organizational goals.** Organizations at this maturity level make sure that all improvement initiatives in the organization directly influence bottom-line results. At least two topics are important at this level of maturity:

The daily management system (chapter 10.1), to communicate problems in reaching these targets between the different parts of the organization, and hoshin kanri, which means cascading KPI targets throughout the organization (chapter 10.2).

Having a clear link between management levels and each of the individual teams creates a situation in which management will pull improvement ideas from the organization. Their KPI depends on the KPIs on each team board, so they will offer their support when a team misses its targets.

Everyone in the organization is working with the system of continuous improvement, and the lean transformation leader can be pulled into leading workshops, kaizen events, and personal coaching sessions when asked.

The four levels of lean maturity are meant to help you reflect on the current way your organization uses lean tools. They do not necessarily reflect the sequence in which these tools are implemented. Though 5S is the starting point for 90 percent of lean initiatives, it is possible for an organization to start by proper KPI cascading and implementing the daily management structure.
When the operations manager does not know the status of the production line, there will automatically be a pull signal for the underling departments to create team boards and show the performance. Performance will be improved when standards are generated, and all workstations are organized properly.

So, wherever you start in the pyramid, at the bottom or at the top, to become a true learning organization, you do need all four levels. The next chapters will explain different tools that are described in each of the four levels, why they are important, how to implement them, and what you can do as a lean transformation leader to teach and coach your colleagues in using the tool.

**Key Points:**
- *The four levels of lean maturity describe how a company grows from an organization that is doing a lean project to a true learning organization in which daily improvements are the norm.*
- *The first level is about setting standards with 5S and SOPs.*
- *The second level is about checking the standards with kamishibai and team boards.*
- *The third level is about improving the standards with kaizen, A3 thinking, and D2MAIC projects.*
- *The fourth level is about linking all improvement activities to the company goals.*

# Chapter 7:
# Level One: Setting Standards

*Every standard describes the current consensus
about the most safe, effective and efficient way of working.*

Standards play a major role in a lean organization. There are different reasons why determining the current safest, most efficient way of creating a good quality product is so important.

First, they describe the current best-known way to perform a task. It is important that team members who perform the same task talk about how the task is done and reach consensus about the way of working, to prevent imbalance. This imbalance of variation can lead to a difference in quality of the output, but also in a difference in process time: the time it takes to perform the task. Needless to say, the specialists who originally designed the way of working (for instance technical engineers, quality engineers, people from research and development) should be included in this discussion.

Second, these standards are the foundation for continuous improvement. Only when the team members have agreed on the current best way of performing the task can they discuss how it can be improved. If a group of people each have their own way of working, they will not always understand each other's improvement suggestions, which makes the discussions longer and the speed of defining improvements slower.

This chapter describes two different types of standards, the workplace organization standards to reduce the 8 wastes, for which the tool 5S is used (chapter 7.1), and the standards that describe how a process step is executed to reduce variability (chapter 7.2).

## 7.1 Setting the Standard with 5S

*5S is about organizing your workplace and the flow of work to improve reliability and productivity of a workstation.*

### 7.1.1 What Is It, and Why Is It Important?

5S is a name for a concept of workplace organization with the goal of reducing all 8 forms of waste, which is described by five stages, all named after a word that starts with S. **Sorting** helps keep only the necessary items at every workstation. **Straightening** prevents having people search for items and limits the quantities of items in a certain area. **Sweeping** helps people in discovering problems at an early stage and prevents dirt from compromising product quality. **Standardizing** helps the team to show and document the agreements at every workplace, which makes **sustaining** these standards possible.

5S is one of the tools used at the first level of lean maturity that helps setting the standards on how a workplace is organized. By identifying and demonstrating how a workstation should be organized to work efficiently, and how the work in process in managed, deviations from this way of working will be shown. When implemented right, a deviation from the standards should lead to action before it leads to delays. 5S is therefore a visual management tool that can prevent waste from occurring.

To be successful, it is important that teams define their own 5S standards. As a team working on a specific workstation, discussing whether a certain tool is needed and when to use it is not only the first step of workplace organization, but it is also the preparation for defining standard operating procedures (chapter 7.2).
Even without calling a set of standards 5S, at least some of those standards of workplace organization can be found in other environments.

I am sure that your kitchen has some 5S standards. You will have a fixed location for everything that you have in there. Pots and pans, cutlery, and glasses—everything is put in the same place every time. And chances are that the things you use most are kept in a place that is easiest to access when you need them. Coffee cups may be close to the coffee machine, and soap and detergent may be next to the sink. Kitchen appliances you need less often might be high up, in the back of the cabinets, or even in another room if you don´t use them that much.

You will also find 5S standards in supermarkets. Fortunately, all vegetables are kept close together, and so are the dairy products. Products are also always placed at the same spot every time to prevent you from having to search for them. Sweets are kept at the cashier. Imagine what would happen if this were not the case. You would have to search the entire supermarket for all your products every time you go shopping.

The concept of 5S is therefore not new to us, and I am sure even at work you already have defined some unofficial 5S standards. So, what does this workplace organization have to do with lean, and what is in it for the organization?

5S directly decreases all three enemies of lean. Waste decreases when we plan our layout in such a way that we do not need to walk or reach that far to find a tool. Overburden is reduced because a standard can prevent people from being stressed because they cannot find the right tools in time to keep takt time. Finally, imbalance is reduced when 5S standards are implemented because not having to search for parts can reduce the variance in cycle time.

Let us take a closer look at the influence of 5S on the eight wastes in the DOWNTIME sequence.

A clean and organized workplace where all parts are straightened and labeled prevents operators from using the wrong parts in production and therefore helps in preventing **defects**.

Having a clearly defined output area with a fixed maximum number of finished products tells the operators of a workstation to stop producing and therefore prevents **overproduction**.

Do you remember how waiting times influence lead times? The lower the quantity of the inventory, the shorter time a part has to wait before it is used. A maximum quantity for every part therefore also reduces **waiting times** for parts. The minimum quantity, on the other hand, can prevent the operator or machine from starvation, thus reducing the waiting time there.

Because people have organized the workplace in a way that they never have to search for parts, tools, or files, they can focus on what they are really good at: performing the actual task they are trained to do. 5S therefore reduces the amount of time with **non-used skills**.

You can apply the 5S principle not only to the workstation level, but to the plant level as well. Defining the standard layout also influences the amount of **transport** necessary to move products and parts within workstations and between workstations or departments.

As described above, when we define a fixed number of products that are allowed to be placed on a certain area, we manage **inventory,** with its fixed quantities for each part, product, and tool. Especially when we start the improvement loop of the 5S standards, one of the goals would be to reduce those inventories and make the workstation work even more efficient.

Within 5S, we focus on having the employee reach for a part, product, or tool with the least physical effort possible. We strive to reduce **motion**.

By reducing defects, 5S also reduces rework and therefore unnecessary effort, or **excess processing**.

So, the eight wastes, easily remembered through the DOWNTIME acronym, are indeed all addressed by 5S, which means productivity should improve when 5S is implemented well.

In addition to directly addressing all wastes—indirectly addressing imbalance and overburden—5S also promotes living according to the fourteen behavioral principles, as described in chapter 6.

Let us start with **principle three, using pull systems**. When our 5S standard has both a minimum and maximum quantity of parts, the upstream workstation or the warehouse can only deliver new parts when the quantity has reached less than the minimum.

One important part of 5S is documenting and sharing the standard (the fourth S), also known as **principle six, working with standards**.

One of the major goals of 5S is to **show abnormalities (principle seven),** such as simply not being able to put a product or part somewhere or finding materials or tools that do not belong at that workplace.

Last but not least, the sustaining step of 5S helps to promote continually checking whether the current standards are kept and if they are still valid. This **hansei,** or **self-reflection (principle fourteen),** should continually lead to small improvements of the standards.

> **Key Points:**
> - *5S is a concept to facilitate workplace organization and improve productivity.*
> - *5S directly reduces all eight forms of waste.*
> - *5S facilitates at least four of the fourteen behavioral principles.*

## 7.1.2 How to Implement 5S in Manufacturing

*Put all machinery in the best possible condition, keep it that way, and insist upon absolute cleanliness everywhere in order that a man may learn to respect his tools, his surroundings, and himself.*
—Henry Ford

Within the 5S concept, one can use multiple tools to work on each of the steps. More significantly, the sequence of working on 5S is important: first, we sort; second, we straighten; third, we sweep; fourth, we standardize; and fifth, we sustain the standard. This chapter shortly addresses all 5 of the stages. More information and examples of each of the 5S can be found in my small book called *Sustainable 5S.*

The first step is **SORT**. In this step we evaluate everything that can currently be found in the work area. Is the part, material, or tool necessary to perform the task? If yes, the part can stay; if no or if you are in doubt, the part is removed from the area.

One tool that we can use for sorting is the **red tag zone** (Tisbury 2012). The red tag zone is one location in the factory or department in which all materials and tools can be put that team members have labeled "unnecessary for my tasks." In this case, all the stuff that is removed from different workstations is identified with a red label and moved to the designated area.

This is a **continual process**. Parts can be moved to the red tag zone at all times, but when it turns out a part is needed at a certain workstation, the part can also be taken back into the work area and should then be included in the standard (step four).

If the tool stays in the red tag zone longer than a defined period, it can go back to a warehouse, which might be able to get it reused by handing it over to another department. If no one can reuse the part or tool, it can be thrown away or maybe even sold (Tisbury 2012). I've witnessed multiple 5S flea markets within our company; items that were tagged out were sold to our employees at very low prices. We donated the profits of the flea market to charity.

Next to sorting out what does not belong on the workplace, one can also think about **what should be added** to it. By doing a waste analysis of the workplace before you start implementing 5S, you can already make a big improvement in productivity if you know what types of wastes occur in the team. My book *Sustainable 5S* (Panneman, 2019) is mainly focused on this topic.

After sorting comes **STRAIGHTENING**, or **SETTING**. This means that after throwing out everything that people do not need at the workstation, the parts and materials that remain can be given a fixed location and fixed quantity. This can be referred to as the **3F principle**: a fixed product at a fixed location with a fixed quantity.

One example of setting these standards is the use of colored lines on the floor to show where something is allowed to wait. Another example is the use of shadow boards on the walls for tools (a board in which the outline of the tool is painted in the form of a shadow to show what tool is missing when the tool is not on its standard location). The goal of marking these locations is to show abnormalities and prevent a decrease of productivity because of something missing. Within three seconds, everybody passing by should be able to see whether something is missing. This is referred to as the **three-second rule**.

Unfortunately, there is no worldwide standard for the use of **different colors** for floor taping. My personal choice for use of colors, which match the recommendations of OHSE standards, would be as follows:

- Yellow shows the boundaries of the workstation.
- Blue shows work in process.
- Green indicates the finished product.
- Red is for defects and the red tag zone.
- Yellow-and-black striped tape is for places where nothing should be put—for instance, an area in front of moving doors or machines.

The third step is **SWEEP**, which the employees partly do themselves, depending on the workplace. Each team or individual should have his or her dedicated machines or workstations to clean at certain intervals. Cleaning by operators is important because nobody knows a machine better than the people who use it on a daily basis (Tajiri and Gotoh 1992).

While cleaning, operators might **discover small abnormalities** before they result in defects.
This is the foundation for lean tools such as autonomous maintenance (Tajiri and Gotoh 1992). Within a manufacturing hall, different zones can be shown with different colors to demonstrate which team or individual is responsible for which area.

Sweeping is a continual process as well. Cleaning a machine only once does not a 5S standard make. It's about defining a cleaning schedule to make sure the machine is always in a good state, preventing possible defects or delays. This transfer of ownership of keeping the machine clean is also the first step of autonomous maintenance (chapter 16).

The fourth S is for **STANDARDIZE**. As with every other agreement on the way of working, the layout and organizational agreements of the workplace should be documented in a standard document.

Usually a **picture** of the workplace or part of the workplace with a sweeping schedule suffices. It is also possible to glue all **3F (fixed place, fixed part, fixed quantity) information on the floor** or walls within the dedicated lines. Again, the main goal of 5S is to spot abnormalities as soon as possible. When a location is empty, we want to know what is missing. The standard fills that need.

We can use the documented standard, which in this case could be a one-pager, as a training document to teach others how the workplace is organized.

Finally, the standard is the starting point for continuous improvement. Only when we have documented the current state of the workplace (as agreed upon by all team members) can we discuss improvements of the standard (J. K. Liker 2004). Improvements might include the need for fewer tools at a workstation, an improvement of ergonomics, or a reduction of the time needed to keep the workstation clean.

The final S represents the **SUSTAIN** stage and is the most difficult to implement in practice. The tool that one can use is the previously mentioned mini-audit tool: **kamishibai**. By writing short questions on a T-card, everyone can do a mini-audit. The cards can include questions such as this: "Are all materials placed at their standard location?" Because kamishibai is the tool to check and sustain all standards (Niederstadt 2013), not just the 5S ones, chapter 8.1 describes it as a tool for that helps bring your organization to a level-two lean organization. For 5S audit inspiration; visit www.mudamasters.com and search for "5S audit Template".

In my experience, the red tag zone (for sorting) and kamishibai (for sustaining) are the most important tools to use to keep 5S an ongoing process instead of a one-time cleanup session. The items that do not belong at a workstation can constantly be moved to the red tag zone. When someone places a found item in the red tag zone, everybody has the opportunity to remove it and bring it back to the workstation where it belongs. Or—when it turns out it did have a function—a fixed location can be created at the workstation where it was found.

To share the success of your 5S event, make sure you measure productivity improvements due to the reduction of wastes that were achieved as a result of using 5S. For more examples about the different tools that can be used within the 5S stages and what they could look like, please read my book: *sustainable 5S*.

> **Key Points:**
> - The 3F principle (fixed product, fixed place, and fixed quantity) can help mark locations on the floor and on shadow boards to make it easily evident when something is visibly missing.
> - All standards should be documented so that they can be taught to others and used as the starting point for improvement.
> - The red tag zone and kamishibai are two tools that help make 5S a continual process rather than a one-time event.

## 7.1.3 How to Implement 5S in the Office

*If the 5S standards are not helping you to solve problems and improve performance, you are not doing it right.*

In the office environment, 5S can improve both the flow of paper as well as the flow of digital information. How do papers flow between and through offices? How long does the paperwork (and the colleague who has to work on it after you) wait before it is worked on? And how long does an employee have to look for the right person or file?

I believe at least three types of standards could be implemented under the 5S umbrella: health-related standards, physical standards, and virtual standards.

Creating an office that is healthy and pleasant to work in increases productivity (Westendorp and van Bodegom 2015). The first of the standards to emphasize is therefore the category of **HEALTH-RELATED STANDARDS**. These can be divided into three categories: ergonomics, general office characteristics, and accident prevention.
In terms of physical safety hazards, the most important part of health-related standards in the office environment is probably **ergonomics**. Do all employees

have desks and chairs that fit their body height? How is the PC or laptop used? Here are a few guidelines for sitting at your desk:

- Legs should be bent ninety degrees.
- Arms should be bent ninety degrees.
- When typing, eight to ten centimeters of the underarms should be supported by the desk.
- The distance between the eyes and monitor should be an arm's length.

Even better than just sitting is switching between sitting and standing while working. After smoking, the next most important health-related topic for improvement is the number of hours we spend sitting down in our lives, (Westendorp and Bodegom 2015). People who have a desk job should be able to change the height of their desk, so that they can have the option to work at their pc standing up. The team board meeting structure (chapter 8.2) is based on the idea of stand-up meetings, where all participants stand up instead of sitting on chairs.

Improving **the general working environment** can include the availability of enough daylight and fresh air and the prevention of noise pollution. These elements do not only influence the physical health of the employees but also the psychological health. A nice, clean, and healthy office is simply more pleasant to work in.

**Preventing accidents** is done by keeping the floor as clear of obstacles as possible so that the risk of stumbling is reduced as much as possible. This means keeping bags and shoes in the cabinets and not on the floor.
Cables should be bound together and neatly positioned on walls and near desks to prevent people from stumbling over them. Electrical appliances should be checked for safe use yearly.

In addition to health standards, 5S is about **PHYSICAL STANDARDS**. These standards contain information about where to put materials and machines so that wastes are minimized as much as possible. There are two categories within the physical standards: the organization of tools needed to perform a task and the organization of how the product or service flows through the office.

One strategy that you can use to define where to put supporting items is **zoning**. In an office 5S event, everything is taken out of cabinets and desks for the sorting stage, during which it is decided what needs to have a place in the office. Figure 5 differentiates between five different zones:

- Zone one is the space that you can reach from your office chair without moving the chair. Within that space are things that are put on the desk and are used continually.
- Zone two is the zone that you can reach using little movement, like stretching an arm to a cabinet of your desk. In this zone are items that are needed daily.
- Zone three is the space that is still inside the office, but you have to get up and walk to the item to get it. This zone is suitable for items that are needed weekly, such as reference material or literature.
- Zone four describes rooms outside the office—for instance, the coffee machine, printing rooms, or break rooms.
- Zone five includes the items that are seldom used, such as archives.

A bigger 5S challenge than organizing the items that are needed to perform a task is the **standardization of paper processes** for paper that flows through the office. Questions that you can ask to help define these processes are the following:
- What is my work in process (WIP)?
- How does the WIP enter the office?
- Where does the work go when the person is finished with his or her task?
- How does the employee know what task to work on next?

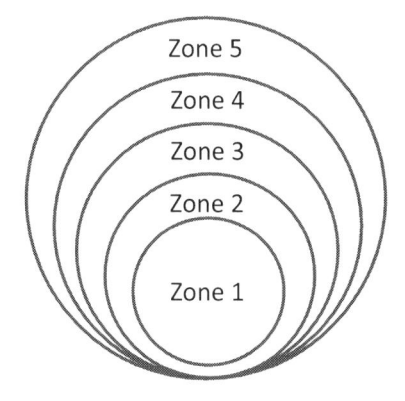

*Figure 5: Five zones of 5S standards*

There are multiple ways of bringing structure in the WIP in an office. You can have a rack or tray on your desk which makes it possible to sort paperwork on its side, which prevents people from stacking paperwork. A second option is to hang a tray on the wall at the entrance for people to bring the next work orders in. This way the team can see how much work is waiting to be processed. To prevent waste, think about where to put the input or output of the flow of paper—on a desk, on a door, or maybe on a team board.

In addition to health and physical standards, many processes are hidden in the computer, and there are **VIRTUAL STANDARDS** for those processes. This category includes a standard for handling e-mail, a standard for folder structures on a server, and a standard for the prevention of having multiple copies of the same file.

In terms of **e-mail**, many wastes can be found. Rereading e-mails, forgetting to respond to them, and searching for older e-mails—it all takes time. A smart inbox system includes only e-mails that are still awaiting actioning (Allan 2001). E-mails that have already been read and e-mails that have led to completed actions should be archived. You will find more information on how to optimize your way of dealing with e-mails in chapter 18.

Time taken spent finding a file on a server is, by definition, a waste. A **standard folder structure** can help prevent time wasted while looking for files. One rule of thumb is to have a maximum of seven folders within a folder, with the seventh one always being an archive folder. Having a maximum of six options to choose from makes it easier for the individual to click through the folders to find a certain document.

Finally, **discourage having local copies** as much as possible, and keep all documents on a shared server so that team members can always find the latest version. This prevents changing two different versions of the same document, which eventually leads to overwriting one version of the two.
We can improve both physical and virtual processes with 5S. When setting 5S standards, think about both safety and flow. If the standard does not affect at least one of those, it might be that it is unnecessary to create it. Marking the location where a monitor is placed on a desk usually improves neither safety nor flow, so I would leave changes like that out of the 5S initiative.

**Key Points:**
- *5S standards in the office can be divided into health standards, physical standards, and virtual standards.*
- *Health standards include ergonomics, accident prevention, and environmental issues.*
- *Physical attributes describe the layout of the office.*
- *Virtual standards describe the use of e-mail software and the folder structure on the server.*

## 7.1.4 Training Tips

> *Good workplaces develop beginning with the 5Ss. Bad workplaces fall apart beginning with the 5Ss.*
> —Hiroyuki Hirano

5S is one of the topics where one can apply the 70/20/10 rule. The **70/20/10 rule** says that the most effective way of learning something new consists of 70 percent doing, 20 percent coaching, and 10 percent classroom training (Lombardo and Eichinger 2006).

For a 5S workshop, plan two whole days with the team should be enough to set the first 5S standards. I would use the first hour of the workshop to explain the theory behind 5S, using the 7 steps of designing a training element described in chapter 2.1. This means explaining first the *why*, followed by the *what*, and then the *how*. The *why* and the *what* parts are described above.

For the *how* part, there are two possibilities. When possible, **visit a department** that already has a mature 5S culture, so that participants could see the benefits in practice.
When 5S is new to an organization, you can use a very short presentation, one slide for each S, with each slide showing pictures of the tools that they can use to

implement each step of 5S.

After the presentation, we would use the rest of the time to put 5S into practice, starting with the sorting-, straightening- and sweeping phase in the rest of the first day. Sorting helps you to remove things at the workstation that you do not need. It does not help you to determine things that are missing already. Therefore, I recommend doing a **waste observation and -analysis** in the area, to be able to add items to the workplace and prevent searching and motion and directly see improvements. Observer people working and focus on the moments where a colleague is searching for a tool or material, especially when he needs to leave his workstation to find it.

For the straightening phase, materials that needed to be built or bought—like shadow boards, furniture, or things that could help in keeping parts separated from one another—could be listed and ordered.

The best way to create lines on the floor—which usually makes sense in the manufacturing environment—is by using plastic tape, which makes it possible to change the layout of the department when necessary. Make sure there is plenty of tape available so that people can make lines on the floor as soon as the ideal layout is defined. It might also be helpful to clean the floor with ethanol before putting on the tape so that the tape will stick well.

The second day would be used to document the standards that had been implemented already, using pictures as much as possible.

The sustaining past of 5S would be a suitable first topic for kamishibai checks. The new team standard would from that moment on include doing regular 5S checks. In the beginning, the team itself could do daily checks at both the beginning and at the end of the shift, to make sure everything is according to standard. Later, people from other departments could do the kamishibai, which improves cross learning. Finally, managers could do the checks as part of their leader standard work (chapter 7.2).

If your organization implements 5S, it could also help if a 5S champion from one department leads the workshop for another department. Or you could have a team leader or group leader of the team training his or her teams. Being able to teach another team what 5S is all about increases knowledge about the topic.

This means the role for the lean transformation leader (as chapter 1 has already discussed) is to train the trainer rather than alone facilitating all workshops.

In the office, the flow of the workshop is similar. The only difference is in the *straighten* part, in which the slides should contain examples of desks where the zoning principle is applied and an example of how to handle the digital folder structure.

A final tip for implementing 5S in the office is to hand out small rewards. For instance, for finding the oldest hard-copy document in the building, the largest number of pens that are found on one desk, or the largest number of documents that can be archived or even thrown out.

**Key Points:**
- *5S training sessions should be 70 percent doing, 20 percent coaching, and 10 percent classroom learning.*
- *Include a gemba walk for a department where 5S is implemented.*
- *Use experienced team leaders or operators from other departments.*

## 7.2 Setting the Standard with Standard Work

*If you can't describe what you are doing as a process, you don't know what you're doing.*
—W. Edwards Deming

### 7.2.1 What Is It, and Why Is It Important?

In addition to 5S, standard work is part of the first level of lean maturity and includes *when* and *how* a certain task is done. In a manufacturing environment, emphasis is put on *how* a certain task is done; in an office environment, the *when* part is the main topic of discussion.

The first reason standard work is so important is that it reduces all three enemies of lean.

**Overburden** is prevented because every documented way of working, also known as the standard operating procedure (SOP), describes *how* a task should be done in a safe way. It can include what protective gear to wear and what tools to use to prevent ergonomically incorrect movement.

**Waste** is prevented because a standard work description should teach the operator how to perform the task in an efficient way for both person and machine. It can, for instance, include how to set up a machine to produce at the right quality from the start and prevent defects. The standard could also document a fixed-batch size (number of products in one batch) to prevent overproduction, inventories, and waiting time for multiple products.

**Imbalance** is prevented when the standard also includes *when* something should be done. Especially for indirect functions, balancing the amount of work on a daily, weekly, or even monthly basis is done using standard work.
In the team board meetings for instance, which chapter 8.2 discusses, a team can decide to discuss bigger topics on different days of the week. The daily meeting can therefore be kept short.
Also, when we define standards on a machine setting level, it can reduce

variability of the output of that machine (the six-sigma approach).

Standard work also facilitates adherence to the fourteen Toyota principles.

**Principle one: Focusing on the long term** is implemented when everyone in the organization (especially managers) has defined his or her standard work. This includes an overview of tasks necessary to create long-term results and, when applicable, how to behave during these tasks. Discussing these lists with their own managers should prevent managers from spending too much time firefighting and focus on what is really important: process improvement.

**Principle four: Leveling of the workload** is done when the standards include when a certain task should be done and the time necessary in which to do it.

**Principle six: Working with standards facilitates continuous improvement**. Only when the team agrees on the current way of working can they start implementing improvements. If different team members have different ways of working (and therefore do not have a standard), it is difficult to discuss possible improvements.

**Principle seven: Make problems visible** when standards are not kept. This chapter covers a way of defining standard work that one can use as a visual management tool at the same time. When someone does not manage to finish his or her standard tasks for the day, this is instantly visible.

**Principle fourteen: The use of hansei (self-reflection)** is encouraged when the standard includes the list of tasks to do each day or week. It will challenge the individual to think about what his or her most important tasks are and when to do them.

The remainder of this section will describe a structured approach to define standard work. This chapter is split in two parts: standard work for manufacturing and standard work for indirect functions.

> **Key points:**
> - *Standards are necessary to document the current best way of working and organizing.*
> - *Standards prevent all three enemies of lean (imbalance, overburden and waste).*
> - *Standard work facilitates at least five of the fourteen behavioral principles.*

## 7.2.2 How to Implement SOPs in Manufacturing

> *Where there is no standard there can be no kaizen.*
> —Taiichi Ohno

To systematically implement standard work in every department, the following five steps can be used: create a SIPOC (an abbreviation for supplier, input, process, output, and customer), create process maps and/or value stream maps, evaluate availability of standard operating procedures (SOPs), create missing SOPs, and build an easy accessible SOP-management system.

The first step in systematically defining standard work is to create a **SIPOC**. The SIPOC is a visual rendering of Deming´s system model (Scholtes 1998), a model that visualizes the complexity of a system, where the word "system" is defined as a combination of processes, methods, and employees who work together toward a common target. The goal of the SIPOC—and systems thinking—is to visualize the patterns in a system by looking at it from a whole instead of from different pieces, such as departments or specific processes (Senge 1990).

The value of the SIPOC compared with the process map or a value stream map is that not only tasks or production steps are visualized, but also the communication complexity between different departments or functions. It helps the team members think about who their customers are and how they know they are serving them well. Finally, the SIPOC helps set the boundaries for a process that will be standardized in the following steps. By agreeing on where the process starts and ends beforehand, you set the scope for the rest of the standardizing process.

The SIPOC usually also plays a big role in six sigma projects, as we will see in chapter 9.3.

The next step after building the SIPOC would be to reduce these complexities, which will lead to higher effectiveness and efficiency in all its processes (Morieux and Tollman 2014). This is why the SIPOC can play an important role in improvement activities, such as kaizen events.

SIPOCs can have different forms, as figure 6 shows below. Personally, I always build the SIPOC with sticky notes on the first day of a kaizen event.

When creating a SIPOC, you do not randomly start filling in the different fields. You first start with a discussion of the goals of the system to get alignment on what is the focus of the process that is being mapped (Scholtes 1998), after which you can start filling in the columns of the SIPOC itself.

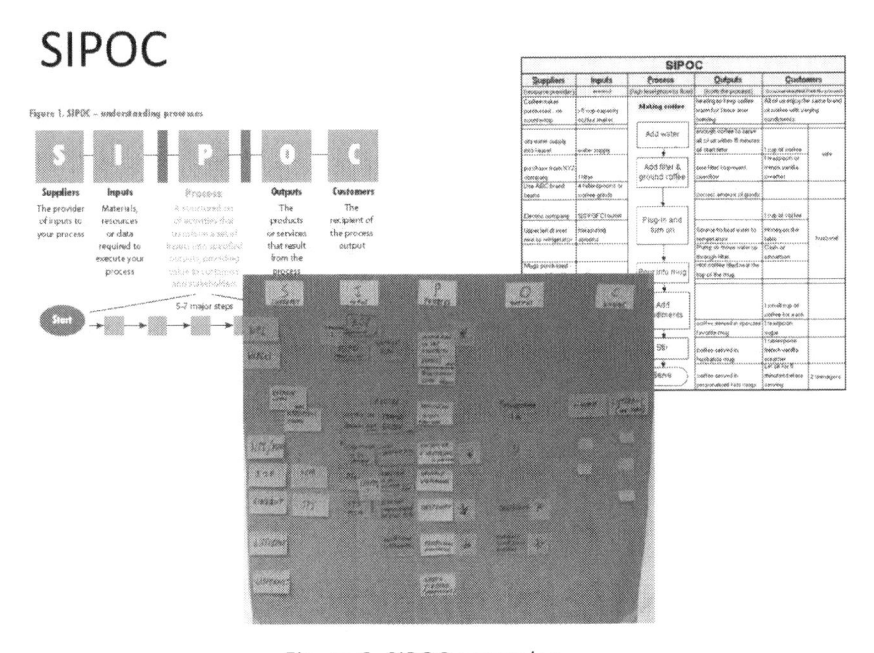

*Figure 6: SIPOC examples*

**The goal** of the system answers the question of which advantages or possibilities the customers get by working with the system (Scholtes 1998). It is the *why* of the process. The goal should describe the needs of the (internal) customers that are served by the system being mapped. Ideally, the goal would be something unselfish and serving, which makes the tasks defined in the system worthwhile for the people who work in the system.

When the goal is defined, one can start with the SIPOC itself, starting on the side of the **customers**.
The only way to measure whether a system is functioning well is to know what the customers are demanding from that system. One system can have multiple customers. Customers can be both internal as well as external; they can be an individual or a group. This depends on the aggregation level for which the SIPOC is defined.

**The output** is the third step in building the SIPOC and describes the output the system creates to serve the customers. Note that, especially in office processes, the output of a sub-step is not always only the part that moves to the next process step. There can be more outputs. In defining this part, discussing the feedback loop is usually interesting. How do the people in the system know that their output is satisfying to the customer? How often and how soon after the output is produced is feedback given? Information gathering is an important part of the system.

Scholtes describes two questions one should always ask the customer: "What are you not getting from us that you need?" "What are you getting from us that you do not need?" (Scholtes 1998).

The next step describes the definition of **processes** in the system. What are the key steps the system performs in producing the output the customer demands? This demarcation can help give direction toward future improvement activities. In this initial stage of setting the standards, I propose you capture the main tasks of the process in 5 to 7 steps. This will prevent the team from going in too many details about the process.

Because the processes in the SIPOC are directly linked to customer demand, it makes sense to have key performance indicators (KPIs) to measure if the output still meets the customers' standards. Feedback loops between teams or departments within the system to discuss KPIs and feedback from customers can be initiated by using team boards (which chapter 8.2 discusses).

After defining how the system produces, one can define the system **input** and, after that, the **suppliers.** For every defined process step, there are different materials, information, or service needs that one should define in these steps.

Just as on the customer side, the supplier can be an individual or a group and internal or external.
Improving the supplier side of the system is important because defects or delayed deliveries can influence the processes and the output of the system directly (Scholtes 1998).

Systems are the reason employees do what they do. If people do something unexpected, it is usually because of a gap in the system (Morieux and Tollman 2014) (Scholtes 1998) (Senge 1990). The SIPOC helps create insight into the complexity of a system, after which you can improve the system with the goal of smoothing the flow from suppliers to customers.

By building in regular feedback loops between different stakeholders of the system with team boards, you can improve not only the efficiency of the system but also the effectiveness. The SIPOC is therefore a valuable management tool that you can use in kaizen events or other improvement activities, such as projects.

The second step in defining standard work is to **MAP THE SUBPROCESSES** the SIPOC defines in a value stream map (VSM) or process map. Both tools have the same goal: to define what the processes or subprocesses in the SIPOC are and to make waste visible. The goal of this step is to describe the process from the product or service perspective and improve the flow of the process (as was explained in part 2).

**Value stream mapping** is used on the factory or even supply-chain level to map the flow, especially the parts that keep the product or service from flowing. For every process box that is drawn, standard work needs to be defined. Chapter 11 describes value stream mapping and how it is used.

**Process mapping** is a tool that you can use at a lower aggregation level, for instance in a department. The process has six different symbols (for process, inventory, transport, decision, check, and delay), that can demonstrate the complexity of a process at a level of detail that is not included in the value stream map. When the process map is made in swim-lane form, it can also show the interfaces between different functions or departments. This is the time to get into more details about the process steps and learn about the different way of working between people.

The symbols of the process map represent the details of each sub-step of the SIPOC. This will help you define which SOPs are needed, because in the end, all steps (hence, all symbols) need to be covered in standard work.

The third step in defining standard work for a workstation is therefore to **CHECK WHAT STANDARDS ARE THERE** based on the process maps that are made. Standard work has to document all symbols in the process map and every process box in the VSM. It is possible to combine multiple steps into one document when multiple tasks are part of the same work cycle.

Step four is to **GENERATE THE STANDARDS** that are not yet defined and update the standards that are already there to take up the least possible number of pages. It is not uncommon that operating procedures are documents of enormous size, which results in operators not using them because of the amount of text. By reducing the size of the SOPs to one page as often as possible, including pictorial examples, people will have the tendency to use them more often.

**Standards for production** usually contain a list of activities (what to do), detailed information on how to execute the different steps (how to do it), and ideally a picture that shows the steps in one visual. Symbols can be used to show what steps or sub steps are critical for safety, quality, or timing elements. Finally, a document number and owner should be mentioned. The best way to document the current way of working is to involve operators who perform the task while documenting the task.

**Standards for products** can contain extra information on what machine settings to use for a specific product. Especially in a production environment where there are multiple products and multiple variables, it can be worthwhile to find out what machine settings work best for which products, because there is a fairly big chance they are not the same for all products.

**Standards for supporting functions** can differ from production standards. Depending on the function, a list of daily activities can suffice, with the possibility for the individual to tick off the activity as it is done.

**Leader standard work** describes a more detailed approach, which not only describes when somebody is supposed to do what, but also includes what behavior is expected of individuals to show when they do it. In this case, the standard not only lists the tasks or standard meetings; it also defines how the person should act within those meetings. The next section further discusses this.

The final step for defining standard work is to describe **HOW TO SHARE** the standards. A system is needed in which all standards are logically presented to the employees (the 5S within the database).

You can facilitate finding the right SOP by building a tree structure of SOPs and a **PowerPoint presentation** to click through the tree to find the SOP you are looking for.
Larger companies may have other **databases** available in which all standard documents are saved and shared; even the number of improvements and different versions are saved and tracked.

Next to the official digital database, it can be necessary to place some of the procedures on the shop floor in the form of **hard copies**. This makes it easier to perform the kamishibai audits that are done to help sustain and improve the standard. They also help training new operators and can be used as reference for these new operators when they start working on their jobs on their own.

Make sure that these hard copies are kept at standard locations throughout your site, so that you can update them when the standards themselves are refreshed. You want to prevent old versions of the SOP wondering around in drawers and cabinets. A good place to keep the hard copy SOPs is on the daily management boards.

Standard work is the foundation for all improvements and therefore the basis of every lean implementation. When current working methods are not standardized, variation might exist in the process. Especially in indirect functions, these variations can lead to problems. When employees all agree on the current way of performing a task, collectively finding improvements is easier.

> **Key Points:**
> - *The SIPOC can help determine what the goals of the team are and what processes should be standardized.*
> - *Value stream mapping and process mapping can help determine what process steps within these processes need SOPs.*
> - *New and updated SOPs should always be shared with the team and should be available for its users.*

### 7.2.3 How to Implement SOPs in the Office

*Cultural change is only possible when the behaviors you would like to see are defined and measured.*

For support functions and managers, defining standard work can be more challenging, especially since their work cannot be planned 100 percent of the time. However, the structural approach for defining standard work in the office is the same as for the manufacturing environment.
In manufacturing, the SOPs will include more technical details about performing the tasks that need to be done, with the use of a lot of pictures. The office environment will usually have more discussion when defining the SIPOC and process map. What is the goal of the department? What are the main processes within the department? With indirect functions, defining what the key processes are and therefore the key customers and suppliers, is more complex than in a manufacturing environment.

And what about management roles? Next to the plannability of their work, there is a tendency in western companies to give managers more freedom and autonomy over their work. They will receive yearly targets and maybe a monthly meeting with the boss, without a clear expectation about what it is that they should do on a daily, weekly or monthly basis.

Not having this clear overview, of what we call **leader standard work**, can be a cause for major disruptions in a site, because a change of site manager or production manager could possibly change the entire way in which the daily business is being run. To prevent these disruptions, we want to document the daily, weekly and monthly tasks of these managers and indirect functions.

When a new manager starts, he or she can start his or her new job by simply following the standard work of his predecessor, which is the most efficient way of running the business at the moment. Based on that standard, the new manager can make changes, as long as they are discussed with his or her boss and team members.

For lean organizations, activities that are typically included in leader standard work are daily meeting structure meetings, kamishibai, gemba walks and activities or reports that people need to hand in regularly.

The next challenge of leader standard work is not to focus only on whether the task or job was done but also on what behavior the person has shown during these activities and meetings.

The first challenge of leader standard work is defining **THE *WHAT* PART**. What tasks does the person put on his or her standard work sheet? Figure 7 shows an example of the leader standard work for a lean transformation leader that I created for myself when I had that role.

**You can plan activities** for different intervals; in this example, they are daily to monthly since one A4 consists of all standard activities for a month. My standard work took about 20 percent of my weekly available time, which left 80 percent of my time available for workshops and training sessions. The amount of work that you can standardize depends on the level of the organization where you work. As a rule of thumb, you can use the following percentages for the amount of work that can be standardized (Mann 2005):

- Shop-floor employee, up to 95 percent.
- Team leader, up to 80 percent.
- Group leader or supervisors, up to 50 percent.

- Area managers or value stream managers, up to 25 percent.
- General Managers and executives, up to 10 percent.

Using white cells as the color to show that something should be done makes it easy to show at a later stage if something is done by **using color-coding**. If the task is completed, mark it green; if not, mark it red.

This type of standard work can capture a few types of activities, starting with the responsibilities a person has in the management and accountability structure. A lean organization typically has a fixed **daily management structure (chapter 10.1)** in which team performance is discussed and problems can flow to the people providing supportive functions and to management in a matter of hours (Mann 2005). These meetings can be both disciplinary and interdisciplinary, depending on the daily business, and people can take part in multiple meetings. In lean organizations, these meetings are usually stand-up meetings that use a team board. Due to my role as a lean facilitator who helps implement the daily management system, there are a lot of team board meetings mentioned in my standard work (figure 7).

A second topic I like to see in leader standard work is **gemba walks and kamishibai**. With **gemba walks,** managers come out of their offices and visit the shop floor to learn about the processes and problems that occur there (Mann 2005).

At the same time, visiting the gemba gives the manager the opportunity to ask coaching questions and promote continuous improvement (Rother 2010). In addition to asking coaching questions, the manager can perform a kamishibai.

**Other activities** that one can add to the standard work can contain everything that is important to the person that needs to be done regularly, which in my example includes communication activities and updating lagging KPIs.

The WHAT part of leader standard work does not help you review standard work—whether you have done a good job. You need, therefore, to define how somebody is supposed to act to be able to review performance (Daniels 2000): **THE *HOW* PART.**

| Activities | Interval | CW 34 M T W T F | CW 35 M T W T F | CW 36 M T W T F | CW 37 M T W T F |
|---|---|---|---|---|---|
| Teamboard FSD (tier 1) | Daily | | | | |
| Teamboard Didi (tier 1) | Daily | | | | |
| Teamboard tier 2 | 2 per week | | | | |
| Lean Steering committtee Meeting | Weekly | | | | |
| Kaizen Escalation Meeting + update Teamboards | Weekly | | | | |
| Lean Certifizierungen (kaizens & 30/60/90) | Weekly | | | | |
| Teamboard Packaging (tier 1) | Biweekly | | | | |
| Teamboard Orderdesk (tier 1) | Biweekly | | | | |
| Teamboard Procurement (tier 1) | Biweekly | | | | |
| Teamboard Prod. Control (tier 1) | Biweekly | | | | |
| Kamishibai | Biweekly | | | | |
| 3C's Support | Biweekly | | | | |
| Newsletter Kaizen | Monthly | | | | |
| Newsletter Lean | Monthly | | | | |
| Update Lead time KPI | Monthly | | | | |
| Maturity Matrix | Monthly | | | | |

*Figure 7: Leader Standard Work example: the What part*

Since Jeffrey Liker wrote *The Toyota Way* in 2004, more and more people learned that lean is about **behavior**. When we would like to review whether leaders have done a good job in the meetings they attended, we therefore need to define what these behaviors are (Webers 2010).

Figure 8 shows another example of the leader standard work for a lean transformation leader, or any one that is involved in coaching. It illustrates the behaviors necessary to facilitate a cultural change by **asking questions** about suggestions for improvement (kaizen) and **positively reinforcing** someone when that person has done a great job.

Figure 8 shows an example that elaborates on the need for behavioral-based standard work as follows: the coach can visit all **team board meetings** as planned (ten a week) and not say a word. In figure 7, the checklist would be green on the entire sheet even though the coach might not have added any value to the meetings.

Figure 8 mentions behaviors for any coach to demonstrate during the team board meetings. How often was feedback about the meeting efficiency given? How often was information about the kaizen events shared with a team?

And how many times did the coach compliment someone on his or her behavior in the meeting? Those are behaviors that can tell, whether the coaching task was done right.
The trick about these behaviors is that they should be **100 percent amendable** by the individual. Using his format, every individual can discuss his or her performance with his or her manager.

It would make sense, of course, to discuss the behaviors with the team and the manager of the individual before you define your standard work to make sure all are aligned on what doing a good job means for that individual.

The next step in being able to review the leader standard work is to add a **scale and weight factor** to each behavior. Doing this makes it possible to quantify behavior and prioritize certain activities or behaviors (Daniels 2000). In the example in figure 8, the total number of points I could earn in one week is five hundred. Counting how often I've shown a certain behavior will give me one through five points, which will then be multiplied by the weight factor.

| Teamboard meetings | Count | 0 | 1 | 2 | 3 | 4 | 5 | Weight | Points |
|---|---|---|---|---|---|---|---|---|---|
| Presence | | 0 | 1 2 | 3 4 | 5 6 | 7 | 8 >= | 5 | |
| Ask or give Team Feedback | | 0 | 1 2 | 3 4 | 5 6 | 7 | 8 >= | 10 | |
| Positive reinforcement | | 0 | 1 2 | 3 4 | 5 6 | 7 | 8 >= | 10 | |
| Action/3C/Kaizen defined | | 0 | 1 | 2 | 3 | 4 | 5 >= | 10 | |
| Status VSM improvements shared | | 0 | 1 | 2 | 3 | 4 | 5 >= | 10 | |

| Kaizen events | Count | 0 | 1 | 2 | 3 | 4 | 5 | Weight | Points |
|---|---|---|---|---|---|---|---|---|---|
| Coaching questions participants | | 0 | 1 | 2 | 3 | 4 | 5 >= | 5 | |
| Personal reinforcement | | 0 | 1 2 | 3 4 | 5 6 | 7 8 | 9 >= | 10 | |
| next steps discussed | | 0 | 1 2 | 3 4 | 5 6 | 7 8 | 9 >= | 10 | |

| Lean Steering Commitee | Count | 0 | 1 | 2 | 3 | 4 | 5 | Weight | Points |
|---|---|---|---|---|---|---|---|---|---|
| Decisions to be made pre-defined | | no | | | | | yes | 5 | |
| Celebrate sucesses | | no | | | | | yes | 5 | |

| Kaizen & 30/60/90 | Count | 0 | 1 | 2 | 3 | 4 | 5 | Weight | Points |
|---|---|---|---|---|---|---|---|---|---|
| Asked individulas for Progress | | 0 | 1 2 | 3 4 | 5 6 | 7 8 | 9 >= | 10 | |
| support in kaizen implementation | | 0 | 1 | 2 | 3 | 4 | 5 >= | 10 | |

Calendarweek:

*Figure 8:* Leader standard work example—the HOW part

Attending at least eight team board meetings per week will give the coach the maximum of five points for this behavior; the weight factor of five will multiply these points to twenty-five.

When feedback is given about the efficiency of the meeting in all eight of them, the coach can earn another fifty points (five multiplied by ten). Note that the weight factor here is twice as high as the meeting attendance.

As with all lean tools, the goal of the tool is to improve performance continually. Thinking about what behavior you should be showing and reflecting on whether you have displayed this behavior helps you improve your personal effectiveness. Even more important is that cultural change is only possible when you define and measure the behaviors you would like to see (Daniels 2000). Using these templates with defined desired behavior can also help you in your coaching dialogues as they were described in chapter 3.

Standard work is one of the most important parts of lean organization. Only when you predetermine how a certain task should be done can you measure whether the job is done properly.

Above is an example of how one can define standard work for managers and people performing supporting functions. Just like standard operating procedures in production, these documents are living documents that are continually subject to changes to maximize the performance of each individual.

**Key Points:**
- *For indirect functions and leaders, standard work should include behavioral-based indicators.*
- *For each what the leader does, you can add a how, listing the behaviors you would like to see exhibited.*
- *A ranking system makes it possible to discuss behavior with one other and use it for evaluation and coaching.*

## 7.2.4 Training Tips

*Creating standard work is a team effort. Supervisors, operators, planners, and engineers collectively agree on the task content and work sequence.*
J. Nicholas

As with 5S, we start with the *why* part of standard work. Why is it important for everyone in the organization to have standard work? When you're leading training on this topic, you could start by asking the group why operators should have standard work. Answers will come up that include assuring safety, quality, and efficiency as described earlier.

The second question to ask is how they know that the managers do a good job. How do they assure quality, make sure that the managers are effective, let alone consistent? If you swap one manager for another one, how do you train the new manager? How do you make sure he or she does a good job? And now my personal favorite question: what are the risks of not embedding a manager's job into leader standard work?

When you think about these questions, the need for having a standard as a manager starts to make sense.

The next step is to define what kind of tasks should be included in the leader standard work. Try not use slides for this topic. Rather, use the collective knowledge of the group by asking its members what kind of information a person needs to do his or her job on both the production and management level. Simply draw a blown-up version of an A4 document on the flip chart and put the different elements that come from the group on it.

At this point, the group mentions all the important information, which is described above. When the group doesn't do this, ask questions until the group mentions most of the important aspects of *what* and *when*.
The main question that needs to be answered is: How do you know you are doing it right in the present moment?
The interesting discussion starts when the group discusses the *how* part. For production, it is widely accepted to take pictures of a single step within the work

sequence and describe how one is supposed to execute a certain part of the job. For people working in supportive functions, around 50 to 70 percent of their job can be captured in how-to steps.

Most discussion, however, usually comes when the group comes to defining leader standard work. How do you determine how a manager should act within his or her role as described above? Usually managers do not even discuss this part of the role among themselves. Each manager gets assigned lagging targets, such as cost reductions within the department, and then can do whatever they want in the way the department is managed.

This scenario makes it very difficult to know for sure whether a manager is doing the right thing today. This is why Daniels (2000) and Webers (2010) both describe the power of behavioral indicators in leader standard work. Define what behavior a manager should show in a way that one can measure it.

The best way for managers to define their standard work is a handshake process between the teams and their managers, which they cannot do in a training session. Managers need to align their own standard work with both their own managers and with their own team members. In addition, the standard work sheet will evolve over time, so don't worry about the details in the first draft. To repeat the 70/20/10 rule from chapter 7.1.4, you should practice and improve the actual leader standard work sheets in real life, on the job (the 70%) after creating a first draft in a classroom training setting (the 10%).

**Key Points:**
- *Start with why production needs standards and then ask why a manager should not have these standards as well.*
- *The content of the leader standard work is not complex. The group can brainstorm what kind of tasks should be listed in the leader standard work.*

# Chapter 8:
# Level Two: Checking the Standard

*We should continually check whether the standards are still followed, to sustain our previous efforts, and to find new improvements.*

We have now covered the two most important tools for an organization to reach level one of lean maturity: 5S and standard work. They are the most common tools within the lean philosophy that help you to gain consensus about the current standard way of working in all levels of the organization.

The second level of lean maturity will be about checking if standards are followed, so that corrective action can be taken when they are not. Before a team can focus on (further) improving its current way of working, it is important to make sure the current way of working is sustained to prevent variability of the output and sustain improvements that are made in the past.

Following a standard can be a challenging thing, especially if people have been using a certain way of working for more than twenty years before it was changed.

There are at least two tools within the lean toolbox that can help us sustain the current level of performance. The first one is the kamishibai, which is a Japanese term used for the tool that facilitates mini audits. For every change that is difficult, a kamishibai might help sustain the change and promote discussion of its importance. Section 8.1 describes the kamishibai in detail.

The second tool that can be used for checking standards is the team board. In the so-called stand-up meetings in which a team meets in front of a physical board, teams can discuss their performance on a daily basis and see if there are any deviations in output that they need to address. Whenever the variation of the output increases, the team board should visualize this change so that the team can address it in their daily meeting. Section 8.2 describes the team board in more detail.

## 8.1 Checking the Standard with Kamishibai

*How wonderful it is to have somebody else come to my workstation
and help me find my next improvement.*
—Gunnar Düvel

### 8.1.1 What Is It, and Why Is It Important?

Kamishibai is an audit tool used for two things: process confirmation and coaching. It consists of small audits that can help you confirm that the current standards are still used, and it helps you engage with colleagues and coaching them in finding the next possible improvements (Niederstadt 2013).

The kamishibai can help managers while they are doing their **gemba walks,** visiting the shop floor to talk to employees about their work, learning about the processes, and learning about the problems the employees have and how the process can be improved. Instead of having only general small talk with an employee, a manager can use the kamishibai card to facilitate a specific, process-oriented conversation about improvement.

One example of a situation in which kamishibai is used for process confirmation is having a kamishibai card for **5S. Regular mini audits** can help sustain a clean, organized, and, most of all, safe workplace. By asking questions like "Do all items have a standard location on this workstation?" and "Is the workstation cleaned to conform with standards?" 5S becomes an ongoing process instead of a one-time cleaning session. When the card also includes questions about how the 5S standards are changing over time to improve productivity, you also link the usage of both 5S and kamishibai towards continuous improvement.

The kamishibai can also check **behavioral performance**—whether people work according to the defined standard work in HOW to perform a certain task. When a person does not work according to standard, there are two possible reasons: either the employee is not trained in the way of working and therefore needs training, or the defined standard is unclear (or even wrong) and needs adjustment. The last one results in kaizen (see chapter 9.1).

Finally, the kamishibai can also check the WHAT side of **standard work**. Even when an improvement is documented into standard work, it is not uncommon for employees to unconsciously slip back into their old ways of working. The kamishibai therefore not only helps sustain 5S, but it helps in sustaining the improvements in all standards (Niederstadt 2013).

In addition to being used to check for deviations from the standard way of working, the kamishibai can be used to check behavior indicators defined at the operational level. Topics could include safety, team efforts in kaizen, and the use of the team board. To be able measure performance this way, it is important for standard operating procedures to describe not only WHAT to do at a certain task but also HOW to do it.

The kamishibai system is shown in figure 9 and includes the following segments: a plan board, T-cards with one green side and one red side, and an attendance list to see who has performed audits. The 3C list (in which the three Cs stand for concern, cause, and countermeasure) on the team board will be used to document outcomes of the kamishibai when necessary, with the reason and the possible countermeasure.

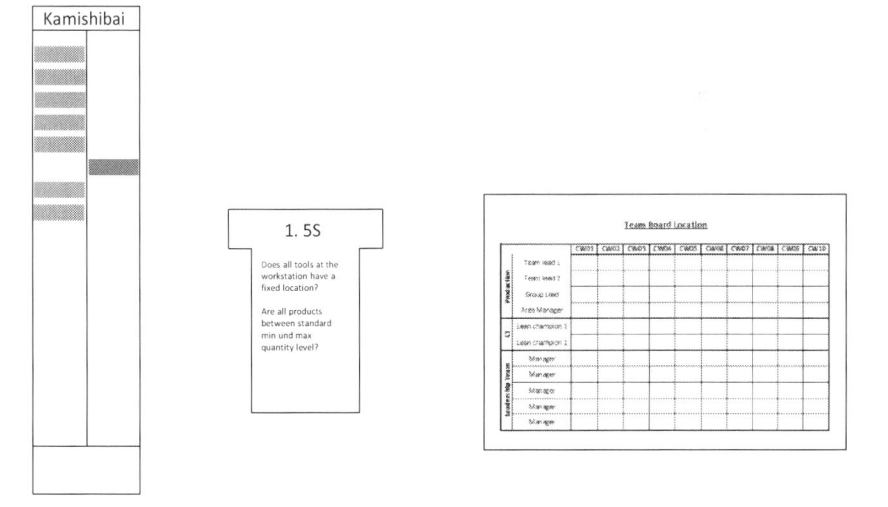

*Figure 9: Examples of a kamishibai plan board (left), a 5S T-card (middle), and an audit history (right)*

The **plan board** contains two columns: on the left side, the cards are placed that have not been run in a particular period. On the right side, the results of the audits performed for that time period are shown, with the green side facing forward when the standard was sustained, and the red side facing forward when the auditor has found something to improve.

Each **T-card** contains a title, such as "5S" or "Standard Work," with a few simple questions the auditor can ask an employee of choice at the workstation (Niederstadt 2013). The other side of the card could contain the answers to the question or a hint of where the answer can be found—for instance, at a server location.

The **attendance sheet demonstrates** who has done a kamishibai audit and signals to the team leader that the results of the kamishibai should be discussed in the next team board meeting. The list also shows who is regularly visiting the gemba and who possibly needs extra training to increase the comfort level when going to the gemba and performing an audit.

When the questions on the card can be answered positively, the card can be returned with the green side to the front. When one of the questions is answered negatively, the card is put back, facing the red side. The deviation of the standard is then written on the **3C list**, with an explanation and possible solution or kaizen to prevent the deviation from happening again. We will come back to this way of working in section 8.2.

You can make kamishibai cards for all (lean) tools an organization uses (including the kamishibai itself) to check whether they are used properly to find the next improvement (Rother 2010). You can also repeat basic knowledge during these kamishibai checks. Here are some examples:

Safety questions:
- How do I know what kind of protective gear I need to wear?
- Where are the first-aid boxes/fire extinguishers/emergency exits?
- What was the last improvement in terms of safety here?

5S questions:
- Does everything at this workstation have a fixed location?
- How do you know when something is missing?

- How do you know you have all the tools available to do your job?
- How would you like to improve the layout of this area, so that you can work more efficiently?

Standard work questions:
- Can you show me the SOP for the job you are working on now?
- Can you do your job solely based on what is shown in the SOP?
- Is there any waste left in you process that you could eliminate?

Team board questions:
- How can I see that all KPIs are up to date?
- Are all red KPIs linked to the 3C list?
- How many of the 3Cs lead to kaizen?
- Which KPIs has been improved since you started using the board?
- What would you like to improve on this board next?

Kaizen questions:
- When did you implement your last kaizen?
- What improvements are you working on now?
- How can I help you solve your problem?

Kamishibai:
- Did everybody do his or her kamishibai according to standard work?
- Are the kamishibai cards leading to kaizen?
- Were the results of the previous kamishibai discussed in the team meeting?

Knowledge questions:
- Can you name the eight wastes?
- Can you name your team goals?

Coaching questions:
- What is your target condition and where are you today on that KPI?
- What obstacles are preventing you from reaching your target condition?
- What experiment are you planning to overcome that obstacle?
- When can we see the results of that experiment?

> **Key Points:**
> - *The first goal of kamishibai is to do process confirmation and make sure standards are lived by.*
> - *The second goal of kamishibai is to engage in coaching conversations with colleagues to find the next improvement.*

## 8.1.2  How to Do a Kamishibai

*When you are out observing on the gemba, do something to help them. If you do, people will come to expect that you can help them and will look forward to seeing you again.*
—*Taiichi Ohno*

The kamishibai should be implemented in such a way that everyone can visit the team and help find the next possibility for improvement. In the ideal world, every team board has a kamishibai board, and every leader in the organization has kamishibai included in his or her standard work. Doing kamishibai checks should be part of the organizational culture.

Going to the gemba and doing a kamishibai will include the following four steps: picking a card at a team board, finding a person with whom to do the kamishibai, using the questions on the card to have a coaching discussion, and updating the team board with the kamishibai results.

One can **pick a card from the board** in different ways. My personal favorites are the kamishibais in which there is a surprise element. You can put the cards in a separate box for instance, in which case you have to pick a random one.

Some team boards implement a so-called wheel of fortune on the team board. In this case, the person doing the kamishibai has to spin the wheel, which tells the person what topic to check or even what person to ask. This way the kamishibai checks are random, which facilitates learning for both the auditor and the auditee.

Another way to use the wheel of fortune is to create one for the level-three meeting in which managers have to spin the wheel to see in what department they will do the kamishibai check during that period.

**Finding a person with whom to do the kamishibai** is an important second step because one of the goals of the kamishibai is to coach team members. You take the card from the team board in a certain department and ask who has some time available for the mini-audit. When no one in the team has time at the moment, ask when you can come back for it.

The **discussion** that takes place can be based on the questions that are written on the kamishibai card, but this is not a must. Both the auditor and the auditee should learn from this experience, so it is OK for the auditor to ask other questions related to what he or she sees while visiting the gemba.

The questions on the card are only the conversation starter, a kick off point for coaching, as chapter 3 discusses. Discussions where improvements are found usually include auditors asking follow-up questions after the auditee has answered the question written on the card. These follow-up questions lead to a better understanding of the current way of working and whether this is the most effective or efficient way.

The last step is to **update the team board**. This means that the kamishibai card is returned to the kamishibai board, and an action (or 3C) is defined with the auditee when the discussion has led to a possible kaizen. By capturing the improvement on the board, you put it on the agenda for the next team meeting, as we will describe in the chapter 8.2.

Since the goal of the kamishibai is to find improvements, strive for a ratio of 50 percent green, 50 percent red ratio. That means 50 percent of all audits lead to a 3C with a possible improvement action. Cards always being returned green can mean one of two things: either the auditor has not asked follow-up questions that have led to improvement, or the standard is at such a high level that no one needs to check it anymore. In the latter case, the card should be taken from the kamishibai board, and a new one can be created.

> **Key Points:**
> - *The questions on the kamishibai card are meant to get the discussion started; the goal of the check is to find a possible next improvement.*
> - *Document the fact that you have done a check (for others to see) and write down the improvement action when one is found.*

## 8.1.3 Training Tips

> *What you do speaks so loudly that I cannot hear what you say.*
> —Ralph Waldo Emerson

The challenge in coaching people on using the kamishibai is not so much in the tool itself, but in how people utilize it.

It cannot be stressed enough, that the goal of the kamishibai is for the person who does the check and the person who is answering the questions to find the next improvement in the process when the check is done.

This means that during the audit, the way people do the kamishibai is more important than how the system works from a technical perspective. The way questions are asked is most important.

First of all, you need to **take your time** on the gemba walk. When you are in a rush and only want to quickly tick off that part of your leader standard work sheet, the chance that you will have a value-adding discussion decreases drastically.

Second, you have to think about how you approach your colleague when asking questions. What does **your body language** say? What about your voice? Are you relaxed? Are you showing a real interest in the process you are visiting? When the person to whom you ask the questions does not feel comfortable with you asking them, he or she might not engage in the discussions about improvement as much as you would like.

Third, if you are in a management position visiting an operational team, do not forget that **you are there to learn** from their experience as well as the other way around. Make sure you can add value to the work and problems they have instead of using the opportunity to give them extra work that solves your own problems.

The best way to practice kamishibai is to do it. Therefore, always go with the people who are new to the kamishibai at least three times until they are comfortable going to different departments on their own.

Do not underestimate what an obstacle it can be if the person in question has not visited a specific department that much or does not know any of the colleagues working there by name. Going to an unknown place like that is really uncomfortable, so it really helps if somebody joins you for the kamishibai and introduces you to the people, if necessary.

> **Key Points:**
> - *Visiting a new department can be scary, so offer support during the first few visits.*
> - *Take your time to have a proper discussion at the shop floor.*
> - *As the person who does the check, make sure you offer support rather than asking for it.*

## 8.2 Checking the Standard with Team Boards

*There once was a leader named Keating,*
*Who fell in love with long meetings.*
*His people were bored,*
*And some of them snored.*
*They wished they could just have a beating.*
—Dan Rockwell, Leadership Freak

### 8.2.1 What Is It, and Why Is It Important?

A team board is a physical board where teams come together on a regular basis for 10 to 15 minutes, to discuss their current performance and how to improve it. It is usually a stand-up meeting, meaning that the team stands in half a circle in front of the board, so that everybody has a clear view on the board, as the different elements on the board are discussed. The team board should consist of at least three elements: people, performance, and continuous improvement.

The team board facilitates performance improvement by improving the flow of problems (Ballé and Ballé 2012). To achieve this, the board offers the team data about performance that are traditionally only available to management. This provides teams with the possibility of solving their problems to improve stability of the processes and even find possible improvements to the standards that directly influence the organizational goals.

Another advantage of having a team board and a team board meeting is that it gives the team leader an opportunity to address the team on a regular basis, address possible resistance within the group, offer personal coaching when requested, and inform the team about what is happening elsewhere in the organization. Having a fixed moment like this on the calendar potentially saves a lot of other meetings or looking for people later in the day.

Whenever the team encounters a problem it cannot solve or finds an improvement that it cannot implement without the help of another team, the problem or improvement should be handed over to another team. Usually it moves up to the next tier level, where it can be assigned to a different department. This is the goal of the daily management system, which is discussed in chapter 10. (Mann 2005) (Webers 2010).

The team board structure directly influences all three enemies of lean: **Imbalance** is reduced because all communication is done in a fifteen-minute daily meeting instead of weekly or monthly meetings that usually run an hour or more. Having a daily meeting balances the communication throughout the week and therefore also the available production time of each line or area.

**Human Overburden** can be prevented when people who are part of the team board meeting may discuss their mood and workload as part of the agenda. This should lead to discussions that prevent overburdening team members. This is especially important in the office environment, where burnout is more and more of an ever-present risk (Westendorp and van Bodegom 2015).

**Waste** can be prevented because the KPIs focus the team on solving the problems directly related to the company vision. When the team cannot solve the problem from within, the issue can flow to another department on a daily basis, which increases the speed of action and therefore reduces waiting time on the problem. It also brings the problem to the attention of the person or function with the right skills to solve it. Solving the problem in a preventive way—preventing it from ever occurring again—avoids rework.

People working with team boards are, when done well, automatically living by the following Toyota principles:

**Principle one: Focus on the long-term philosophy.** The performance part of the team board includes the team's key performance indicators (KPIs). These should directly cascade down from the organizational strategy and vision and therefore the long-term philosophy. We will discuss this more in chapter 10.2, about Hoshin Kanri.
Problems that arise that lead to a red KPI red should lead to actions and improvements that improve the performance of that KPI to help the organization reach its long-term goals.

**Principle two: Create continuous flow of problems that are being solved.** The third part of the board includes a physical list of problems that need to be solved.

The focus on these problems directly relates to the interval of the meeting. A daily stand-up meeting in front of the team board will therefore remind the owner of the problem of his or her action on a daily basis.

**Principle seven: Make problems visual.** The entire team board is a visual management tool, in which everybody can grasp the current performance of the team within a few seconds. Everyone should be able to see whether it is a good day or a bad day for the team. You can do this by using colors in which all KPI are shown with red and green.

**Principle eight: Use only reliable, tested technology.** In terms of using technology to keep the boards up to date, I can strongly recommend using handwritten forms only. Two advantages of using the power of the pen are that it minimizes the time it takes to update the board and it increases personal accountability for the people updating the forms. It also prevents people from having to wait for a new print of a form, or the need to update the file after a software update has messed up the layout of the form.

**Principle twelve: Go see for yourself.** By taking the meetings out of the meeting room with its computerized lists and information, the team board meeting structure encourages people to come out of their offices and to the gemba, the shop floor. This is a big change, especially for managers in levels two and three of daily management, who are traditionally used to managing the company by staying in their offices and reading numbers from a PowerPoint presentation.

**Principle fourteen: Use hansei (self-reflection) and continuous improvement to become a learning organization**. The team board is structured in such a way that all abnormalities in the KPIs are directly linked to the 3C (concern, cause, and countermeasure), of which the countermeasures are focused on improving the standards—hence, kaizen.

Because the daily management structure includes different departments and teams, team boards are used in both production and office areas. You will find the difference of the boards in the KPIs that are tracked and the frequency of the team board meetings themselves. In production environments and their supportive functions, daily level-one, level-two, and level-three meetings are common. In office environments on a higher aggregation level, a biweekly or even a weekly meeting might be satisfactory.

> **Key Points:**
> - *The goal of the team board is to provide the teams with data to help them solve problems and improve standards.*
> - *A good team board makes it possible for anyone to see within a few seconds whether the team is having a good day or a bad day.*
> - *The daily management structure is a structure in which team boards are connected to one another to make information flow between teams and departments.*

## 8.2.2  How to Implement the Team Board

> *The team board should tell me*
> *whether it is a good day or a bad day today*
> *- Gerard Luijten*

Team boards are used for communication within shifts, between shifts, and between departments. By seeing important events from every shift on the team board, people visualize the information flow, which prevents them from forgetting to share information with their peers (Suzaki 1993). Team boards should include the following three elements: people, performance, and continuous improvement and there are multiple ways of designing these boards to include these three elements. I will explore the different possibilities in this chapter.

The three sections of the team board form the agenda of the meeting; you simply address all parts of the team board from left to right and from top to bottom. The goal should be to have the meeting last no longer than fifteen minutes when it is a daily meeting and maybe half an hour when it is a weekly meeting.

There are usually different levels or *tiers* of boards within the organization.

Chapter 10 will discuss the daily management system with the different tiers of team boards and what that means in more detail, but to understand the examples in this chapter it is good to know that:
- tier 1 boards are used by work teams to discuss performance and improvements with their shift leader,
- tier 2 boards are used by shift leaders to discuss their performance and improvements with their functional manager, and
- tier 3 boards are used by the team of functional managers as they discuss performance and improvements with their site manager.

This is important because the level of detail of the performance that we visualize on the board depends on the team that is using it.

Figure 10 shows the first of three examples or a team board. In this example, each of the elements of the board (people, performance and continuous improvement) are represented as separate columns.

The **PEOPLE part** includes the topics of safety, presence, and/or mood and a training matrix. You can use a **safety cross** to show performance in terms of safety. It shows at a glance whether accidents or near misses (an observed unsafe situation that could have led to an accident, but fortunately did not... this time) have occurred.

When a shift or day is colored red, the event should be written down in the 3C list at the continuous improvement part to improve the manner of working and prevent the situation from happening again.

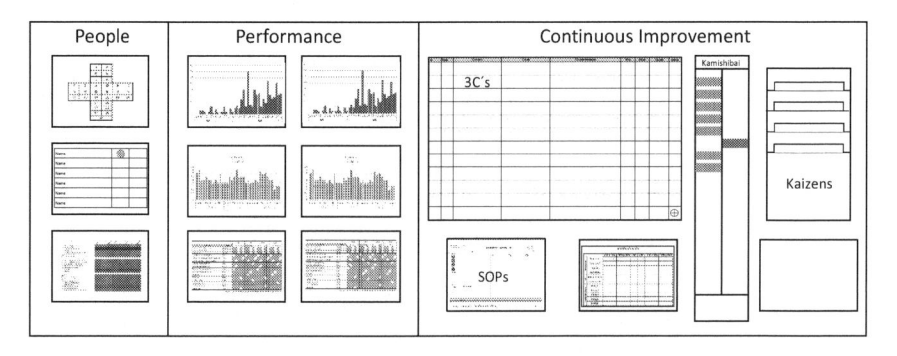

*Figure 10: Team board example one (tier one)*

In an office environment, you can use a **mood board** in which all team members can address their current moods if they wish to. This way, topics such as workload and number of overtime hours can be put on the team meeting agenda.

The people part of the team board should include a summary of the employees' skills in a **training matrix**. By using different colors for different levels of training, the training matrix demonstrates the need for training within a team. The goal of the training matrix is to show the gap between the current skill level for a certain skill and the goal for skilled employees.

Part 2, **PERFORMANCE,** includes KPIs for that specific workstation or department. The KPI section should at least include the following categories: **quality**, **delivery**, and **reliability** (Ballé and Ballé 2005). We will see more elaborate KPI categories in the examples to come.

There are different ways of demonstrating performance on the team board. You can demonstrate KPIs using graphs, tracked per shift and including a target line (Ballé and Ballé 2005) (Suzaki 1993). The example in figure 10 above shows a team board in a process environment. In this case, the performance KPIs were focused on the overall equipment effectiveness (OEE) because this was the one KPI that had the largest impact on product costs. Other KPIs measured in the example above are the results of preventive quality checks. The team should again mention deviations from the target on the three 3C list at the continuous improvement part of the board; and they should implement preventive actions for future prevention of the deviation using kaizen.

Every KPI should have **a target**, but different theories exist about how these targets should be set. The first theory is that targets should be stretching, which means the target is set in such a way that the target is achieved 50 percent of the time. Doing this shows that the target actually can be achieved but is not met the other 50 percent of the time. This scenario shows there are still possibilities for improvement (Webers 2010).

The downside of this strategy is that 50 percent of the time the red KPI should be addressed on the 3C board, which leads to a fast-growing list of entries. You can solve this by adding another layer of data entry to the team board structure, as figure 11 shows in the second example of a team board.

The example in figure 11 is from a tier 2 team board, which means this is a board where performance of multiple other boards comes together for a management team. In this case, we do not want managers to define actions when a KPI is red and an action is already defined at the lower level. Instead, the team decided to create a visual overview in the first row (red and green), a breakdown of the red days in the second row, and a Pareto chart of possible causes in the third row, and actions targeted for this KPI in the fourth row. This means that you still record all red days in the first row, but you only define an action when the cause of those red day reaches a certain number of hits.

Another way to manage the number of actions that need to be recorded in all the team board meetings is to use a different target-setting strategy. You could set the target in such a way so that the KPI is achieved 90 percent of the time. This way only 10 percent of the time does a red KPI have to be addressed on the 3C list. This also gives the team's manager many more opportunities to positively reinforce his team members for achieving the targets (Daniels 2000).

Now if we look deeper into the example of figure 11, we can see that the top row in the performance column represent four categories of key performance indicators instead of the three we had in figure 10. Safety is included as a separate category so that we now have 4 categories: safety, quality, delivery and productivity. Each category represented by the shape of the safety cross, and the first letter of the other three categories in which the shapes are split into 31 smaller squares to represent the calendar days of each month.

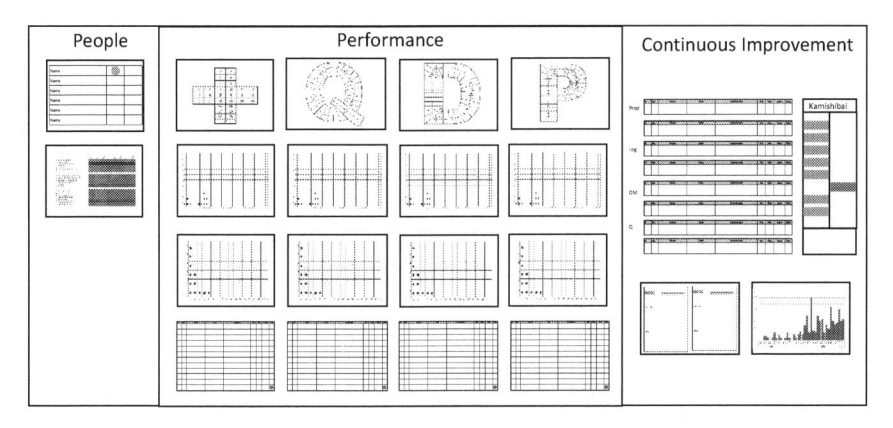

*Figure 11: Team board example two (tier-two and tier-three boards)*

The teams can color those shapes with red if it is a bad day, and green if it is a good day. As the month progresses, we can see within a few seconds how green or how red the month is.

In addition to the discussion about whether the target is set to be achieved 50 percent or 90 percent of the time, the challenge with the KPIs is that they have to be **leading indicators** which means that the team can use the indicator to adjust their way of working to make sure that at the end of the day, all targets are achieved. The pitfall of this is, that KPI's are very easily defined as **lagging indicators**, meaning the team looks back on yesterday to conclude whether or not the target was achieved and presents that value in a way that is not meaningful to the team, and does not directly give the team an opportunity to do something about it.

Let's look at an example. For the delivery column for instance, what you want to measure in a broad sense is whether all products that left the department were send to the customer on time. Asking that question after the day has finished already; provides no opportunity for the team to reach and change the outcome of the KPI. After all, the day is already over!
On-Time-In-Full (OTIF) is one example for measuring the delivery performance of a factory. It is a percentage calculated over the number of shipping to the customer that were send on time. This percentage, usually a monthly number, does not help a production guy in a molding department to find improvements. He needs a KPI that he can influence, that is related to the OTIF.

For our delivery column on tier 1 (operating team level), we could use a metric which reflects his machines production schedule, in which case data is added to a chart every hour, or every batch, informing the team about the **progress of the teams work during the shift**. This way, the team can use this information to act before the shift is over. When the team is one hour behind schedule, they may either working through breaks, or try to get support from another department. Or, in the case of running ahead of schedule, the team could decide that now is the right time to do that 5S audit, or work on that kaizen.

Having a leading indicator also means that the team can influence that KPI a hundred per cent. Having a Quality measure that is red every day because of reasons that are not within the influence of the team does not help the team improve their processes. Measuring these kinds of indicators are therefore not value adding for a team.

So, every board should have only leading indicators, indicators that can be influenced by the team, in such an interval that the team has time to respond to deviations when they are below target.

When the pitch (the interval in which production orders are released) of a value stream (see chapter 13) is twenty minutes, **the interval** in which the team measures performance should probably be shorter than that. When the cycle time of a product is more than one day, a two-hour interval might be enough to show problems.
Finally, the stability of the process can determine the interval in which the KPIs are measured. The more stable the process becomes, the shorter the interval should be (Mann 2005).

Examples of leading indicators are the following:
1. Number of safety observations done in the shift (safety)
2. Number of quality issues discovered during production (Quality)
3. Deviation from production plan in hours (or minutes?) per shift (Delivery)
4. Number of hours waiting due to material availability, or people availability (Productivity)

One step further than the above leading indicators is to track performance with **behavioral indicators**, which could be the behaviors that the team should show to lead to better results (Daniels 2000) (Webers 2010).

Examples of measurable behavior in a production environment are the following:
1. Performing a 5S check on the workstation before starting the shift
2. The number of proper root-cause analyses done on defined problems
3. Percentage of nonconformity processes started compared with number of quality issues
4. Documenting newfound solutions in the standard work
5. How often kamishibai cards are changed to sustain new improvements.

Examples of lean behaviors that could be part of a leader´s standard work or supportive functions include the following:
1. The number of 3Cs the leader solved for the production team

2. The number of kamishibais the leader has done and the number of improvements (kaizens) that resulted from them
3. How often the leader gave positive reinforcement to team members

Chapter 7.2 already described examples of leader standard work in the form of checklists. We can, however, also show a similar list as a KPI for an entire team (see figure 12). In this example, we defined three behaviors that we would like our managers to show at least once a month: perform a kamishibai, solve a kaizen for the team, and solve one problem that the team could not solve itself. Each manager can simply tick the box (with a green marker) whenever he or she has shown the behavior.

**CONTINUOUS IMPROVEMENT** is the third element of the team board. This part of the board, of which figure 11 is an example, includes the 3C list, the kamishibai, and a kaizen loop.

On a **3C list** (concern, cause, and countermeasure) all problems that occur within the team are listed. We usually talk about countermeasures instead of solutions the same way a homicide detective would say a case is closed rather than solved. The countermeasure does not necessarily eliminate the problem completely, but it should be satisfactory (Shook 2008).

Most important of all, 3Cs should be started when there a KPI that is below target. That way, when the KPIs directly link to the company vision (as chapter 10 will discuss), the teams help the organization achieve its vision by daily problem solving.

| Month | Kamishibai / gemba walk | Kaizen supported | 3C solved |
|---|---|---|---|
| Manager 1 | | | |
| Manager 2 | | | |
| Manager 3 | | | |

*Figure 12: Behavioral indicators, KPI example*

| No | Date | Concern | Cause | Countermeasure | Who | When | Kaizen | Status |
|----|------|---------|-------|----------------|-----|------|--------|--------|
|    |      |         |       |                |     |      |        | ⊕      |

*Figure 13: 3C*

Figure 13 shows an example of a 3C entry that includes the following:
- The follow-up number and date the 3C was opened,
- The concern or problem description linked to the KPI or kamishibai that led to the definition of the problem,
- The cause of the problem—ideally the root cause—which should be either a missing or incomplete standard or somebody not being familiar with the standard,
- A corrective or preventive countermeasure—corrective measures are quick fixes that bring the process back to standard; preventive measures are improvements of the standards to prevent the problem from happening again,
- The owner of the countermeasure,
- The deadline date for implementation, which is the date the 3C should again be discussed in the team board meeting,
- The possible kaizen number when the countermeasure is preventive and therefore can be recognized as an improvement,
- A small wheel on the right of each 3C to demonstrate the status of the 3C— the first quarter shows us that the problem has been identified. The second quarter means the countermeasure has been found. The third quarter means the countermeasure has been implemented and the fourth quarter can be checked when the problem has been solved preventively.

Finally, the continuous improvement part of the team board includes the **kaizen loop**. Every employee should be capable of implementing incremental improvements in his or her standard way of working. These improvements can evolve from not meeting targets, input from the kamishibai, or improvements based on a waste that were discovered that did not directly influence the KPIs. (See the chapter on kaizen, 9.1)

Another tip on the topic of team boards is that it helps when all team boards in the organization have the same **STANDARD FORMAT**. This way everyone in the organization knows how to read all the boards of the different departments. This system makes it easier to cross-train people for multiple workstations and facilities. An employee could also possibly implement kaizens in other departments (after discussing his or her ideas with the current operator on that workstation, of course).

Figure 14 shows a third example of a team board, this time at tier 3. In this company, we designed the boards to include all three elements, people, performance and improvement that were described above, but the layout of the board was different. There are **5 different columns: safety, quality, delivery, cost and people** on the board, of which the sequence was chosen carefully:

- Without healthy people to work in your teams, you cannot produce anything, so safety is always the first category of KPI to discuss.
- Second, you want to produce high quality products. Quantity doesn't matter if the quality of what you produce is bad, therefore quality is the second column.
- Third we can discuss delivery. Did the team produce the volumes that the customer has ordered? This looks at the schedule adherence, not yet at efficiency.
- Then comes the cost of satisfying the demand. This is the efficiency part. What resources did we need to fulfill the production schedule? Productivity plays a big role here and using this same principle on tier 1 boards includes measuring one specific waste that is common in the team.
- The final column is for people and it includes the engagement of the workforce. Next to all problems that we have captured in the previous 4 columns, were you able to do a proper job or was something missing?

In figure 14, you can see barometers on the first row, in which either all numbers of different areas are combined in one red or green indicator (in the safety, quality and people columns), or with the possibility to split the indicator for different departments (the first row of the delivery and cost column in Figure 14).

At the second row of charts, we see some different examples of visualizing KPIs with trends. There is a year to date performance measure of different safety risks the safety column, a yearly trend of monthly quality numbers in the quality column, a yearly trend of weekly delivery numbers in the delivery column, a detailed OEE breakdown in the form of a waterfall chart in the cost column, and a 5S audit score in the people column.

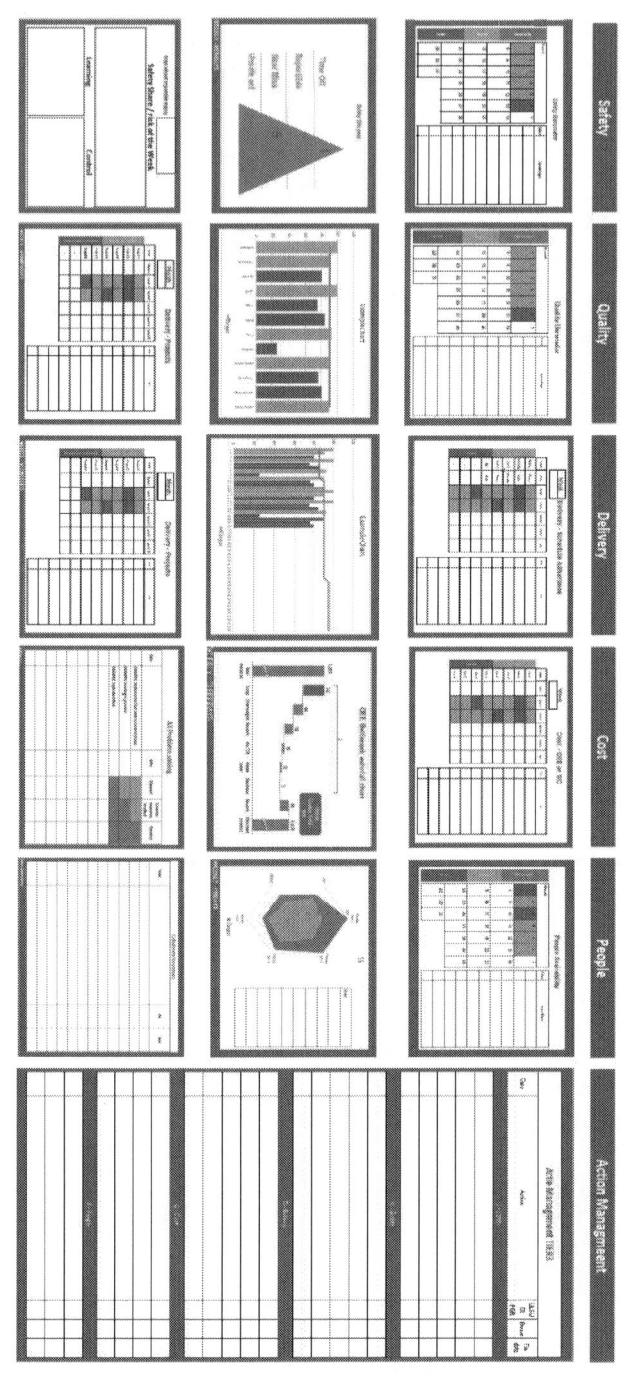

*Figure 14: Team board example, tier 3*

Where the first row depicts the daily barometers of the site, and the second row the trend of these KPI's to see whether the site is improving towards its targets over the year, the third row contains some examples of other topics that could be included in the tier 3 meeting.

A safety share in the safety column, a visual overview of the progress of D2MAIC projects in both the quality and delivery columns, progress of A3 problem solving in the cost column, and a list of recognitions in the people column.

Note that all three examples in this chapter are just that: examples. It is up to each company to define their own board standard and define the standard lay-out that works best for them and their unique circumstances.
Each team then has the challenge of defining the leading indicators for themselves, linking them to the KPI on a higher tier. Chapter 10 will contain more tips on this topic.

We will now first look into situations where the examples above will probably not work: the project environment.

**Key Points:**
- *A team board is about discussing and improving team performance.*
- *The team board should include the following elements: people, performance, and continuous improvement.*
- *The people part shows safety behavior and needs for training.*
- *The performance part shows behavioral indicators.*
- *The continuous improvement part is about improving the standards to prevent a red KPI tomorrow.*

## 8.2.3 Obeya and governance board: Team Boards for the Project Environment

*The face-to-face communication in the obeya improves the commitment and therefore speeds up the decision-making process in the project.*

The setups described so far are especially useful in an environment where there are cycle times of seconds, minutes, or hours. They do, however, become more difficult when the cycle time is longer than a day. If a task or a group of tasks takes you longer than a week, how can you discuss the daily KPI within the team?

**Project work** (for instance, engineering, quality departments, and research and development) is known for its repetitive cycles of work. The cycles are similar due to the fact that they all have project milestones, yet every project is different. For these departments, the *obeya*, also known as the war room, can be a valuable communication tool (Gort 2015).

The obeya was first developed at Toyota in 1994, when the first Toyota Prius was developed (Morgen and Liker 2006). Takeshi Uchiyamada was responsible for the project and he thought the obeya would be a logical first step in creating a place where all experts would meet regularly and talk about concepts to make sure both the expert and his team members could **make good decisions** (Morgen and Liker 2006).

Within lean, we always focus on the process creating value. In a project environment, the value that is being produced is the **packages of knowledge** that make it possible to produce high-quality products that the customer is willing to buy. Making the right decisions about these packages of knowledge is therefore the main focus for project teams (Barnhart 2013). The obeya supports this need, with the primary goals of collecting and managing project information (Morgen and Liker 2006).

The **OBEYA ROOM** for an R&D project consists of a few standard parts that (except the prototype) all hang on the walls of the room.
For starters, **the prototype** of the product that is being developed is put in the middle of the room. A visual of the actual end product for everybody to see helps

the team better understand the challenges of the designing process. It does not need to be a functioning product; sometimes a scaled model of the product suffices.

Second, **the design goals of the product** are hung on the wall. What are the goals of the design, and how are these linked to the organizational strategy? These questions can help in making decisions during the project.

You can find the **vision of** the final product next to the design goals. What are the expectations in terms of what the product should look like?

Then it is time for the **KPIs**. Just like products in a production process, projects can be measured in terms of costs, quality, and expected delivery. The project team should continually be focused on these to make sure targets in all three of these areas are achieved.

**The project value stream map** describes all tasks that need to be done to be able to make decisions and achieve different project milestones. Figure 15 shows an example of a project VSM in which a 5S implementation is mapped; part 4 is dedicated to this topic.

The **decomposition table** is an overview of the product with the possible subsystems that need to be designed. Showing subsystems within the product helps focus on modular design and identifies what specialists are necessary for the design.

Then there is the **action list**, which includes all problems that arise during the product that need to be tracked, similar to the 3C list on a team board. Finally, a **projector** is available to project information on the wall that can support further exchange of information.

The largest waste in R&D processes is probably waiting for information (Morgen and Liker 2006); it is also the most important reason projects are delayed. To prevent this delay from happening, the team should meet regularly in the obeya to discuss who needs what information to be able to make the relevant decisions in time. Within Toyota, teams **meet three times a week**. This short cycle facilitates the efficient exchange of information between disciplines.

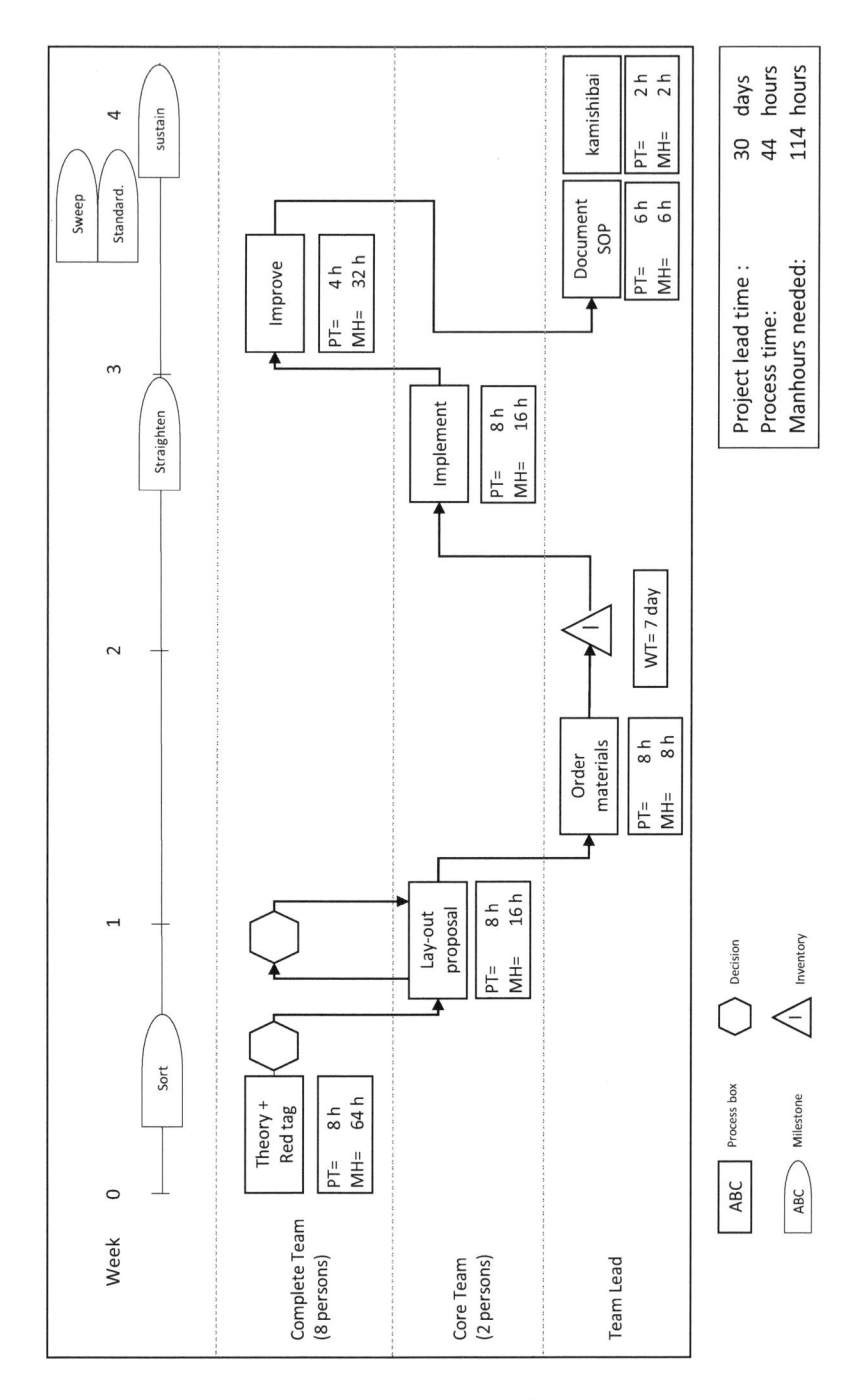

*Figure 15: Example of a project value stream map*

The go-and-see principle is embedded in the obeya when the **obeya is mobile**. When it is easy to move the posters or boards around, the obeya meeting takes place wherever the R&D process takes place, first in the R&D department and later in production.

A second example of a board where project leaders meet to discuss progress of their projects is a **PROJECT GOVERNANCE BOARD**. This board or wall is a visual representation of the projects that are currently being run in a department to reach a specific target.
In this weekly meeting, the sponsors and project leaders meet all together to discuss the progress of each project, in about 5 minutes per project. Detailed discussions should be done outside of the team meetings.

Where the A4 paper on the tier 3 board example of figure 14 shows just the status in red and green, this governance wall could contain more information about each project. At a minimum, the information that is posted here are the project charter and a progress-report if each project.
The **project charter** of each project shows, among other things, what the goal of the project is and an introduction on how a specific problem is addressed.
A **progress report** can be used for weekly or monthly updates. One example is a four-blocker report in which an A4 paper is split in 4 blocks. The four areas include the summary of the successes of the project to date, the trend of the KPI that is being improved, the next steps of the projects, and the support that the team needs to succeed in achieving its goal.

> **Key Points:**
> - *An obeya is a team room used in project management.*
> - *Just as a team with a team board, the project team meets in the obeya on a regular basis to discuss the progress of the project.*
> - *Clear goals, KPIs, and action lists ensure the team prevents the project from being delayed.*
> - *A project governance board is used to visualize the progress of a number of projects that are done within an area.*

## 8.2.4 Training tips

*Who is not interested in cutting the meeting time in half, while improving the effectiveness of the meeting at the same time?*

The best way to get to the *why* part of the team board and the daily management structure, is to start the discussion based on Karin de Galan's effect, situation, and behavior principle (de Galan 2008) discussed in chapter 2. She describes the importance of helping people relate to the problems you would like to solve with a tool before you introduce the tool.

The idea is that you start with discussing **the effects** of having a bad structure, which in the context of a missing daily meeting structure could lead to discussions about the following questions:
- How do I know if I have done my work correctly on a daily basis?
- How do I know that I am working on the right tasks at the moment?
- Do we share important things learned between team members or departments?
- When I ask for support from my manager, do I get it?
- When I get support, how long does it take?
- Are we discussing all relevant topics in our team?
- Are we discussing non-relevant topics within our team?

Usually the answers to these questions lead to a common understanding of a gap in communication, the negative effects, so to speak.

The second step is to discuss **the situations** in which the teams can try to influence these effects. The simple answer in this case is the regular team meetings, official moments in the day or week where the team comes together and discusses its performance and, more importantly, its improvements.

This already leads to the question of whether the team meetings are addressing the right topics.

The final and most important step is to discuss what **behavior** the group sees in the current way of organizing the team meeting. There are themes such as the following:

- Having a clear agenda that states all important topics
- Having an action list that itemizes actions with the owner and the end date
- Discussing team goals and progress to reach those goals
- Discussing whether improvements are documented and shared

In my experience, when the daily management structure is not implemented in a department or organization, all participants are keen to hear what you can offer as a solution to their problems to prevent the negative effects discussed above.

I have yet to meet someone who tells me he or she is enthusiastic about all the meetings that he or she attends over their week.

After discussing the effect, situation, and behavior regarding current communication, the group becomes ready to discuss the tool—the team board—that supports lean behaviors in keeping the long-term vision, creating a continuous flow of problems that are being solved, making problems visible, using only reliable technology, going to the gemba, and practicing self-reflection.

So, how do you make your team familiar with the tool – in this case the team board? Here are three ideas: visit another site that has already successfully implemented the board, organize a classroom training, or plan a workshop.

First, the best way to convince a management team to use the daily management structure and its team boards is to **GO ON A PLANT VISIT** where they have already implemented it and see the benefits at the gemba and on the site KPIs. Many managers get optimistic when they learn that by having a short meeting every day, they get an accurate overview of what is happening in their organization and how they can help solving problems.

In one of the companies where I worked, a training structure is in place with different levels of lean training: a two-day basics training and an eight-day advanced training. In both types of training sessions, **practicing** how to use the team board is part of the course.

The second option is to practice the use of team boards in **CLASS ROOM TRAINING**. In the two-day course, we play a paper plane folding game in which participants have to improve the process by eliminating wastes. After every round, the team comes together and has a team board meeting. The team board is already set up in advance with the basic parts: people, performance, and continuous improvement.

The eight-day course is more complex. Starting at day two, different teams have to build their own team boards and have team meetings every day as part of their teach-back sessions, in which they present what they have learned to other groups. During the eight days, the teams figure out the best way to show KPIs and what KPIs they should measure to track the performance of the team. In this case, as a trainer, do not go through the creation of the team board in detail as you would do with tools like value stream mapping or using the SIPOC. Focus on the *why* and the *what* in the theory. The participants have to figure out the *how* for themselves.

A teach-back session is then followed by feedback from other groups and from the trainers, which helps the teams improve their team boards as the training continues.

Finally, there is the **WORKSHOP** itself in which one or multiple teams built the first version of their team board. This workshop ideally includes as little theory as possible (30 min maybe) and then gives the teams the time to define their leading indicators for each of the columns of the performance part of the board.

I like to include multiple teams in one workshop, preferably even of different tier levels, so that the teams can discuss not only their leading indicators, but also how they relate to each other and to the other tiers. We will come back on this linkage of KPI's in chapter 10, where I describe the KPI tree.

**Key Points:**
- *Start with effect that you would like to prevent, then move to situations that led to that effect, and finally the behavior that got people into the situation in the first place*
- *Practice in a training environment.*

# Chapter 9:
# Level Three: Improving the Standard

*Never ignore the standard. When you know how to do it better: discuss it with your team and improve the standard.*

So far, we have used lean tools to define the current way of working with 5S and standard work and to make sure the use of kamishibai and team boards sustains the current level of performance. In the next level of maturity, the organization moves in the direction of continuous improvement: improving the standards in such a way that performance improves.

At this level, three tools can help us improve our standards. The first one is kaizen. *Kaizen* is the Japanese word for "change for the better." It means that everybody in the organization should be challenged to implement small changes in his or her current way of working. In time, doing this results in major performance improvement. Chapter 9.1 discusses kaizen.

In addition to the small incremental kaizen improvements, a team can use A3 problem solving to solve larger problems, for which one person can be responsible. When a new target is set on the team board, a team is challenged to analyze how this target can be achieved using the scientific method. The A3 tool supports that need, and chapter 9.2 is dedicated to it.

Finally, there is the D2MAIC (discovery, define, measure, analyze, improve and control) project described in chapter 9.3.
Projects can be chosen as problem-solving tool for even larger problems and are selected based on the profit and loss statement of the organization. The projects last about six months and are done by a team.

## 9.1 Improving the Standard with Kaizen

*Do it better, improve it—even when it is not broken, because if you don´t, you won´t be able to compete with organizations that do.*

### 9.1.1 What Is It, and Why Is It Important?

Kaizen is the Japanese term for having a mindset of continuous improvement, which in a lean organization is lived by everyone at all time and in all departments (Imai 1986).

Kaizen means continuously improving the current way of working. It means **bringing the current standards to a higher level**. This is not the same as finding a quick fix for a problem to make the symptom go away over the short term and keeping the underlining standard as it was. A famous metaphor within the lean community is the firefighting metaphor. Whenever there is a fire, you not only want to put out the fire in the short term, you want to understand how this fire occurred in the first place and prevent it from happening again in the future. In most production environments, my experience is that people spend way too much time firefighting, and too little time preventing fires.

If we want to include everybody in this process, as Imai suggests, we need to put kaizen on the agenda. This is the reason it is part of the team board. When kaizen is part of the daily management system, employees discuss the problems that have occurred in the team and whether the action taken to solve the problem was corrective or preventive. This in turn should lead to more preventive actions, changes in the process that prevent problems from occurring in the future, which is kaizen.

The kaizen mind-set requires a lot from the people in the organization; employees are required to look outside their contractual roles to find improvements that they think contribute to organizational goals (Brunet and New 2009) (S. Covey 1989).

To facilitate this, we need to look at how we can influence employee participation in the continuous improvement activities. Fenkner (2016) performed a case study on this topic to find the drivers and barriers of participating in lean initiatives.

One of the findings was that employees need to be equipped with **motivation, opportunity, and ability** (MOA) to be able to participate (Fenkner 2016).

Motivation is defined as desire to participate in the lean initiative. Opportunity means the employee has the supplies, time, working conditions, and information needed for them to work on the improvements. Ability means every employee has the knowledge and skills to be able to do so. Fenkner's research proved that training skills alone are not enough. We need to also create the opportunity for people to work on the improvements, which includes providing them with the time, working conditions, and information they need (Fenkner 2016).

This is one other reason why kaizen should be part of the team board, and it explains why the team board meetings are so important. They not only place focus on discussing improvements with the team, but they also equip team members with the information they need to think about improvements that are important for the organization.

A third reason for putting kaizen on the team board meeting agenda is to share improvements within the team and even between teams or departments. By sharing knowledge with one another, **everybody gets smarter** (Tichy 2002).

When you give away money, you reduce the amount of money you own. When you give away knowledge, you create the possibility for discussions and feedback, which actually **increases your level of knowledge** and therefore increases the knowledge in the organization (Aslander and Witteveen 2010).

So why focus on this aspect of lean? Why do we need everybody in the organization to engage in these improvement activities?

The kaizen mind-set helps to focus on reducing all three enemies of lean. An identified **waste** is the best target for a kaizen, and who can identify the waste better than the person who encounters it day after day? When an employee identifies a waste in his or her process—and that person is equipped to eliminate it—performance increases. A second link to the waste is a red KPI on the team board. Whenever a KPI is red, chances are that one of the wastes is the cause for this situation. Focusing on preventing this waste from occurring again will also increase performance. As described in earlier chapters, waste is usually caused by **overburden** and **imbalance**.

The most important management principles that kaizen facilitates are the following:

**Principle ten: Develop exceptional people and teams.** By focusing on improvement in the team board meetings and sharing information about what is important in the organization, you develop your people, so they can solve problems and improve organizational performance.

**Principle fourteen: Practice hansei (self-reflection) and kaizen (continuous improvement).** Having the kaizen loop on the team board puts the actual improvement of the standards on the agenda of every meeting. Every day, all teams should discuss whether they have been firefighting or improving standards.
This is why there is a column for kaizen on the 3C list, as figure 13 in 8.2.2 already showed. It helps people focus on creating countermeasures that solve the problem in a preventive way by raising the standard.

**Key Points:**
- *Kaizen is the mindset in which people think about whether they have improved something or just put out the immediate fire.*
- *Sharing improvements makes everyone more knowledgeable.*

## 9.1.2 How to Implement Kaizen in Manufacturing

*Are you too busy for improvement? ...Look, you'll stop being busy either when you die or when the company goes bankrupt.*
*—Shigeo Shingo*


This section describes the use of the physical space dedicated for kaizen forms on the team board. If you do not wish to add another type of template to your toolkit, you can also choose to add a column to your action list (3C list) on the team board and indicate there whether the action is a corrective action or a kaizen. You can use the example shown in figure 13 in chapter 8.2.2 for inspiration.
A third option is to have a separate action board for long term improvements. In this case, for each problem you could have two types of actions: one short term action of the action list to contain the problem and reduce the symptoms that occur in the team, and one longer term action for the actual improvement.

I believe it is important to have this split between short term actions and actual improvements, because it visualizes the maturity level of problem solving that a team has. Do they only have quick fixes on their action lists? Then they are just working on managing the daily business, not on improving their processes.

When you have a separate template on the board for kaizen, you can provide the team the option to document more details about the problem, its expected root-cause, and the countermeasures needed to prevent this problem from reoccurring than the 3C list does. If the team needs support from another department, the physical paper itself can move up the team board structure to the next level of management, where these supportive resources can be planned. In this case, the kaizen form is used as suggestion system.

Even though what we are talking about here is the first and simplest form of problem solving at this level, the kaizen form could evaluate more in the direction of the A3 problem solving sheet described in chapter 9.2 as the teams become more mature in problem solving.

Let's now look at the **kaizen loop**, in which we have these separate forms on each board in more detail. The kaizen loop is present on all team boards in the form of a **box or ring band** that contains empty forms and the kaizens that are in progress or implemented.

If you want to focus on measurable improvements, you could set the rule that all improvement actions or kaizens should be focused on reducing at least one of the **eight wastes**. When we can quantify a reduction of waste, and the effort or cost of implementing the kaizen is reasonable, we should implement the kaizen.

Some authors even say all improvement suggestions should be implemented, whether they are improving bottom-line results or not. The reason for this is simple; if you don't listen to your employees today, they might not share their ideas with you tomorrow. The first 9 ideas that a person has may not be that impactful, while their 10$^{th}$ idea could be that million-dollar breakthrough idea that the company needs! So, listen to your team members, implement as many ideas as you can to positively reinforce the team to bring you even more and better ideas (Tichy 2002).

The **kaizen form** should be standardized and available for everyone to document his or her improvements. What to put on the kaizen suggestion form varies among firms. I like to keep it as clean as possible to minimize bureaucracy:
- Name/department of the person writing the kaizen
- Problem statement with the identified waste (quantified when possible)
- Root-cause of that problem (for instance after using the 5why method described in 9.1.3)
- Countermeasure that prevents the waste from reoccurring

There is room left on the form to make notes about implementation. For instance, this part of the form may show who is keeping the form and working on implementation.

The goal of kaizen is to have everybody participating in implementing improvements, not just suggesting improvements. Otherwise, the suggestion system will just lead to a long list of suggestions for R&D, engineering, or the technical staff to work on.

The secret to Toyota's impressive seventy thousand implemented kaizens per year is that all employees focus on improvements they can implement themselves. It can therefore help to add a small checklist on the kaizen form that asks the individual whether he or she can implement the idea and if it can be done within that day or week.

As kaizen is part of the team board structure, it is also part of the daily team board meeting. Therefore, you can also use the **daily management structure** (the structure that connects all team boards to manage the entire organization, chapter 10) to discuss kaizens if the person or department cannot implement them. The kaizen is then taken to the next-level daily management meeting to be discussed or handed over to another department that is able to implement it. This, however, should be the exception not the rule. Teams should focus on ideas that they can implement themselves; it will help them think about how they themselves can influence the situation. It helps them act in their circle of influence (S. Covey 1989).

The input of the kaizens can come from wastes that team members identify. These wastes can be identified randomly, but they can also come from the **KPIs on the team board**. Chances are, when a KPI (and therefore the standard) is not met, one of the wastes has occurred and led to the deviation.

We can then use the KPI to identify a goal for improvement, a target (Rother 2010). This means the target identified through the KPI is changed in a way that it will turn up red regularly, in which case the deviation from the standard is mentioned on 3C and eventually leads to kaizen.

Another way to find deviations from the standard is to use the **kamishibai** as input for 3C and kaizen. These mini-audits are used to check any standard that might be of interest. If there is a process where a lot of waste occurs, or a process that has changed recently, a kamishibai check can be put in place as a temporary check to see if the standards are kept. Deviations from these standards can lead either to training on the standard or training on an improvement of the standard and therefore kaizen.

Note that kaizens only result from kamishibai and team board meetings if the tools are used properly, as chapters 8.1 and 8.2 describe.
The last step in implementing the kaizen loop is the **monitoring of kaizens** handed in and implemented. Usually, a database which contains the list of kaizens or a physical list on a team board on which all kaizen forms are listed is

enough. This is the measurement tool that the facilitator uses for multiple reasons.

First, we it would be useful see what teams and/or individuals are implementing kaizen to show possible coaching needs.

Second, we can see how many kaizens are handed in, how long it takes to implement these, and how many are still open. These are indicators of the types of kaizens that are handed in. If the kaizen is a small improvement that the individual can implement alone, it should be implemented quickly and easily, which results in a short list of open kaizens.

> **Key Points:**
> - A team board should have a visual representation of improvements: on the 3C list, a separate action list, or a kaizen form.
> - When on the board, they are automatically part of the agenda of the daily stand-up meeting.
> - Reflect on every action: is this an improvement of the standard or a back-to-standard action?
> - Kaizens should link to KPIs to increase performance.
> - Kaizens can also result from kamishibai.

### 9.1.3 Training Tips

*Root-cause problem solving involves asking 5x Why, not 5x who.*

This section elaborates upon two aspects of the kaizen principle. First of all, with kaizen, it is important to focus on what you can do yourself. Simply writing down ideas for others to implement is way too easy. is actually one of my favorite topics of personal growth. To be successful in life, the first of seven habits of highly effective people is to **BE PROACTIVE** (covey 1989).

Second, the best way to improve organizational goals (which is the eventual goal of the whole kaizen idea) is to solve problems in a way that they result in a kaizen – an improvement of the standard.

The difference between acting reactivity and proactively can be explained by the circle of concern in which there is a smaller circle of influence (see figure 16). A reactive person will focus on the circle of concern and on aspects that he or she cannot influence.

Proactive people are focused on the smaller circle of influence, in which they can hold actual influence over a situation. The interesting thing about focusing on the circle of influence is that it usually makes it bigger, which means that using your influence usually grows your influence (S. Covey 1989).

Another difference between reactive and proactive people is described by the verbs "to have" and "to be." Reactive people who act in their circle of concern think in terms of *having.* For instance, they might say, "I wish I had more time," or "If only I had a diploma." The circle of influence is based on *being*, which focuses on how one can be in the future. In that circle, a proactive person might say, "Maybe I can be more patient in the future" (S. Covey 1989).

We should think about our circle of influence not only in our private lives but also in our professional lives. Pointing to other departments or colleagues is not going to solve our problems.

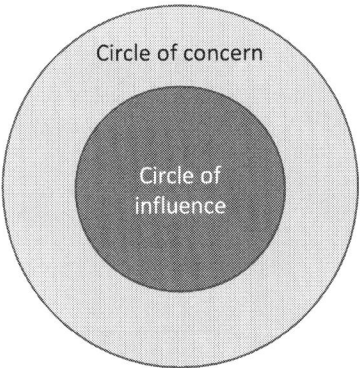

*Figure 16: The circle of influence and the circle of concern (Covey 1989)*

We need to take a look at how we influence our own outcomes and what we can do to improve them. If a friend is unhappy or has a problem, and you ask your friend how he or she influenced the situation, there is a chance that your friendship might end right there. (Just imagine asking friends who are unhappy about their weight about what they did or did not do to get to that weight.) Within a business environment however, as a mentor or coach, you are allowed (or even expected) to ask these questions: How did you influence allow this problem to occur? And how can you prevent this outcome from occurring again?

The second topic of interest is **PROBLEM-SOLVING**. A meeting is only truly valuable when problems are solved. The focus of any team board meeting should therefore be on problem-solving, but how do you really solve a problem?

Lean places focus on continually improving standards, on kaizen, and it is therefore the goal to have as many 3Cs linked to kaizen as possible. The ratio of 3Cs with kaizen to the 3Cs that are not linked to kaizen is one measure of lean maturity.

To improve this ratio, and to improve the number of 3Cs linked to kaizen, a root-cause analysis is necessary. This is where the 5x Why comes in. The idea of this tool is that you keep on asking *why* until you have found the root cause of a problem. The number five is just a hint. It could be that you need six times to get to the root cause, or just three.

The following example explains the use of the **5X WHY** to help you find the real root cause of the problem:

> *As a Dutch guy, I like taking my bike to work. As a standard, I decided that my tires should always be filled with air up to a certain pressure.*
>
> *On Monday morning, I planned to take the bike to work when I realized I had a flat tire. I did a very quick 3C, without analysis, pumped up the tire, and cycled to work to make sure I did not miss my early-morning meeting.*

This clearly is a quick-fix solution, a **back-to-standard** countermeasure.

> *On Tuesday morning I wanted to cycle to work again but realized the same tire was flat again. Apparently, I did not analyze the problem properly the*

> day before, so I asked myself why the tire was flat. I found there was a puncture in the tire that needed patching. After I patched the tire, I quickly cycled to work.

Even though I did more than the day before, this countermeasure was still a back-to-standard action because I only looked at the symptom: the puncture.

> On Wednesday morning, my tire was flat for the third time that week. I was starting to get annoyed but did take the time for a slightly better analysis than the day before.
>
> Why was my tire flat? Because there was a puncture in the tire.
>
> Why was there a puncture in the tire? Because a piece of glass was stuck in the outside tire.
>
> Solution: I removed the glass from the outer tire, patched the puncture, pumped up the tire, and cycled to work.

I would ask the group at that point whether I had raised the standard or if the countermeasure was a classical back-to-standard action. Just like Monday and Tuesday, even though I asked *why* a couple of times, removing the glass and patching the tire was still a back-to-standard countermeasure, as I was to find out on Thursday.

> On Thursday morning I found myself with a flat tire again. This time, however, I was motivated to do a real root-cause analysis.
>
> Why was my tire flat? Because there was a puncture in it.
>
> Why was there a puncture in my inner tire? Because a nail punctured it.
>
> Why was there something puncturing my tire for the second time that week? The outer tire might not have been protective enough to cycle through the rough streets of Hamburg.
>
> Solution: over the weekend I invested in new tires that couldn't be punctured.

This last solution is the first solution of the week that actually described an **improvement of the standard (kaizen)**. Monday through Wednesday, I only executed some short-term quick fixes to get my bike functioning again. Only on Thursday did I find a possible root cause for my problem, the reason I got so many flat tires. This led to a proper solution, buying a better tire, to prevent something from puncturing my tire again. Figure 17 shows the 3Cs described in this example.

Problems in keeping the standard are just one aspect of what team boards can address. There are three in total:
1. The standard is not good enough (like the flat-tire example).
2. The standard is not bringing the correct results anymore, reflected by a KPI that is red.
3. A team member has identified a waste and would like to prevent it from occurring again.

When all teams in an organization solve problems like these on a continual basis using root-cause analysis, the performance of the organization improves drastically. When the 3Cs are only used for firefighting—which means the standards are not being raised—there will be no measurable improvement of performance in the long term. A thorough root-cause analysis is therefore one of the most important points to address in any (lean) organization.

The 5x Why in this example has only one *branch*, meaning that in this case, each time we ask 'why' for a cause, we identify only one cause each time.

| No | Date | Concern | Cause | Countermeasure | Who | When | Kaizen | Status |
|----|------|---------|-------|----------------|-----|------|--------|--------|
| 1 | Dec. 1 | Flat tire |  | * Pump up the tire | Thijs | Dec. 1 |  | ⊕ |

| No | Date | Concern | Cause | Countermeasure | Who | When | Kaizen | Status |
|----|------|---------|-------|----------------|-----|------|--------|--------|
| 2 | Dec. 2 | Flat tire | Puncture in the inner tire | * Patch the puncture, * Pump up the tire | Thijs | Dec. 2 |  | ⊕ |

| No | Date | Concern | Cause | Countermeasure | Who | When | Kaizen | Status |
|----|------|---------|-------|----------------|-----|------|--------|--------|
| 3 | Dec. 3 | Flat tire | Puncture in the inner tire because of a piece of glass | * Remove the glass from outer tire * Patch the puncture. * Pump up the tire. | Thijs | Dec. 3 |  | ⊕ |

| No | Date | Concern | Cause | Countermeasure | Who | When | Kaizen | Status |
|----|------|---------|-------|----------------|-----|------|--------|--------|
| 4 | Dec. 4 | Flat tire | Puncture in the inner tire because of sharp object. The tire is too thin | * Buy 'unbreakable tire' * Install and pump up the tire. | Thijs | Dec. 7 | 3207 | ⊕ |

*Figure 17: Documented 3Cs, number four being the most desirable because it is linked to kaizen*

For daily meetings, this is the way to go, since we are talking about defining countermeasures for one specific situation that made the KPI red in the last shift. This one situation should also lead to one countermeasure which is then listed in the action list.

In the other two levels of improvement, A3 thinking and D2MAIC projects, the 5x Why analysis can become a *tree* in which every cause can have multiple other causes in turn. The 5xWhy analysis will then lead to not just one, but possibly multiple root-causes, all of which may need a different set of countermeasures.

We will now first look at the A3 thinking in chapter 9.2, and then at D2MAIC Projects in chapter 9.3.

**Key Points:**
- *With kaizen, we focus on what we can improve by ourselves to improve the situation.*
- *Really solving a problem means it won´t reoccur in the future.*
- *The 5x Why is a simple tool that helps you find the real root cause of a problem.*

## 9.1 Improving the Standard with A3 Problem-Solving

> *I want to hear about your thinking, tell me about your plans.*
> —John Shook

### 9.2.1 What Is It, and Why Is It Important?

The 3Cs on the team board help us to focus on finding the root cause of a problem and to think about preventive countermeasures. There are, however, many problems for which the root cause or countermeasures cannot easily be found. For these more complex problems, we can use A3 problem-solving.

**The name** *A3* refers to the size of an A3 paper that managers use to coach their team members while they are solving problems (Rother 2010). While traditional managers hand out tasks and care only about the results, a lean manager likes to hear how a mentee has arrived at a particular solution. The A3 facilitates that process. Within Toyota, the A3 is therefore considered not only a problem-solving tool but also a management tool (Shook 2008).
In addition to helping to lead to an understanding of a mentee's way of thinking, the A3—which is not about the form itself—facilitates some sort of standardized storytelling, which we use to communicate facts and meaning in a commonly understood format (Shook 2008).

Rother (2010) summarizes the **PURPOSE OF THE A3** in the following five points. First, it is important to challenge the mentee to think about the problem so deeply that he or she can distill his or her knowledge down to only one A3 piece of paper. If you have a big, complex problem at hand, it will take some effort to be able to bring it down to a report of only one page.

Second, the A3 creates a story line. This makes it possible for the mentor to follow the thinking steps of the mentee. It shows the mentor the next step for the mentee to think about and what skills the mentee might need to develop.

Third, the A3 brings structure to the coaching conversation by going through the steps one by one. This avoids a vague discussion in which the conversation jumps between problems, causes, and countermeasures.

Fourth, using an A3 generates consensus and helps define clear actions. When interviewing different people for a certain problem, the interviewer can use the A3 for continual updates with the latest insights, and in the end, it can represent the consensus of the group.

Finally, it can provide milestones for process checks.

In summary, we can say that in terms of **imbalance**, A3 thinking creates some sort of standard problem-solving method using the same storytelling template. When all managers use the same A3 format, variance among the way managers coach their team members and how problems are solved is reduced.

**Overburden** is reduced when there are some rules about the A3s. There can be a maximum number of open A3s per person to prevent overburden. The structure of the A3 and all the conversations about the problem can prevent a person from feeling overwhelmed by the complexity of the problem.

Finally, **waste** can be prevented when the A3 helps to find the real root cause of the problem and prevents the team from dealing with the same problem again in the future. When used as part of the strategic planning process (hoshin), the templates help prevent setting unachievable goals and all the rework that follows because of that.

In terms of management principles, the A3 facilitates at least the following:
**Principle four: Leveling out the workload** happens whenever there is a maximum number of A3s defined for a person to work on.

**Principle six: Use standard work** for project reporting, problem-solving, and coaching as part of leader standard work.

**Principle nine: Grow your leaders internally**. When you use the A3 as a coaching tool, as Rother (2010) suggests, you are building problem-solving and coaching capabilities when solving problems. These are two important traits of the next generation of leaders.

**Principle ten: Develop exceptional people and teams.** The same holds for this principle. By asking everybody in the organization to reflect on the problem and challenging those people to find the right problem definition and root-cause analysis, you really develop the workforce.

**Principle thirteen: Make decisions slowly using consensus.** As the A3 is changed over and over again during the problem-solving process, it always reflects the latest consensus view on the problem. By starting every discussion with the latest description of the problem and its breakdown, there is more consensus about the chosen countermeasures later in the process.

**Principle fourteen: Use hansei and kaizen.** The more complex the situation or problem, the more difficult it is to summarize the results on only one piece of paper. Boiling all information down to one A3 requires a lot of reflection.

> **Key Points:**
> - *The A3 tells a problem-solving story that unfolds during the process.*
> - *Documenting the story makes coaching easier.*

## 9.2.2 How to Use A3 Thinking

*If you can't explain it simply, you don't understand it well enough.*

Different authors describe the **CONTENT OF THE A3** differently, but the general idea always includes the different steps of the problem-solving process. Figure 18 shows one example. The different fields of this sample A3 are the following:

A **problem statement** describes what the problem is and also what it is not. This step alone can take quite some time and can include multiple revisions (Shook 2008).

*Figure 18: Example of an A3 document*

The **breakdown of the problem** helps a person dive deeper into the problem. The breakdown describes the different subproblems that possibly lead to the general problem statement. The more complex the problem that needs to be solved, the more useful this field is.

The **goal** or the target condition of this A3 summarizes what the mentee has to achieve in terms of measurable results. This ensures that the mentee knows up-front when the manager or the team will accept later-defined countermeasures. Preferably the goal is defined in such a way that it has one measurable KPI, with a 'from ... to' definition, and a time frame.

The **root-cause analysis** is the next step on the A3 form. This is where you can use fish bone diagrams, 5x Why, or a problem-analysis tree to clarify where the root cause(s) of the problem can be found. The 5x Why analysis will be more complex in the A3 than in a Kaizen or on a team board. Every cause could have multiple causes, and therefore the results of the 5X why could lead to multiple root-causes.

Then it is time to determine the **countermeasures**. What can be done to preventively solve the problems? It is important to note that one problem can contain multiple root causes, and one root cause may need multiple countermeasures to reach the target condition (Shook 2008).

The sixth field gives you space briefly to mention information about **implemented countermeasures**, after which the results of the countermeasures are measured in field seven.

When the countermeasures are successful in solving the problem, the mentee can use the last field of the A3 to address what **standards** need to be updated and shared and to make sure the points learned are embedded in the standard work of colleagues, whose work might have changed due to the countermeasures.

The last two fields of the A3 form are what Barnhart refers to as the **learning plan** (Barnhart 2013). This term highlights the fact that the A3 is a useful way to guide the learning process. You cannot be certain that the countermeasures defined will actually solve the problem preventively. It is very possible that the countermeasures will change during the problem-solving process, and that different standards will need to be updated than what was initially expected.

Here are some examples of **WHEN TO USE THE A3**. Because the A3 structures thinking and facilitates reporting with as little text as possible, the A3 is a perfect tool for **one-on-one coaching** in the daily improvement process (Rother 2010). Imagine having multiple team members all working on different improvements. It could be difficult to remember in what stage of problem-solving your mentees are. The A3 makes it possible to repeat the status of the improvement and to keep focus on the target condition (usually reducing one of the three enemies of lean), which is the reason we are doing something at all (Rother 2010).

The same applies to coaching within the daily management structure for **problem-solving** (Jackson 2006). In this case, a defect occurs somewhere in the process, and it is the task of the mentee to learn why this problem has occurred and how to solve it.

In a broader sense, you could also use the template within **project management**. In a project management environment, it is not uncommon to have long meetings in which certain causes or countermeasures are discussed without clearly repeating the project's goals and whether the countermeasures are actually helping to achieve those goals. The project as a whole should have a project charter that includes the same structure as an A3 document, and within each project, every subproblem could be documented on one A3 as well. More information on projects, and especially the D2MAIC structure, can be found in chapter 9.3.

In terms of **process design**, you can use the A3 template when the kaizen events are defined after a value stream mapping event. The eight steps of creating a future-state VSM (described in chapter 13) will lead the team to a list of necessary improvements in the design of the process, and for each of those you can use an A3 template.

Finally, on a **strategic level**, you can use A3 documents during the *catch ball* process of policy deployment (Jackson 2006), during which the targets for each department and team are defined based on the organizational goals. In this case you can capture every tactic listed in the X-matrix, the tool to use for policy deployment, on an A3 template. Chapter 10 discusses the X-matrix.

The A3 is a simple tool that can bring huge benefits to the company. Forget PowerPoints or reports that have a countless number of pages. By challenging everybody in the organization to condense all information necessary to one single A3 page, we can increase our problem-solving, our improvement, and our coaching capabilities at the same time!

The best way to learn how to use A3 problem solving is by doing it. Lead by example and start practicing the principles yourself to see both the difficulty of answering the questions as well as the benefit of talking about the different blocks with your colleagues.

**Key Points:**
- *The A3 is a tool that standardizes coaching conversations, standardizes storytelling, and reduces paperwork.*
- *The fields on the A3 can be different in each company, but they all include the different steps of problem-solving.*
- *One can use the A3 in daily management, for projects, and for strategic planning.*

## 9.2 Improving the Standard with D2MAIC Projects

*If a person is going to spend six months on a project, you better be sure it helps you reach your company goals!*
- Perry Kuijpers

### 9.3.1 What Is It, and Why Is It Important

Projects are an important part of every lean program. First, you have the small problems that can be solved within the team using the kaizen approach described in chapter 9.1; then you have the larger problems that can be solved with the use of A3 thinking described in chapter 9.2. There are, however, bigger structural problems that cannot simply be solved within a few weeks. These can be solved through *projects*.

Projects can take up to six months to complete, and one structure that can be used is the D2MAIC structure described by Abramowich (2005), which includes six phases: discovery, define, measure, analyze, improve, and control (Abramowich 2005). This is a slightly different version of the most common used DMAIC abbreviation, which is the same as the D2MAIC, except for the discovery phase. I like the addition of the discovery phase by Abramowich, because it makes sure you link your projects clearly to your organizational goals (fourth level of lean maturity).

When done well, the project reduces all three enemies of lean. By looking at the profit and loss statement in the discovery phase, you only select projects that directly reduce the largest **waste** in your organization.

The measure and analyze phases will make sure that the root-cause analysis leads to the root cause for the waste. Chances are that **overburden** is at stake. Why did a machine have to wait for material? Why was the downtime of a machine so long? These are all related to the way the operators have defined their standard work and how the machine settings are standardized.

These root causes will lead the project team to imbalance. What standards do we need to define or to change to prevent these variations from happening—the variations that lead to these losses found in the discovery phase?

So far, the overburden and the wastes mentioned above can usually be reduced in what is commonly known as *Yellow Belt projects*. There are several types of *belts* within the six-sigma community, *yellow, green* and *black*, which describe the level of complexity of the projects that the project leader can lead.

Yellow belts are the simplest form of projects and these are usually focused on reducing an observed waste or overburden as described above. This is the level of D2MAIC that will be described in this chapter.

*Green-* and *Black Belts* are project leaders that focus more on reducing **variability (imbalance)** of a process, with the help of a variety of statistical tools. These are then called the *Green- or Black Belt Projects*. This book will not include these statistical tools, but an introduction of these can be found on my blog: www.mudamasters.com.

## 9.3.2 How to do a D2MAIC project

> *The D2MAIC approach directly affects what customers buy and hence the organization's revenue and margins.*
> —E. Abramowich

The **DISCOVERY PHASE** is part of the strategic plan of an organization and takes place before the actual start of the traditional DMAIC project. There are three tools to use in this phase that will help define the goals and scope of the project, that are needed in the define phase: The X-matrix, a loss analysis, and the Pareto analysis.

The **X-matrix** is part of the hoshin kanri process, in which the next year's targets are defined. Within this X-matrix, you move from strategies, to desirable results, to processes that need to be changed, and finally to tactics that are defined to make that change happen. In this case, the future project is the tactic, which could for instance focus on achieving a downtime reduction, which directly reduces conversion costs (results). The X-matrix will be described in more detail in chapter 10.

Now, the strategic part of the project is set. We know that we have a realistic opportunity for improvement that directly leads to measurable results.
The next step is to start working on **the project charter**. In the discovery phase, you only define the first two parts of the charter: the problem statement with the improvement goal, a rough benefit calculation including monetary benefits, an expected time line, the scope of the project, and the team structure, including roles and responsibilities.

Questions that need to be answered before the hoshin is complete, and before the project starts, are: What is the gap that we wish to close? What is the number one KPI that we are going to measure to make sure our project is a success? and can we express the expected improvement of that KPI in monetary savings? Who is going to be in the team and what are the risks?

Having just **one main KPI** will help the project team to focus. Even better is when you can describe the possible savings in monetary terms that are linked to that one KPI. Showing the financial benefit will help you get the support from higher management that you may need to start, continue and finish your project. The loss and waste analysis will help find this one KPI.

Since we would like every project to directly influence bottom line results, we should define our projects based on where most of the losses occur. This is where a **loss and waste analysis** is helpful. There are many ways in which you can visualize the different wastes in a process. One of them is a waterfall chart as shown below.

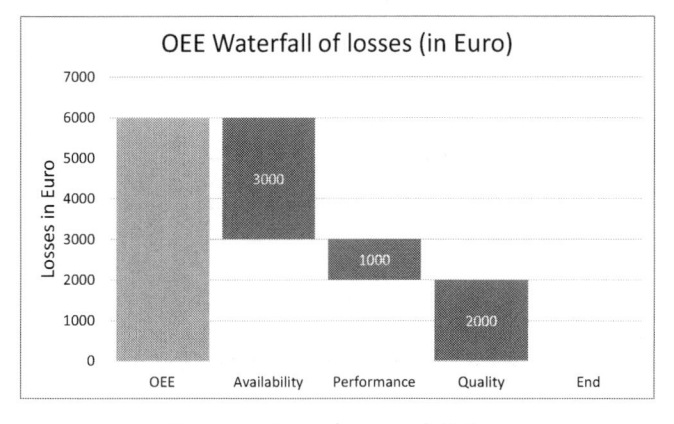

*Figure 19: Sample waterfall chart*

Figure 19 shows an example of a waterfall chart breakdown for a machine part in a factory. By splitting OEE numbers into different categories, the chart shows that most losses occur in the machine availability category.

Of course, you can split losses in any other possible way that helps you in your organization; the OEE is just one possibility. Other examples include the breakdown of quality issues per product family, the yield loss per machine, or a breakdown of the fixed manufacturing cost of a product over different departments.

After this waterfall chart, it is possible to break down one of the aspects of the problem at **a deeper level**. As a next step, we could create a waterfall chart for availability only, to see what factors influence this indicator the most.

When creating these charts, keep them **money focused**. The deeper you go into the waterfall chart, the smaller the individual parts will be. In the end, we would like to select an indicator to improve based on savings that are worthwhile and based on the resources necessary to complete the project.

**The Pareto analysis** can then help to define what improvement gaps there are. Figure 20 shows a sample Pareto analysis of downtimes for seven machines. In this example, we can see that half of the OEE losses were due to availability of the machines. It makes sense to see what the difference is between the different machines in the factory.

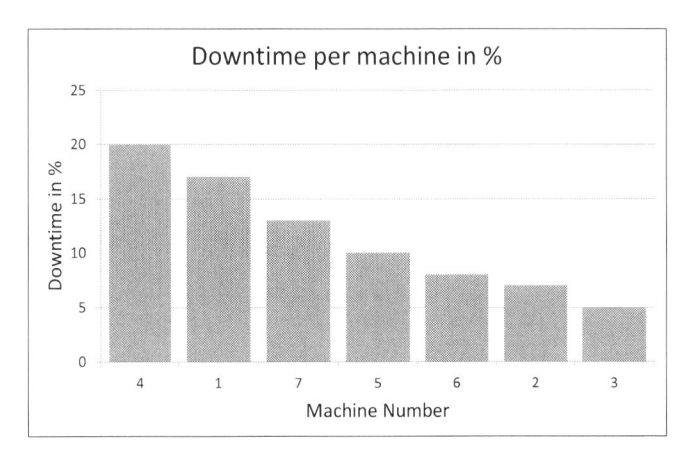

*Figure 20: Sample Pareto chart*

Assuming these are seven parallel machines, this graph shows that machine four has a downtime of 20 percent, while machine three only has a downtime of 5 percent. Because machine three proves that it is possible to have downtimes of only 5 percent, it could be worthwhile to define a project that reduces the downtime of machine 4 from 20 percent to 5 percent, with the possible benefit of moving the same positive results to the other machines. Before we start the project, we **calculate how much we would save** by reducing the downtime of machine four.

Finally, the discovery phase should include a **risk analysis**. What are the possible risks for this project? Different risks are mapped on three scales: the chance that it would happen, the impact that the risk has on the organization and how well we can detect the risk when it occurs (Abramowich 2005). This is also referred to as a Failure Modes and Effect Analysis (FMEA).

The next project phase is **THE DEFINE PHASE**. This phase has at least two goals: understanding customer requirements and gaining a general understanding about the process. Each of these goals can be achieved using a variety of tools. Tools to use in this phase are the SIPOC and the critical-to-quality analysis based on the voice of the customer (VOC).

**The SIPOC**, as was already explained in chapter 7.2, is a model that is used to show the complexity of a process. The SIPOC helps to **identify the different stakeholders** of a process (suppliers and customers), which helps the project team determine its communication plan and the nature of the voice of the customer.

In the **critical-to-quality (CTQ) analysis**, the project team defines the customer requirements and how the product and/or process delivers those requirements. The voice of the customer (which can also be the voice of the business) can be both internal and external. In its simplest form, the CTQ analysis can take the form of a table that lists the most important criteria for each customer, but this is not a given. The goal of this exercise is not to create this table, but to make sure that you keep the discussion going about what it is the customer expects from you. The project team can list different stakeholders, their most important topics or indicators, and the critical requirements that need to be met by the process, which helps the project team in fine-tuning the project goals.

The critical to quality analysis is also known as the critical-to-satisfaction analysis, which is a name that is used for the same analysis but acknowledges that a certain level of quality is not the only thing that a customer may require.

At the end of the define phase, the **project charter** that was started in the discovery phase is continued. The project team has now gathered more information about the project and can update the problem statement, which includes the goals and scope of the project with the project sponsor(s).
After doing the SIPOC and CTQ analysis, a more precise business case can be built to show the value for the business when this project is done, not only moneywise but also with respect to improvement in customer satisfaction.

Just like within A3 problem solving, the goal of the project that is defined in the charter should have one measurable KPI, and a from ... to statement, and a deadline for when this improvement should be reached.

The define phase is followed by the **MEASURE PHASE**. This phase has three goals: gaining a detailed understanding of the process, defining what metrics can be used to measure the capability of the process, and defining a system to collect and measure the process capabilities. Tools that can be used during the measure phase include the value stream map (VSM), the metric selection table, and control charts.

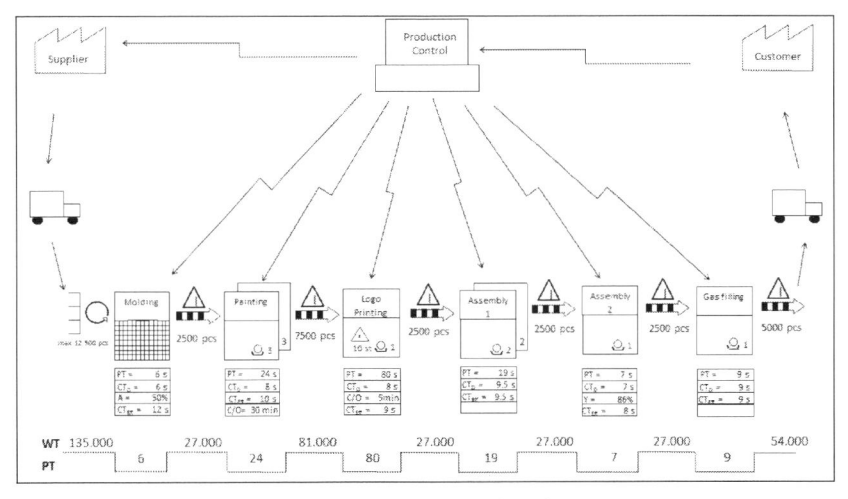

*Figure 21: An example of a VSM*

**Value stream mapping** is a lean tool that can be used to map processes in detail, based on both the flow of material and the flow of information. Data boxes make it possible to list important aspects of each process step, such as changeover times, cycle times, and machine availability. This makes value stream mapping a great tool to use in designing or redesigning a value stream. In traditional lean initiatives, a current-state value stream map is drawn first, after which a future-state map can be designed. An example of a very simple value stream map is shown in Figure 21. Value stream mapping is further described in part 4.

The value stream map should help the team in **defining the correct metrics** to measure the success of the project. When the VSM is done well, all important information of the process can be found in the data boxes, so the team can select the metrics based on these.

To close the loop with the previous phases of the project, a metric selection table can be created to link the metrics that were selected from the VSM to the CTQs. Those metrics were obtained through customer feedback earlier. A simple table with three columns – measure, description and CTQ – suffices to make this link.

**The control charts** can be used to track the performance of a specific metric. The control chart is an illustration of the results of one metric, where a certain bandwidth of variation is allowed between an upper control limit (UCL) and a lower control limit (LCL).

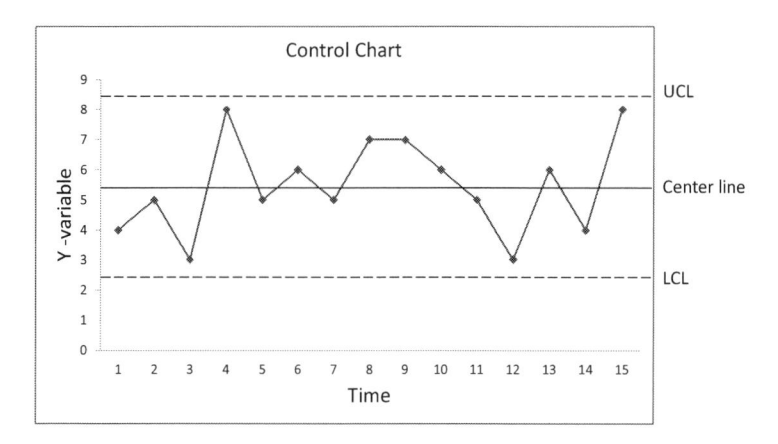

*Figure 22: Example of a control chart*

When the process is unstable and acts outside these two limits, action is required in terms of analyzing the process criteria that led to this result. The control chart is shown in the figure 22 below.

After the measure phase comes the **ANALYZE PHASE**. This is the phase in which the data that is collected is used to find the root causes for the problems defined in the discovery phase and the define phase. Tools that can be used in this phase are flow analysis and different root-cause analysis techniques, such as the 5x Why.

The main difference between the projects, the A3 (chapter 9.2), or kaizen (chapter 9.1) is that in these complex projects, root causes need to be validated using the measurement system defined in the measure phase.

Remember from chapter 9.1.3 that the **5x Why** analysis is the easiest tool that helps you to continue questioning the possible cause of a problem to make sure you get to the root cause. The root cause can only be one of two possibilities: either there is a missing or incorrect standard, or the standard is not known to all who have to work with it. In both cases, it is clear what the countermeasure options of the root cause would be: either you have to update or create the standard, or you have to train people in using it.
Within technical projects, examples of standards that need to be set are machine settings, short interval control standards, or cleaning standards. Again, it is important to check whether the actions that derive from the countermeasures impact the metrics defined in the measure phase.

**The Ishikawa diagram**, also known as the fishbone diagram, is a brainstorming tool that can help identify the possible root causes of a problem. When a simple 5x Why analysis does not help you find the root cause, the project team can brainstorm possible causes using this structure, of which figure 23 is an example. Every bone of the fish represents one category of the possible cause, and the bones are traditionally grouped in either four or six words that all start with "M."

In this example, the fishbone diagram is also a 6M diagram, with the categories of measurement, material, machine, mother nature, man power, and method.

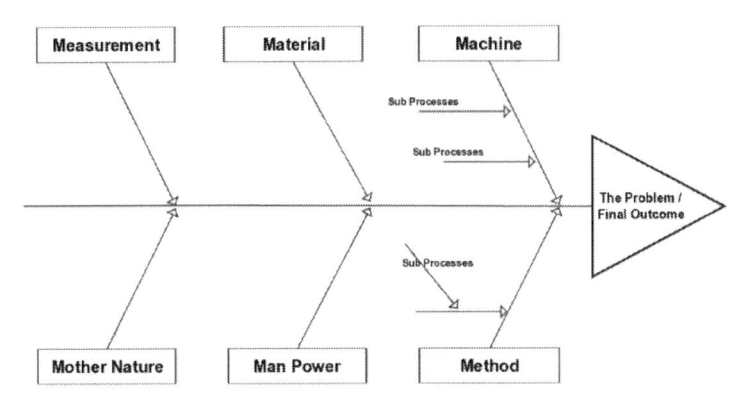

*Figure 23: An example of an Ishikawa (Fishbone) diagram*

Together, the measure and analyze phases are the phases that make the project fact based. Measures are selected to quantify the problem that is to be solved. The metrics are also used to validate improvements in the future. In the analyze phase, data is analyzed to be able to set a direction for action. These actions will be described in the final two phases: the improve phase and the control phase.

The **IMPROVE PHASE** of the project is about implementing countermeasures that can solve the problem described and analyzed in the previous phases. There are three goals in this phase: to generate improvement ideas, to select the right countermeasures, and to implement the countermeasures.

For idea selection, an easy tool to use is the **benefit-effort matrix**. Simply put, it includes all the generated countermeasures in the graph based on the estimated implementation effort (technical effort, costs, resources) and the benefit they bring in terms of achieving the project goals determined in the define phase. An example of the benefit-effort matrix is shown in figure 24.

When it is determined what you need to implement, it is time to determine when it will be done. This is where the **implementation plan** comes in. The plan should include the actions that were defined in the previous step on a timeline that schedules the tasks for specific days or weeks. Usually, there are two rows per action, the planned timing and the actual timing. Of course, the actions can be broken down into smaller actions and can have different owners.

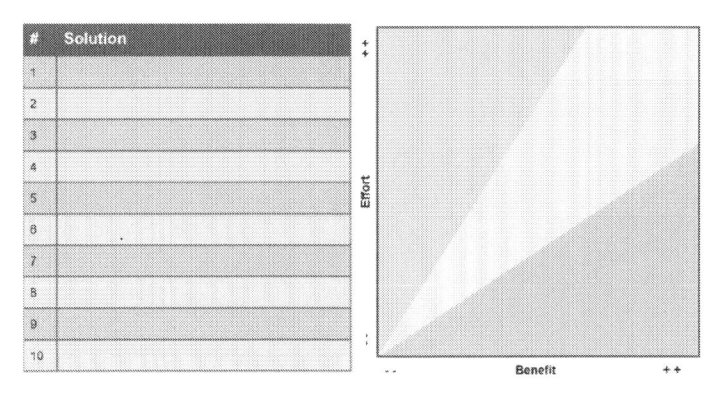

*Figure 24: An example of a benefit-effort matrix*

A planning tool that will bring your project plan to the next level is **the PERT chart**. PERT is an acronym for program evaluation and review technique. In the PERT chart, you not only show the tasks on a time line, but you show the critical path of the project. The example in figure 25 shows the basics.
- The dark gray actions show the critical path; the lighter actions show the other actions.
- Each activity has six variables—three on the top and three on the bottom.
    - The top row shows the day the action starts, the number of days the activity takes, and the end day of the action. Take activity E, for example: this activity takes five days, starts on day ten, and will therefore be finished on day fifteen.
    - The bottom row shows us what the maximum delay of a task can be without delaying the entire project with, from left to right, the latest possible start date, the maximum number of days delay, and the latest possible finish date. When we look at activity B, for instance, we can see that it has to be finished at day ten for the project to still be on track. The difference between ten and six (top right) is four days of maximum delay. This means that the activity should start at (0 + 4 = 4) day four at the latest.

Even more detailed than the PERT chart is the **project value stream map**. This type of value stream mapping, which will be further discussed in chapter 14.3, includes the project milestones, the decisions that need to be made to achieve those milestones, and the actions that are needed to be able to make those decisions.

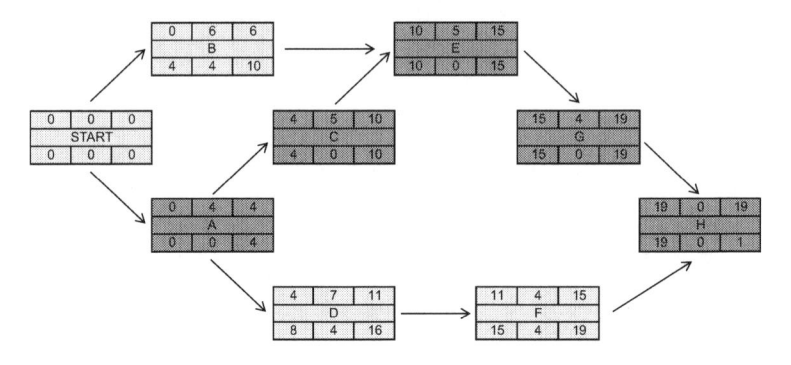

*Figure 25: An example of a PERT chart*

The final phase of the project is the **CONTROL PHASE**. This is where it is validated that the actions undertaken during the improve phase have led to the improvements that were originally targeted for this project, the sustainability of the results are assured, and success is celebrated.

One easy way of showing improvements is using **Statistical Process Control (SPC)**. With this tool, process charts can show the behavior of a process in statistical terms. Figure 26 shows one example of the process chart in which improvements have been made at the end of the first quarter of the year, which led to measurable improvements at the second and third quarters. We can see that the average value has been reduced to 10, and the variation of the process has been reduced, moving between 25 and -2 (the upper and lower control limits).

To sustain the results of the project, it is important that new ways of working are documented in **Standard Operating Procedures (SOPs)** which are also vital tools to inform or train the workforce about the new way of working. In my dream factory, every team has papers with SOPs on workstations where the task is performed. Whenever there has been a change in the way of working, the new SOP is distributed to the people during the **daily team board meeting.**

The process chart shown above can also be posted on the team board (chapter 2.2) to keep tracking the results for a certain time frame.
To make sure the new instructions are followed, you could choose to create a temporary **kamishibai check** on this topic.

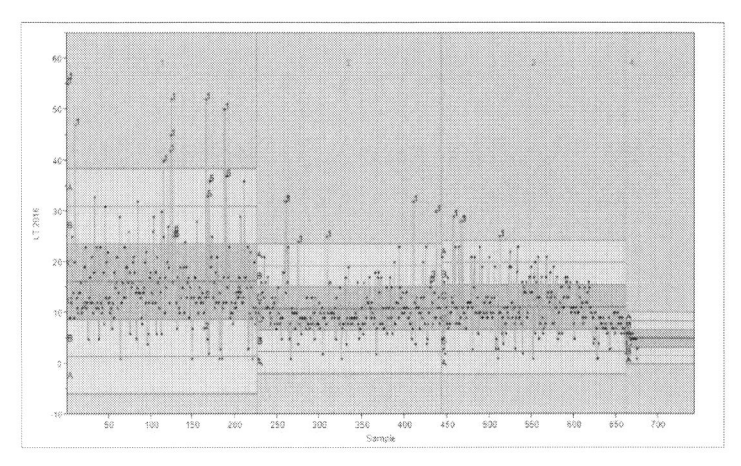

*Figure 26: An example of a process chart*

Next to kaizen and A3, projects are a way of improving your business. Ideally, they are directly linked to your organizational goals and take about six months to complete.

D2MAIC, in turn, is a way of managing a project and is commonly used within a lean- or Six Sigma program (though many organizations do not add the discovery phase as an official step; they only use DMAIC).

Following the phase structure helps both the project team and the management team track progress of the project to make sure the yearly targets of the organization are met. D2MAIC is therefore a very valuable tool.

**Key Points:**
- *The D2MAIC project structure describes six phases of a project.*
- *The discovery and define phases make sure the project directly improves bottom line results.*
- *The measure and analyze phases make sure the project is fact based.*
- *The improve and control phases ensure the actions taken are solving the problem defined in the define phase and that the countermeasures are sustained.*

# Chapter 10:

# Level Four: Linking Improvement to Company Goals

*When you would like to measure success of your lean journey, make sure that everybody is improving to achieve the same goal.*

So far in this third part of the book, we have discussed the first three levels of lean maturity. 5S and standard work set the standards that everybody works with at level one. Then kamishibai and the team boards check whether standards are being followed at level two. In level three, we have discussed kaizen, A3 thinking and D2MAIC projects to be able to improve the standards, taking them to a higher level to improve performance. This chapter will discuss the highest form of lean maturity: level four - linking improvements to organizational goals.

An organization achieves the highest level of maturity when all members of the organization not only improve their own processes but also link them to the company goals. This is where the daily management system (chapter 10.1), the linkage between the team boards in the organization, becomes important.

Using the tool hoshin kanri to cascade the KPI throughout the organization, we make sure all departments are improving in the same direction, the vision of the company (chapter 10.2). Team board meetings discuss progress and problems, which can be escalated to different levels of team boards when necessary. This is the topic of the following chapter.

## 10.1 The Daily Management System

*Seeing how efforts influence the performance of the company gives everybody a sense of contribution and meaning in their working lives.*

### 10.1.1 What Is It, and Why Is It Important

There are multiple reasons why the daily management system is important. First of all, it improves the flow of problems, because a problem can flow from one department to another using the standard meeting structure.

Second, KPIs are cascaded throughout the company, which means every team knows exactly how its performance influences the organizational performance in general. This increases the sense of personal contribution and thereby increases employee satisfaction.

To improve the flow of problems, you need a team board structure in which problems have the chance to flow between departments without much waiting time in between (Mann 2005).

In the meeting structure, the following hierarchy levels are differentiated within Toyota: team of employees, their team leader, group leaders to manage the team leaders, and an area manager to manage the group leaders.

A **tier 1 meeting** takes place every shift or day in which the production team discusses the last shift's performance with their team leader, as well as details for the upcoming shift and possible employee input. All problems are listed on the 3C and solved within the team as much as possible.
One example of a tier 1 meeting is a meeting in which a team of operators in a packaging department that reports the progress of 5 different packaging lines.

**The tier 2 meetings** are the daily meetings between the team leaders and the group leaders in which they discuss the top three problems of different departments from the last twenty-four hours that the teams could not solve themselves. Improvement activities are defined to prevent these problems from ever occurring again. One example of a tier 2 meeting is a production meeting in which the team leaders of logistics, production, packaging and quality discuss progress of all their departments with the group leader for their product group.

**The tier 3 meeting** is the daily meeting between the group leader and the value stream *owner* (the person who is responsible for the performance of the value stream) in which the escalated problems for the entire value stream are discussed. This meeting is focused more on achieving the weekly targets.
One example of a tier 3 meeting is a meeting in which multiple group leaders who each have their own production groups (and tier 2 meetings) report back to the area manager on progress.

It is also possible that the teams collect information on machine level, OEE numbers that are collected every 5 minutes, or production output levels that are collected on a shorter interval than published on the tier 1 board. These boards and measurements provide the input for the tier 1 meeting where the team (that possibly run multiple machines) discussed them. I sometimes refer to these machine level KPI as **tier 0**.

The greatest strength of having a meeting structure like this is that the entire organization discusses organizational performance. And higher management is involved in problem-solving on a daily basis.

**Imbalance** is reduced because all teams in the organization have similar team meetings that discuss KPIs that directly link to the organizational goals. This means all teams discuss the same KPIs, and silo thinking is reduced. With silo thinking, each department only focuses on their own performance, using their own team KPI, which at its worst is counterproductive to the KPI of another team. Having the same KPIs for all teams therefore reduces the risk of silo thinking and improves cooperation between departments. That's because the teams are now working toward the same performance targets.

**Overburden** is prevented because problems and improvements are discussed daily at different organizational levels, which means the problems can be prioritized within the meetings. This prevents teams from spending too much time on problems or improvements that do not impact organizational goals.

When there is too much to solve or improve, the higher level can either support the solving process or set priorities to prevent the lower-level team from becoming overburdened.

**Waste** in all communication between individuals and departments can be reduced. A problem that cannot be solved within the team can flow to another department, which increases the speed of action and therefore reduces the waiting time associated with the problem. It also brings the problem to the person or job function where there are the right skills to solve it. When the problem is solved in a preventive way, it prevents rework in the future.

The daily management structure facilitates living the following lean management principles:

**Principle one: Making decisions based on the long-term vision.** When the KPIs of all team boards are cascaded correctly and they are directly related to the organizational goals, the team will use these visual representations to guide their decision making. If a problem in a team prevents the team from reaching its target, the organizational goals are also at stake. The daily management structure creates the possibility for management levels to support the level-one teams in solving their problems so that they can stay on track in achieving their goals.

**Principle seven: Make problems so that they are demonstrated visually.** One important aspect of the daily management structure is that the organizational goals are shown on the team boards at the management level and therefore they are transparent for everybody to see. Whenever there is a red KPI, everybody can see and should understand that there is a problem and that actions are necessary to improve performance again.

**Principle fourteen: Take time to reflect and continuously improve.** The daily meeting structure gives all teams in the plant the opportunity to reflect on how communication happens. What happens if an important topic in the company is not discussed or a problem that occurred is not addressed? Are we then still discussing the right topics in each team? Or do we need to adjust the KPIs or meeting rules?

> **Key Points:**
> - *The daily management structure is the tool that links all improvements to the company goals.*
> - *KPIs should be broken down to different levels of the organization, referred to as tiers, or levels.*
> - *The daily management structure facilitates the flow of problems in which every problem can move up to a management-team level within twenty-four hours.*

## 10.1.2 How to Implement the Daily Management Structure

*By noon all levels in the organization should know what problems exist in each of the levels and know what is being done to preventively solve these issues.*

Chapter 8.2 already described what a team board should include in terms of people, performance, and continuous improvement. This chapter focuses on linking the different team boards together using the daily management structure. This is a structure of meetings that make it possible for problems to flow to any department that can solve it.

The foundation of the daily management structure is the **KPI tree**, in which each department has a lead indicator that is directly cascaded from the organizational goals. The KPI tree is also an important step of hoshin kanri, which is the topic of 10.2.

One example is the cascading of the cost value 'cost per kg' or 'cost per unit' measure that is being used on site level (tier 3) to measure costs of producing one unit or one kg of product. On operator level (tier 1), this is not a helpful way to find improvements, since this is a general number that includes many other aspects that are outside their circle of influence.

However, the tier 1 team could measure specific wastes that occur in their team that impact the cost of the product. They could measure waiting times, or the rework that they had to perform to get the product up to a certain quality level. These indirectly improve the production costs of the product but are within the circle of influence of the team. Every team can define their own leading indicator for each lagging indicator, meaning that one team could define the time it waits for material as their biggest loss, while another tier 1 team has identified the amount of machine downtime as their biggest loss. Both leading indicators then become the branches, the cascaded values, of the cost part of the KPI tree.

Now, let's look at the meeting structure itself. First, the meetings of the daily management structure should be planned in such a way, that **within a few hours,** problems can move up to the right person to solve them. In one of the factories where I worked, all meetings for levels one through three took place between eight and ten in the morning, which meant that important unsolved problems were discussed at the management-team level every day and were assigned to a person or department to develop a solution.

Second, the **problems of multiple meetings can flow into one meeting** at a higher level. Figure 27 shows an example meeting structure. The number of meetings necessary at every level depends on the organization. Each meeting should be no longer than fifteen minutes. As we learned, coaching is an important part of the duties of a lean transformation leader. However, it is not just the lean transformation leaders who do the coaching. Remember from chapter 1 that all managers and leaders are potential coaches, and coaching team board meetings can be part of their leader standard work.

Two tools that make it easier for anyone to assess a team board meeting are the terms of reference (TOR) and a maturity scale that can help you start asking the right questions.

**The terms of reference**, or TOR, are on a document that includes all information about the meeting, time and place, participants, responsibilities, agenda, etc. The terms of reference also contain the meeting rules, such as being on time, sticking to the agenda, and letting each person speak when that person has something to say.

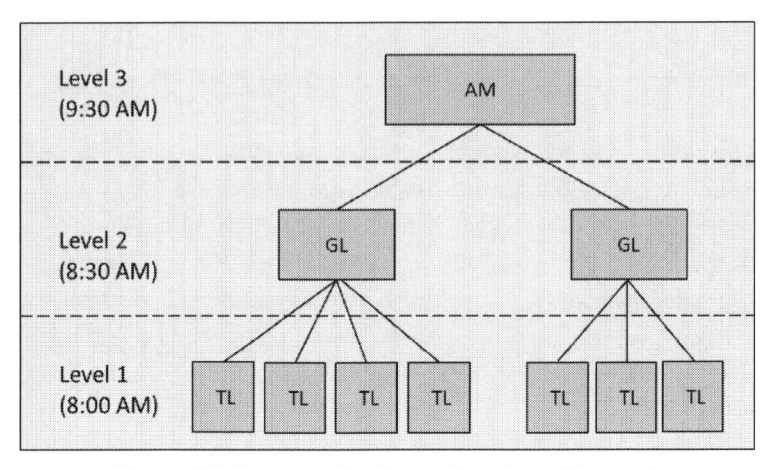

*Figure 27: An example of meeting times for levels*

Having a TOR can also help you as a facilitator to subsequently judge whether the meeting was good or requires improvement. The coach in this case simply takes the TOR for the meeting and checks if the actual meeting was what was described in the TOR, and then the coach provides feedback at the end of the meeting.

At one factory that I worked for, we also used a template to **determine the maturity** of the team board meeting at the site. There are five levels of maturity:
- At level one, there is a team board, and people meet in front of it.
- At level two, the people, performance, and continuous improvement parts are found on the board. KPIs are clearly defined, the three-second rule is applied and all KPIs have an owner and a backup.
- At level three, the team follows the TOR and uses the team board structure to address problems in the team using 3C and A3.
- At level four, the board is linked to a higher-level board, and when problems are not solved within a certain timeframe, the higher level provides resources to make sure the problem is solved.
- At level five, red KPIs start the problem-solving process, and these problems lead to kaizen that improve the KPI.

In my experience, it can take a team between one and six months to achieve the fifth level of maturity. Coaching and management attention are the most important factors that can positively influence this time span.

The coach is there to help the team address the rules or agenda point that is on the TOR but that was not used while the coach was present at the meeting.

It is the manager of the department who has to want his team to use the team board the way it is designed and ask for input for his next-level meeting. In this case, it is the site manager who has a major role to play in the daily management structure. When he or she asks his or her team members to deliver KPIs and follow up on red KPIs, each of the team members will ask the same from their teams.

Remember, from chapter 7.2.3, that **positive reinforcement** is the key to motivating people. So, the best way to motivate people to use the daily management structure is to reward their good behavior. Make it worth their while for them to use it.

The easiest way to positively reinforce this as a coach, is to compliment the team, or a member of the team, for a specific instance of using the structure or following the agenda.
Even better is to make sure that, **when a problem is moved up to the next-level meeting, it is acted on quickly**. This will be rewarding to the team that moved the problem up, which increases the probability that the team will do so again.

The key to making the daily meeting structure work is to link the KPI of every team directly to the organizational goals. This principle is called **hoshin kanri**, or **policy deployment** in English (Jackson 2006) (Webers 2010), which is discussed next.

**Key Points:**
- *Assess team meetings using the TOR or a maturity score system.*
- *Start the daily management structure from the top down to create a pull for information from the bottom.*
- *Positively reinforce the proper use of the daily management structure.*

## 10.2 Hoshin Kanri

*Before the calendar year starts, each department should already know what their most important target is going to be, and how they are going to achieve it.*

A complete hoshin kanri cascades the organizational goals from a strategic level, to a tactical level, and then to an operational level, as Figure 28 shows below.

Within this cascade, the types of KPIs change from lagging on a strategic level to leading on an operational level. We will discuss two different types of KPIs: control indicators at the tactical level and behavioral indicators at the operational level.

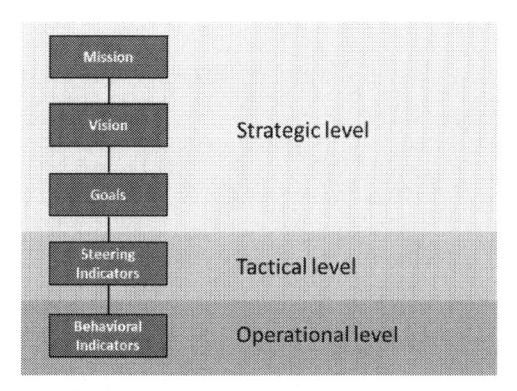

*Figure 28: Hoshin kanri, cascading from strategic to operational goals*

At the **STRATEGIC LEVEL,** the organization needs to determine its mission, vision, and goals. The combination of these three can be referred to as **the strategic intention** (Floyd 2010). In most organizations, the intentions of the organization are not clear to all employees. Sharing the strategic intention on the team boards might therefore be a good idea to help employees understand why management has certain expectations.

**The mission** describes the *why* for the change. This could include things like "improving customer satisfaction for our product" or "employee job fulfillment."

**The vision** describes the future state of the organization necessary to complete the mission. This answers the *how* question. How will we achieve higher customer satisfaction or higher job fulfillment for our employees? One vision could be "being a learning organization that continually reduces costs and quality issues and increases the reliability of deliveries." As I described in chapter 1, having a clear and motivating vision is one of the five important elements of change. Phrases that are often used in the vision are "perfect factory", "#1 in the state/country/world", "best place to work", "cheapest" and so forth.

**The goals** are then the measurable targets that are necessary to be able to achieve the vision. As we learned in chapter 4, one measure improves quality, costs, and reliability at the same time: the lead time (Krafcik 1988). One goal at the strategic level could therefore be to reduce the lead time of the value stream by 50 percent in the following calendar year.

In a strategic workshop, I like to spend one hour analyzing the vision of the organization, and do the exercise of defining the KPI that they use measuring the success of getting closer to achieving that vision, and identifying the lean tools that they can use to achieve that goal.

At the **TACTICAL LEVEL,** KPIs with targets are cascaded down to **control indicators**. Every department or workstation within tier 1, 2 and 3 should have a cascaded form of the goals. The indicator should be manageable, and the people at the workstation should be able to influence this indicator. These are the lagging indicators for each performance categories: safety, quality, delivery, cost and people.

A tool that can help create the cascading of KPIs into control indicators at the tactical level is the **X-matrix**. The process of hoshin kanri starts at the top of the organization with the goals the management team wants to achieve. Jackson (2006) describes four steps for filling the first X-matrix on a strategic level, as figure 29 shows.

The first step of the strategic planning process is deciding on the three-year to five-year **strategies** (on the left part of the form). What does the organization want to achieve in the next three years or the next five years? One example could be to speed up the response times to a changing market.

The second step is deciding on **the results** that the strategies should lead to. These usually are cost related and can be divided into development, material,

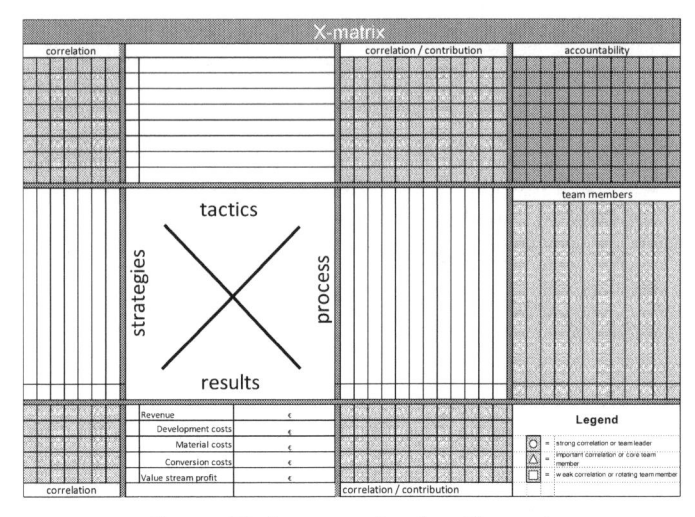

*Figure 29: An example of an X-matrix*

and conversion costs (Jackson 2006). What are the bottom-line results that we want to improve with this strategy? For example, let´s say we would like to reduce conversion costs by 10 percent this year.

After we decide on the results for the coming year, we decide on the **process goals** that should lead to those results. In our lean example, we could copy the strategic goals and set the target to reduce lead time of a value stream by 50 percent.

The final step of the top-level X-matrix is to define the **tactics** needed to achieve the process goals. In our example, you can a current-state and future-state VSM event where we define the kaizen event necessary to reduce our lead time by 50 percent. These tactics can be summarized in project charters and even published on a wall for everyone to see that these are the most important projects or workstreams that we as a site need to work on to achieve our organizational goals. You could even add a regular update of each of these projects on the wall to discuss and share how we are getting on with achieving our yearly targets.

The third and final level of cascading is the **OPERATIONAL LEVEL,** where control indicators cascade down to **behavioral indicators.** The theory behind these kinds of indicators is that operator performance is the direct result of his or her behavior (Webers 2010), as we discussed in chapter 10.1.2 when I described the

KPI tree.

Traditionally quality checks at the end of the process are in place to check for abnormal output. This is a lagging indicator, since you can no longer influence the quality of the item that you check. Its already produced. A better way of measuring a process is to check the behavior employees show while doing their task. In other words, that means checking on whether the standard work has been followed in the process. By now, the word *kamishibai* should pop into your head immediately. Imai (1986) describes six categories of process indicators that one can use to figure out which behavioral indicators lead to the control indicators: discipline, time management, skills development, participation and commitment, morale, and communication (Imai 1986).

When we are talking about creating a lean culture in which all employees continually check and improve their processes, one example of a behavioral indicator could therefore be whether a team has done a kamishibai. A second behavioral indicator could be measuring whether the kamishibai has led to a kaizen. A third example is the 5S check. The best way to prevent problems within the production process is to check the working environment beforehand (Shingo 1986). A behavioral indicator could be whether the 5S standard has been checked for abnormalities before starting to work.

A change of culture can only be achieved if the behaviors you would like to see are properly defined and measured (Daniels 2000). When these behaviors are linked to strategic goals, they form the foundation for the kaizen mind-set and show where the team should focus its next improvement (Jackson 2006).

**Key Points:**
- *Cascade KPIs from the strategic, to the tactical, to the operational level.*
- *We do not want twenty KPIs on each team board; the hoshin kanri process can help determine what KPI to focus on.*
- *Operational KPIs should be based on behavior and can be fully influenced by the team. Operators cannot be held accountable for a machine availability of 100 percent, but they can be held accountable for following their standard work.*

# PART 4:
# PROCESS REDESIGN TO IMPROVE FLOW

So far, this book has only described lean tools that help an organization create a culture of continuous improvement in four levels of lean maturity: standardize processes, check if standards are kept, improve the standards, and link improvements to company goals. The tools that part 3 describes help every team contribute to envisioned targets from the bottom up.

This fourth part focuses on process redesign in a more top-down approach. Next to the kaizens and A3, a central team can focus on redesigning processes to implement larger flow improvements. Using value stream mapping, the flow of a process can be mapped and help a team define the next improvement to implement.

First, we start with an overview of what value stream mapping is in chapter 11, which includes a summary of the different times that are used within value stream mapping, three different pull strategies, and the value stream mapping event. These help us to create and understand the current-state value stream map with all its different symbols (chapter 12) and creating the future-state value stream map in eight steps (chapter 13).

Chapter 14 then describes two practices that are usually needed while creating the future state value stream map: line balancing (chapter 14.1) and load leveling (chapter 14.2).

Finally, chapter 15 will discuss how you can use value stream mapping in the office environment.

# Chapter 11:
# Introduction to Value Stream Mapping

*It's hard for most managers to even see the flow of value and, therefore, to grasp the value of flow.*
—J. P. Womack

A value stream is the combination of all actions (value adding and none-value-adding) done today to bring a product from raw materials to the arms of the customer (Rother and Shook 1999). **A value stream map (VSM)** is visualization of the value stream. It is a lean tool that maps the flow of material and the flow of information of a value stream.

The goal of the VSM is to improve the flow of the process and thereby reducing the lead time. Since lead time is the number one KPI within the lean philosophy (as described in chapter 4.1), value stream mapping is part of many lean initiatives and the tool is described in many lean books (Duggan 2002) (Floyd 2010) (J. K. Liker 2004) (Rother and Shook 1999) (Womack and Jones 1996).

Remember from part 1 that the efficiency of every process is measured in terms of time and that generating flow can improve lead time. The VSM helps map that flow and offers a structural approach to **improve the flow**.

Value stream mapping helps in eliminating all three of the enemies of lean.

**Waste** is reduced because the primary goal of the mapping exercise is to reduce the lead time of a process by eliminating waiting times between process steps. It is not unusual that the lead time of a process is reduced by 50-90 percent (Womack and Jones 1996).
Linked to this improvement is the reduction of overproduction and over processing in the line because the more pull the process has, the fewer products are produced before they are needed.

**Imbalance** also will be reduced when VSM is used. The one way to reduce waiting times between workstations is to improve flow; flow can only occur when the different process steps are balanced. This means the variance between cycle times and/or process times is reduced. Second in improving the information flow, the variance in the content of the production schedule is reduced when balancing is done.

Finally, **Overburden** is prevented when all the work cycles of both people and machines are planned in a way that they will always meet customer demand. Taking the takt time into account at all steps of the design process facilitates this.

Using value stream mapping in the way that is described in this chapter also helps you live the lean management principles. Here are some examples:

**Principle one: Focus on long-term goals.** The leadership team can use value stream mapping to define the next improvement projects necessary to achieve the company goals. Ideally, a new current-state VSM is created every six months to help the leadership team make strategic decisions.

**Principle two: Create flow.** By splitting the lead time in process times and waiting times in the lead time ladder (part of chapter 12), the VSM shows exactly where the flow is obstructed, which will point us to opportunities to eliminate these waiting times.

**Principle three: Create a pull system.** While developing your future-state value stream map, you will put all inventories within the value stream into pull systems to prevent overproduction.

**Principle four: Balancing the production line** is also part of the future-state value stream mapping exercise because balancing workstations and production schedules will reduce the need of extra buffers between the workstations, and that will help you implement principles two and three.

**Principle seven: Make problems visible.** Value stream mapping is a visual tool that shows where most of the waste is piling up in your processes. Ideally, the VSM is used as a management tool that the management team uses to identify the next improvement projects.

**Principle twelve: Go to the gemba.** The best way to map the current state is to follow the process real time from the customer side back to the supplier side. We start from the downstream side of the VSM because we want to optimize flow. A good example of flow in nature is a waterfall. If we would like to increase the speed with which water flows downstream, we observe the process from the bottom of the waterfall and look upstream to see where rocks or ponds obstruct the water from flowing (Ballé and Ballé 2012).

Finally, **principle fourteen: Self-reflection** is being served by value stream mapping because it continually challenges you to find the next improvement opportunity.

Before we discuss value stream mapping in detail, there are two basic topics that should be understood before starting the value stream mapping task: understanding the different times, and the different types of pull systems.

**Key Points:**
- *Value stream mapping maps the flow of a process.*
- *Value stream mapping helps identify what obstacles to work on next.*

## 11.1  Takt, Cycle, Process, Waiting, and Lead Times

*How fast can you deliver to your customer?*
*How much of your work is adding value?*
*How much of the work that you do is unplanned?*
*Lean is all about time.*

As we learned in chapter 4, lean distinguishes itself from other methods by focusing mainly on time. With tools like value stream mapping, yamazumi (for line balancing), and heijunka (for load leveling), different time metrics are used to help you find your next improvement opportunity. All these times are interconnected.

This paragraph explains five different measures of time:
1. The takt time: the time between two products that are sold.
2. The cycle time: the time between two products that are produced,
3. The process time: the time needed to produce the product.
4. The waiting time: the times that products are waiting to be worked on.
5. And finally, the lead time: the sum of all process- and waiting times.

Figure 30 shows a breakdown of these five different times that are important to distinguish when analyzing and improving the flow of value streams. We will first discuss the horizontal lines in the diagram and after that the times in the stacked barchart.

First, we start with the **TAKT TIME**, which is the interval in which customers request products from the production line. This is a calculated time based on the available production time for a period and the requested number of products in the same period:

*Takt = [Available Production Time]/ [Customer demand for product X]*

For example, when we take a typical workday in a factory, the available time in Western Europe is seven and a half hours (from eight hours, subtract thirty minutes for a paid lunch break, and the available production time is seven and a half hours). When there is customer demand for fifteen units per day, takt time is seven and a half divided by fifteen, which is thirty minutes per unit. Thus, there should be a minimum of one good-quality finished product coming off the line every thirty minutes to be able to fulfill customer demand.

How this is achieved is not relevant to the customer. So, the fact that operators have other tasks to do within the seven and a half hours—for instance, attending team board meetings or working on kaizens—is not important for the calculation of takt. The operators are available (and paid) for seven and a half hours per day.

The takt time is the top horizontal line in figure 30, and if the sum of all other times in the stack stay below that line, customer demand can be fulfilled.
In designing or redesigning a value stream, it is unwise to design your process in a way that it would meet takt time exactly. It is common to build in small time buffers to compensate for small failures of processes that can lead to variance in cycle time (Duggan 2002). A defect can occur, or somebody might ask the operator something that would cause the operator to leave their workstation for a few minutes. These small interruptions should not lead to a late delivery, which is why we usually would design a buffer into the system, by designing a cycle time that is below the takt time.

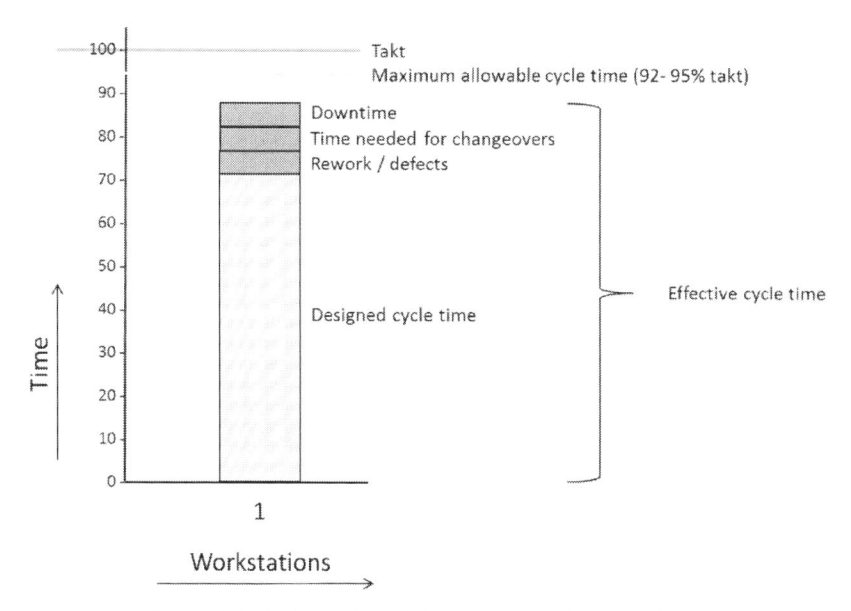

*Figure 30: A visual breakdown from takt to cycle times*

The second type of time is **CYCLE TIME**, which is the average measured time of two products coming out of the process. There are at least three different forms of cycle time to consider.

**The maximum allowable cycle time** describes the maximum cycle time the engineers should design into the system, to take the buffer described above into account. It is usually set at 92–95 percent of takt time (Duggan 2002). The lower the takt time is, the larger the buffer needs to be to prevent being unable to deliver in the customer's time frame. Figure 30 shows this in the second horizontal line.

The **designed cycle time** is the calculated time it takes for a workstation to produce a product when there are no interruptions (Stamatis 2011). The light-gray stack represents this time in figure 30.

The **effective cycle time**—or actual cycle time—is the measured time between two good-quality products produced in practice (Stamatis 2011) and represents the designed cycle time plus interruptions. These are actual measured times and include interruptions like the overall equipment effectiveness (OEE) which include the variables machine downtime, delays because of changeovers, and defects. These OEE-related factors are shown in figure 30 with the darker-gray stacks.

The effective cycle time is the sum of the designed cycle time and the OEE interruptions. Whenever a workstation produces in batches with parallel machines or is a shared resource, the effective cycle time also changes.

When we discuss effective cycle time, a person can measure the time between two good-quality products at the end of the workstation. When drawing a value stream map, multiple intervals should be measured to get a reliable measurement.

The third type of time is **PROCESS TIME**. This is the time a product spends within a process step. You can measure the process time with the so-called red-dot principle. You mark a random product with a red dot and measure the time from the moment where the part moves into the machine or workstation until the moment it comes out on the other side. When there is only one operator on one workstation and that person is working on only one product at a time,

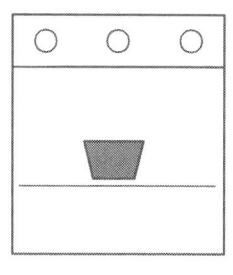

|                |        |   |                |        |
|----------------|--------|---|----------------|--------|
| Process time:  | 40 min |   | Process time:  | 40 min |
| Cycle time:    | 40 min |   | Cycle time:    | 20 min |

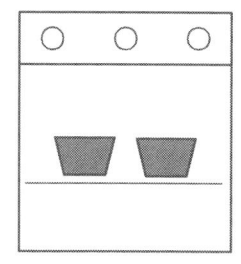

*Figure 31: The difference between cycle time and process time in batch production*

the process time equals the cycle time. When the workstation produces in batches or on parallel workstations, or when there are multiple people working in a work cell, the cycle time differs from the process time, as visualized in figure 31 and figure 32.

Figure 31 shows two ovens in which cake is baked. On the left, there is only one cake in the oven. It takes 40 minutes for the cake to be ready for brunch, which means the process time is 40 minutes. The cycle time in this case equals the process time and is also 40 minutes.
On the right-hand side, we bake two cakes at the same time, a so-called batch production. It still takes 40 minutes for the cake to be ready, which means the process time is still 40 minutes. The cycle time however has been cut in half, because now two cakes are ready every 40 minutes, which means the average interval between two products is 20 minutes.

The same holds true for parallel workstations. When there are two ovens in parallel, with each oven only one cake in it, the process time would still be 40 for each cake, while the cycle time is 20 minutes.

When there are multiple people working in a line, the cycle time reduces as well, even though the process time stays the same. Figure 32 shows us a work cell with 8 process steps, that each take 10 seconds to complete.
On the left, only one operator does the work, which means he needs 8*10 seconds to finish one product, and every 80 seconds, one product is finished. On the right however, two operators work in the same cell.

```
PT 10s   PT 10s                    PT 10s   PT 10s

PT 10s           PT 10s            PT 10s           PT 10s

PT 10s           PT 10s            PT 10s           PT 10s

PT 10s           PT 10s            PT 10s           PT 10s
```

Process time:   80 sec              Process time:   80 sec
Cycle time:     80 sec              Cycle time:     40 sec

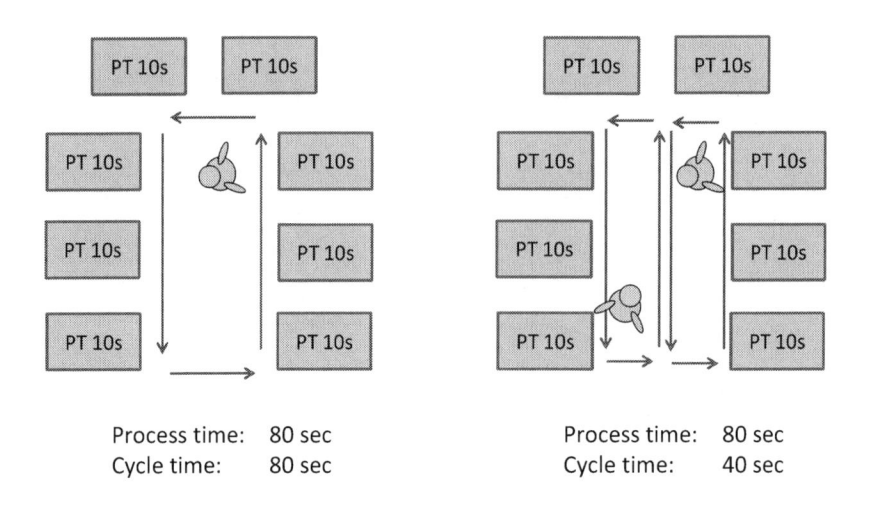

*Figure 32: The difference between cycle time and process time (both in seconds) with multiple operators*

The work that needs to be done on each product is still 8*10 seconds, but because the two operators divide the work in two, the cycle time is reduced to 40 seconds.

From the above examples we can conclude that splitting the work between two people has the same impact on the cycle time as investing in a parallel machine. The one big difference being that the first option does not require any investments to buy new machinery, space to put that new machinery, and people available to maintain the new machinery.

The fourth type of time is **WAITING TIME**. As one of the eight wastes, waiting time can be found both before and after a workstation, as well as while the product is being worked on at a workstation (multiple machines, multiple people, or batch production).

In a value stream map, the waiting times between process steps are shown with specific symbols for unstructured inventory, first in first out (FIFO) lanes, and supermarkets, the topics of chapter 11.2.

Finally, the fifth and final measure of time is **LEAD TIME**, which measures the general efficiency of the value stream. This can be understood as the process time of the entire value stream or line using the red-dot principle mentioned before. It is the sum of all process times of the process steps plus the sum of all waiting times between the process steps.

When there are parallel processes in a value stream with different process times, the longest one is considered for the lead time calculation.

So why are these times interesting to us and why would we spend time measuring and calculating them? These different times help us to evaluate the process in terms of both efficiency and effectiveness.

The **efficiency** of a value stream is measured based on lead times, for which you need process time and waiting times because they tell you how fast you can deliver to your customers.

The **effectiveness** of the value stream is calculated by comparing effective cycle times with the takt time. It tells you how well your process is designed to meet actual customer demand.
Knowing the different times and the goals for which they are used can prevent long discussions at value stream mapping events. It is therefore advisable to define each term before you start mapping, especially because different organizations may use different definitions of the terms.

**Key Points:**
- *Takt time is the calculated time between two products being sold.*
- *Process time is the time a product spends in a process step and can be measured using the red-dot principle.*
- *Cycle time is the measured time between two good-quality products coming off the line.*
- *Waiting time is the measured time a product spends waiting between process steps.*
- *Lead time is the total process time plus the total waiting time.*

## 11.2  Pull Production: Three Strategies

*When you only produce what your customer needs right now,
you never overproduce again.*

As part 2 briefly mentioned, creating a pull system is the third of five steps described by Womack and Jones (Womack and Jones, 1996). This chapter will explain in more detail the nature of pull and three strategies to implement it, one-piece flow, first in first out (FIFO) and the supermarket.

A **PULL** process is a process in which a workstation starts to work on the next order only when there is a signal from the customer side. This means the trigger for producing anything on the workstation comes from a downstream workstation. The customer pulls orders through the process instead of the process being driven by a traditional push connection in which products are produced no matter what happens on the output side of the workstation. Because inventories between workstations are managed by a pull system, and lead times are therefore minimized, pull always has a preference over push.

There are **THREE TYPES OF PULL CONNECTIONS that** help achieve different levels of pull in the system based on three factors: having a maximum of one piece of inventory between two process steps, having a fixed production sequence, and having a maximum number of parts waiting.

The **one-piece flow** connection has the highest level of pull because all three factors are included. Products are worked on one by one with a maximum inventory of one between the workstations. A workstation can only work on the one product that is waiting in front of it at that time (the fixed sequence), and it can only produce when the inventory behind it is less than one (no inventory). Multiple workstations with continuous flow between them are also known as work cells, a U-cell, or a one-piece flow line.

The **first-in-first-out (FIFO)** connection is the second-best possible pull connection. In this case, the work orders are worked on in the exact sequence that they arrived. Because a fixed quantity is determined, and the sequence of product movement is defined, the workstation does not need a production schedule to know what to produce next. The operator will simply take the next product waiting in the buffer in front of that workstation. To buffer for variance, the FIFO lane has a defined maximum, which means the upstream workstation must stop producing when the FIFO lane is full.

**The supermarket** is the third and last pull option and works the same as a regular real-world supermarket. There are different products on shelves and whenever a specific number of products are sold, a signal is sent to the supplier to replenish that product.

The supermarket has a maximum capacity, which means the upstream workstation must stop producing when the supermarket is full, but it is unknown which type of product will be used at the workstation. This has two important implications. First, the inventory kept at a supermarket is bigger than in a FIFO lane, because all possible product parts need to be kept in stock just in case it is needed. Second, the workstation downstream of the supermarket needs a production schedule to know what order to work on and what products to take from the supermarket to build it.

Figure 33 summarizes the differences between the three types of pull connections.

As we will see in chapter 13, **CHOSING THE RIGHT TYPE OF PULL CONNECTION** is one of the steps in designing a future-state VSM. This decision depends on a few process- and product variables. Figure 34 shows a discussion table with variables that I find might help you decide for what type of connection you should aim for.

|  | one-piece flow | FIFO lane | Supermarket |
|---|---|---|---|
| Max 1 part inventory | x |  |  |
| Fixed sequence | x | x |  |
| Maximum number of parts waiting | x | x | x |

*Figure 33: Difference between one-piece flow, FIFO lanes and a supermarket*

|  | Process reliability || Changeover times || Lead time || Demand variation and part usage || Part cost ||
|---|---|---|---|---|---|---|---|---|---|---|
|  | Low | High | Low | High | Low | High | Low | High | Low | High |
| One-piece flow |  | x | x |  | x |  | x | x | x | x |
| FIFO |  | x | x |  | x | x | x | x | x | x |
| Supermarket | x | x | choose FIFO | x | x | x | x |  | x |  |
| Push |  |  | x |  |  |  |  | x |  | x |

*Figure 34: Discussion table, when to use what type of connection*

In the discussion, follow the topics from left to right and move from top to bottom. The goal of the table is not to discourage the use of a certain pull system, but to give direction in pointing out what variables need to be worked on to be able to implement a higher level of pull within a specific situation.

**Process reliability** is the first factor that influences the type of pull connection that can be used. When the reliability of the output of the upstream workstation is low, a buffer is needed to prevent the entire flow from stopping. Since in this case all products need to be buffered, the sequence cannot be held anymore, which results in the supermarket being the only viable option at this point.

**Changeover time** is the second variable. In situations where more than one product is produced within a family, short changeover times are needed to produce in sequence and per order on a workstation. Whenever changeovers are high, it would make more sense to batch products, which means a buffer is needed in front of the workstation. This buffer would be a supermarket because the products are sorted by type, and therefore sequence cannot be kept.

**Lead times** also influence the type of pull connection that one can use. One-piece flow can only be kept if the upstream process can respond to downstream changes. When the lead time is higher than the cycle time of the machine, a buffer is needed to prevent starvation. The same holds for takt time. Only when the upstream machines can deliver on all takt times (which can vary, for instance, with seasonal products) can one-piece flow be implemented. When some takt levels cannot be achieved upstream, a buffer is needed.

The fourth variable is **variation in demand of products**, which limits the options for a pull connection the other way around. The higher the demand variation or product mix is, the less desirable a supermarket becomes, because the number of buffers and the number of products per buffer increase. Load leveling should minimize this variation (and is described in chapter 14.2).

This also holds true for the **price of the part** or product, the fifth factor. The more the part costs, the less desirable the supermarket option becomes. This is a tough one because it might be necessary to have a supermarket to keep the pull system running even though the costs are high.

The interesting thing about these five factors is that there are situations where an **unstructured push connection** might be the only option left and having push connections in a future-state value stream map is really not desirable. In these situations, kaizen events need to be defined to change one or more of the above five factors to make it possible to implement one of the three pull connections.

The table shown in figure 34 is meant for discussion only. It is not black and white and does not include all possible factors that might influence the choice of connection type. It is the task of the team that develops the future-state value stream map to decide what connection type is suitable for each specific situation.

**Key Points:**
- *There are three types of pull strategies.*
- *One-piece flow is the most desirable connection, with no inventory between process steps and a fixed sequence by which products are worked on.*
- *FIFO lanes have a maximum number of products waiting between process steps, and it is known in what order they will be worked on.*
- *Supermarkets have a maximum number of parts between process steps, but it is unknown what product will be worked on next.*

## 11.3  The Value Stream Mapping Event

*The value stream mapping event should deliver an integrated plan for overall process improvement.*

The value stream mapping exercise is a complex one. To go through the entire current-state and future-state steps thoroughly as described in the following chapters, you would usually need at least four hours to make sure everybody understands the theory including the use of a variety of symbols and the different steps of the value stream mapping exercise.

It might not be necessary for everybody in the organization to gain a full understanding of this tool, however. In a value stream mapping event, there should always be an expert present who understands the tool in detail. For the rest of the participants, it suffices when they understand the different symbols.

In a factory environment, a value stream mapping event in which both a current-state and future-state VSM are created, takes, in my experience, four to five days. Of course, this depends largely on the process complexity and the preparation work—for instance, data gathering—that has been done before the event. The more data for each machine you have, for instance the earlier described waterfall charts and Pareto diagrams on OEE, the better.

For the success of the kaizen event, it is important that the **PREPARATION** of the event be done well in advance. Usually, since a team of people is required to work on the event for four or five days, it should be **planned about a month in advance**. This means that a month before the actual event, the list of participants needs to be complete.

The team members can already **collect general information** and data about the value stream they will map, that are already available from data reports. The data from those reports might be added to the data boxes. Since the participants might not be aware of the value stream mapping tool before the event, it is important that the facilitator of the event has a preparation meeting with the team or part of the team and actively sets out this action. In general, the four-day VSM event could look like this:

**DAY ONE**: This starts with an **introduction to the VSM** tool in general. In one to two hours, the current-state VSM example of the lighter factory in chapter 12 can be explained. The goal of this time slot is that all participants of the workshop understand that there are different symbols and how the VSM is created in the six steps described in chapter 12.

In the second half of the morning, I like to give a general overview of the process. This is where the **SIPOC** discussed in chapter 7.2 is created. It's also where the team discusses the scope of this VSM event (including the start and end) and the goals of the process that is being mapped.

The afternoon is used to start **walking the process** from the customer side to the supplier side and generating an overview of all the process steps. Map the value stream in terms of steps and connections but leave the detailed data for day two. This way there is a clear overview of the process steps at the end of day one.

In **DAY TWO,** we continue gathering data for the process steps. In day one, ask the person who is performing a task how long it takes. When process steps take longer than thirty minutes, we split the team up in day two and have different pairs of team members **measuring different process times** to collect the data for the data boxes.

When there is **variability in product portfolio and quantities**, part of the team will also collect this data on day two. Since we are still mapping the current state, rough numbers are enough at this stage. There is no need to spend four hours on data analysis when we are not sure whether we need to improve this workstation in the future state.

By the end of day two, there should be a complete current-state VSM.

**DAY THREE** starts with an **explanation of the eight steps of future-state value stream mapping**. Using the lighter factory example described in 13, this takes about one to two hours to make sure everybody understands what steps we will execute on our created VSM.

The rest of the day and the beginning of day four are spent following the eight steps to **create the future-state VSM**. The complexity of the process determines how much time is necessary to go through all the steps.

**DAY FOUR**: When the future-state VSM is not finished on day three, we first finalize it and then **create an overview of all the kaizen events** needed to achieve it.
Depending on what kind of kaizen events are necessary; there can be more **theory** on this day. Topics such as line balancing (chapter 14.1), load leveling (chapter 14.2), autonomous maintenance (chapter 16), and SMED (chapter 17) can be introduced here so that the kaizen event owners have an idea of what they need to implement.

At the end of the day, every kaizen event should have one **A3 document** in which the first draft of the problem statement and breakdown are documented. Also documented should be the improvement targets and which team members are going to help achieve the goal.

**Key Points:**
- *A value stream mapping event usually takes four to five days.*
- *Determine who needs to be at the event and what data to collect a month in advance.*

# Chapter 12:
# Mapping the Current State

*Begin at the shipping end and work upstream....This way you will begin mapping the processes linked most directly to the customer, which should set the pace for the other processes further upstream.*


To get to know different symbols of value stream mapping and when to use which one, this chapter includes an example of a process in which most of the basic icons are used. It will illustrate how to create the current state value stream map it in six steps:
1. Drawing the process steps
2. Drawing the data boxes
3. Drawing the connection methods between the process steps
4. Drawing the links with customers and suppliers
5. Creating the lead time ladder with all process and waiting times
6. Drawing the information flow

The following is a production example of a lighter factory that produces different colors of lighters. I based this example on my experience in an actual lighter factory in the Philippines where I wrote my master thesis. When I use this example in training, I share the story about my trip and how I found the factory when I arrived, and how I improved the flow and the lead time using the 8 steps of future state value stream mapping in the next chapter.

The story of my graduation in the Philippines is real, but the numbers used in this process are changed to fit the purpose of the training, in the name of storytelling (remember from chapter 2?).

To map the process, we start with mapping the product flow first, followed by the information flow.
We will get to know more about this process as we go through the different types of icons.

The first step in value stream mapping is drawing the **PROCESS BOXES** for the different process steps, starting from the customer side and going upstream to the supplier side. Six types of process boxes exist for different kinds of production steps, all of which are shown in figure 35. All process boxes may include the number of employees working on that process step.

From right to left, we first find the gas-filling station. This is one station with only one production step: filling the lighters with gas. One production step with inventory before and after it can be defined as a **regular production step** and is drawn as a "normal" process box.

When we move upstream, the next workstation we find is in the assembly step. This step contains five different production steps and adds all the small parts on top of the lighter. However, since there is no inventory between these steps, the cell is designed as a **one-piece flow line**, the second type of process box.

To show that the process box contains multiple production steps in a work cell, a U is added to the symbol. The U represents the ideal form of a cell: the one-piece flow line shaped in a U as the example of Figure 32 showed in chapter 11.1. In this example, five people work in the cell, which is shown on the bottom right of the process box in figure 35.

Further upstream, the third process step found is a logo-printing station, which prints customized logos on the lighters. This is still one machine; however, the machine prints the logos on the lighters in **batches** of ten. We can visualize that on the VSM with a triangle inside the process box, which shows us that this is a batch process, the third type of process box.

A little further upstream, we find the painting station, where white bodies are sprayed with a certain color. Coloring the molds of the lighters is a relatively long process, which is why five machines are working in parallel. You can visualize **parallel machines**, the fourth type of process box, in the VSM by drawing a second box behind the first one and indicating the number of machines on the bottom right of the second box.

The most upstream workstation is the molding step, where standard white bodies of the lighters are molded. However, it is not only lighters that are molded here; the factory also produces pens. Because pens are a different product family, the molding machine is a **shared resource**, a resource used for multiple product families. A shared resource is shown by adding a grid to the process box.

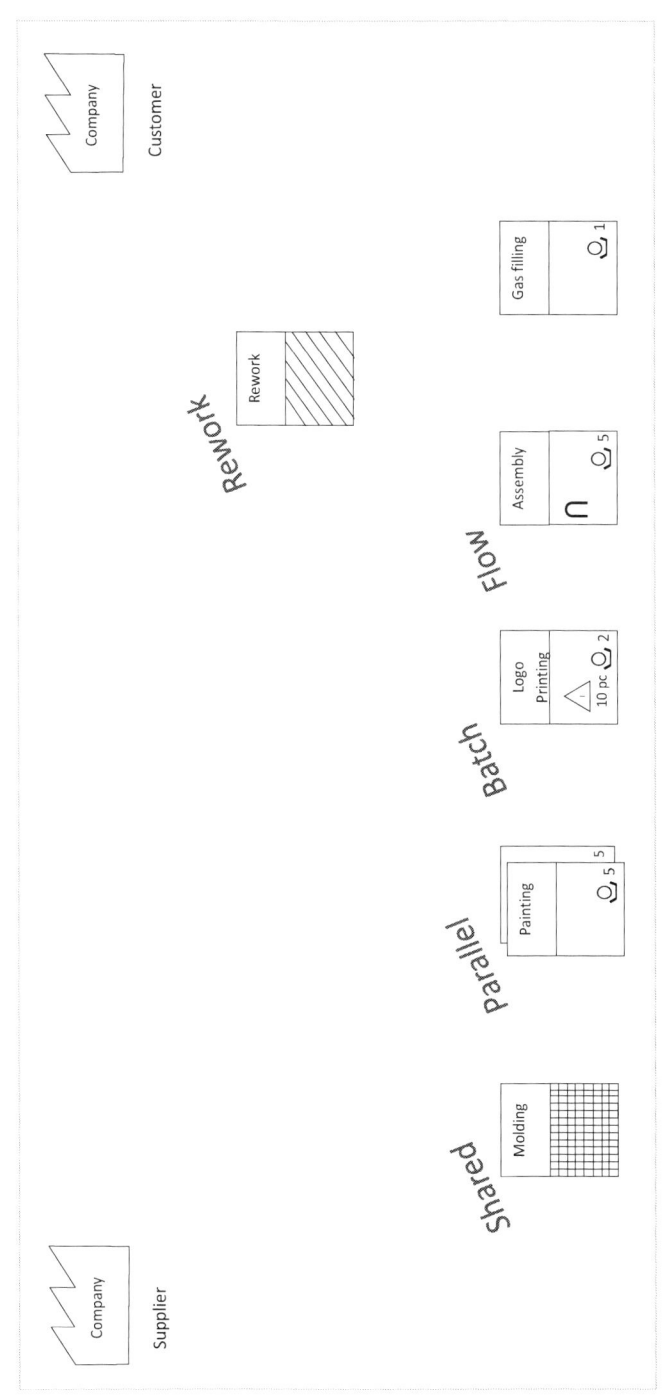

*Figure 35: VSM step one—process box icons*

**Rework is the sixth and final type of process box.** In this example, rework is sometimes necessary after the assembly step. Whether the rework step is included in the VSM depends on the amount of time it takes to do the rework (which results in it being an important influencer on the lead time) and the percentage of products that need rework.

Now that all process boxes of figure 35 have been explained, we can move to the second step in value stream mapping: to add **DATA BOXES** to each process box. The data boxes capture data for each of the process steps that are drawn in the map. Everything that prevents flow in the process should be written here. In figure 36, different numbers are added for the different process steps. In this and following figures, some measures are shown in %, and all times are recorded in seconds (s).

**Process time (PT)** is the time one product spends in a process step. The red-dot principle described earlier in chapter 11.1 helps to determine it.

**Designed cycle time (CT$_D$)** is the time between two good-quality products leaving the process step according to design. For regular and one-piece flow boxes, the cycle time and process time are the same. For batch and parallel processes, the cycle time is shorter than the process time because multiple products are worked on at the same time. For shared resources, the cycle time is longer than the process time because the machine is not producing products for this value stream all the time. Chapter 11.1 already described more information and examples about the different measures of time.

**Effective cycle time (CT$_{Eff}$)** is the time between two good-quality products being delivered. As discussed in chapter 11.1, this time considers the OEE of a machine and availability of the shared resources. This is the value that will be compared with takt time when the future-state VSM is designed.

The following are four measures that could be included in the databoxes that explain the difference between the designed- and the effective cycle times. It is in these four where you might also find your improvement options.

**You can use overall equipment effectiveness (OEE)** to show how often the machine produces high-quality products. This measure includes machine availability, machine performance, and output quality.

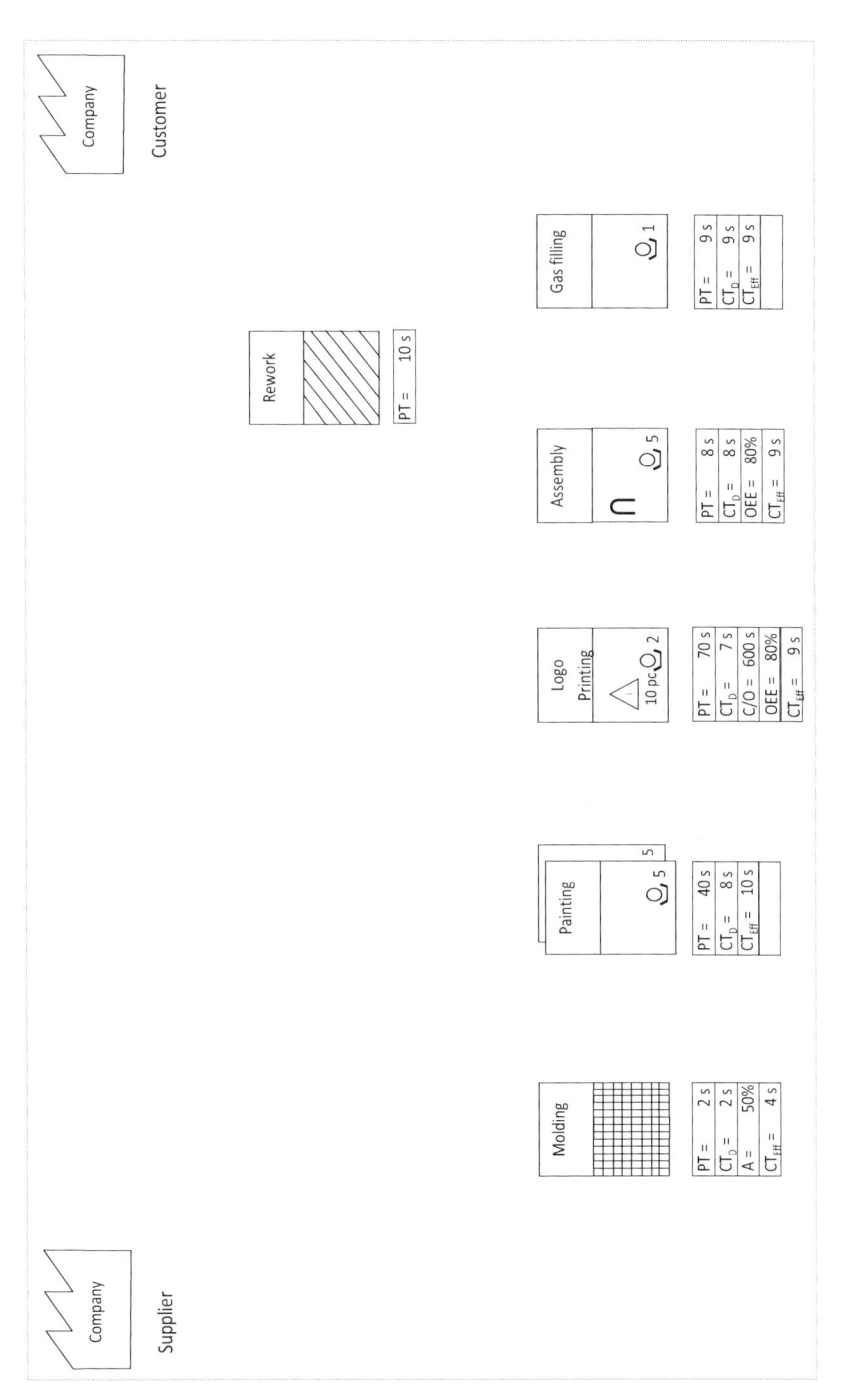

*Figure 36: VSM step two—data boxes added*

Depending on the situation, you might also decide to put one or more of these aspects in the data boxes individually—for instance, you might insert only the defect rate.

**Machine availability (A)** shows how often a shared resource is available for this particular value stream. In our lighter case, an availability of 50 percent for our value stream would mean that our cycle time should be 50 percent of takt time to be able to meet customer demand.

**Changeover time (C/O)** can log how long it takes to change over from one product in the product family to another. In the lighter example, this is valuable information in the painting stage, where changeovers are necessary to change the color of paint.

**Batch** can show how many products are worked on at the same time, and **EPEI** (every product every interval) can show the maximum lead time for one product within the family. We will come back to the EPEI in chapter 13, which addresses mapping the future-state VSM.

The third step of current-state value stream mapping is to draw the **CONNECTION METHODS** between the process boxes. Remember from chapter 11.2 that there are four possibilities (only three have their own symbol, because one-piece flow is drawn as a type of process box) and figure 37 shows them all. Notice that the supermarket and the FIFO lanes are two of the pull strategies that chapter 11.2 describes. The one-piece flow strategy is captured in a type of process box and not in a connection method because a true one-piece flow cell does not have inventory between two steps.

**The first type of connection method is the push (uncontrolled) inventory**. Between molding and painting, a traditional push method is used. The shared resource is very expensive to use, so when it is available, it just produces as many products for our product family as possible. This type of inventory is drawn with a triangle and a dotted arrow. It means the inventory has no maximum number of products and no sequence in which the products are used at a later stage, which is why it is considered a push system.

The number of products waiting in an uncontrolled inventory vary over time. The triangle in figure 37, the 10.000, is therefore a snap-shot value, a value that was

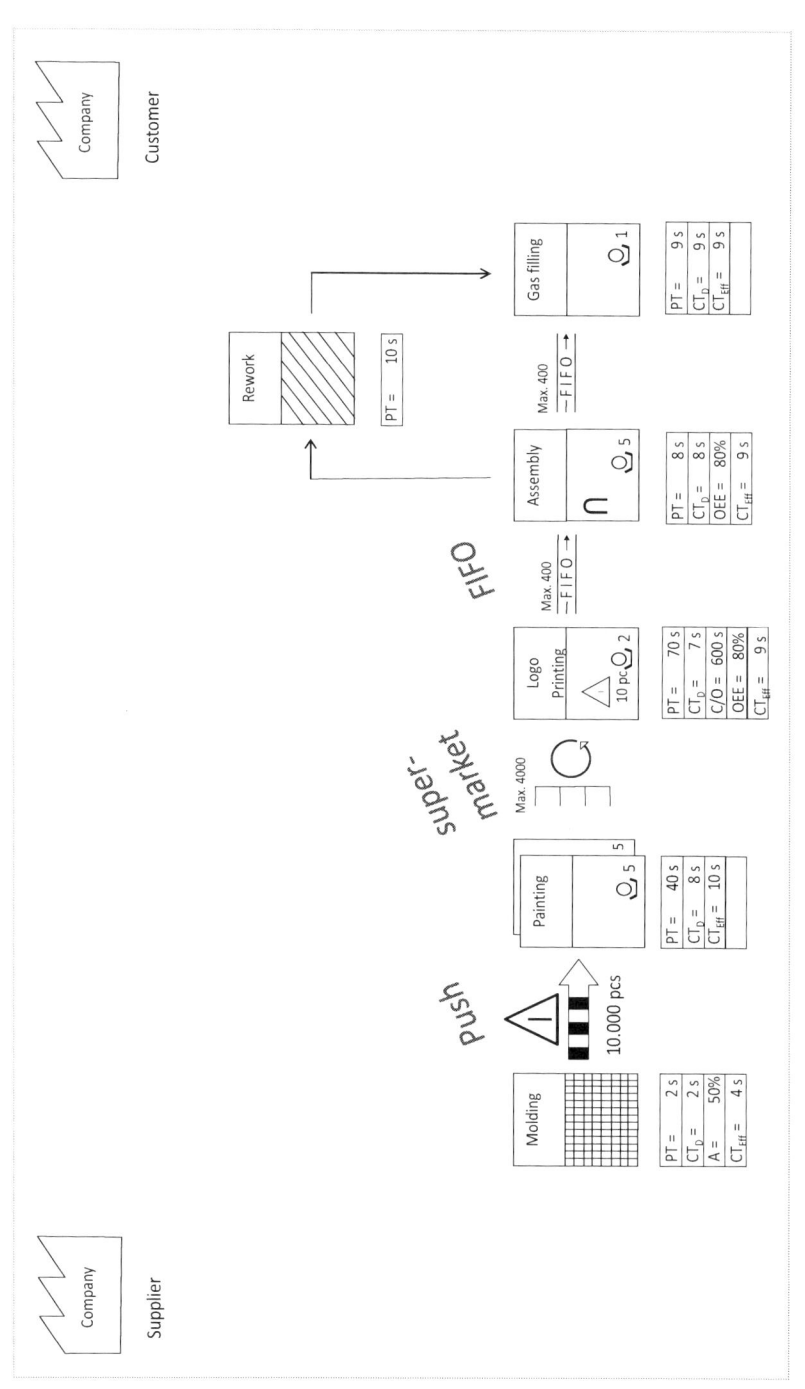

*Figure 37: VSM step three—connections added*

counted on the day the VSM was made. In theory it could be any number.

**The supermarket** is the second type of inventory and can be found between painting and logo printing. In the example, different colors of lighters can be sold, and the supermarket contains each of those colors. Only when a certain color is taken out of the supermarket by the logo-printing station, will the paint shop produce new products with that color.

The machine filling up the supermarket only produces when there is room in the supermarket, which means there is a pull signal. The supermarket is preferable over a push inventory because it has a maximum number of products allowed in it, therefore preventing too many parts from waiting before they are being worked on.

The number of products that are held in a supermarket depends on two factors. The first factor is the number of different products you have, in the lighter example 5 colors, and the second factor is the time you wish to buffer for. If you would like to buffer for 4 hours of production to make sure the workstation downstream of the supermarket Is never idle, you will keep 4 hours of stock per product in the supermarket.

In the lighter factory case example, the takt time is 10.8 seconds, and there are 3 different colors of lighters. To prevent the printing station from idling it was decided to keep 4 hours of inventory in the supermarket. This means each color should have a stock of 1333 items, in case it is necessary to produce only one color those 4 hours. Multiply this by the 3 different colors, and we end up with a supermarket stock of 4000, as shown in the figure.

**The FIFO lane** is the third type of connection. In the lighter case, we find one between logo printing and assembly. After the logo is printed on the lighter, it is customer specific, and therefore the sequence in which the orders are worked on can be determined easily by the sequence in which the orders are sent. The FIFO is also a pull system because the upstream machine can only produce when there is room in the FIFO lane. Having a fixed sequence also reduces the variance of lead times within the process steps because the different orders can no longer overtake one another.

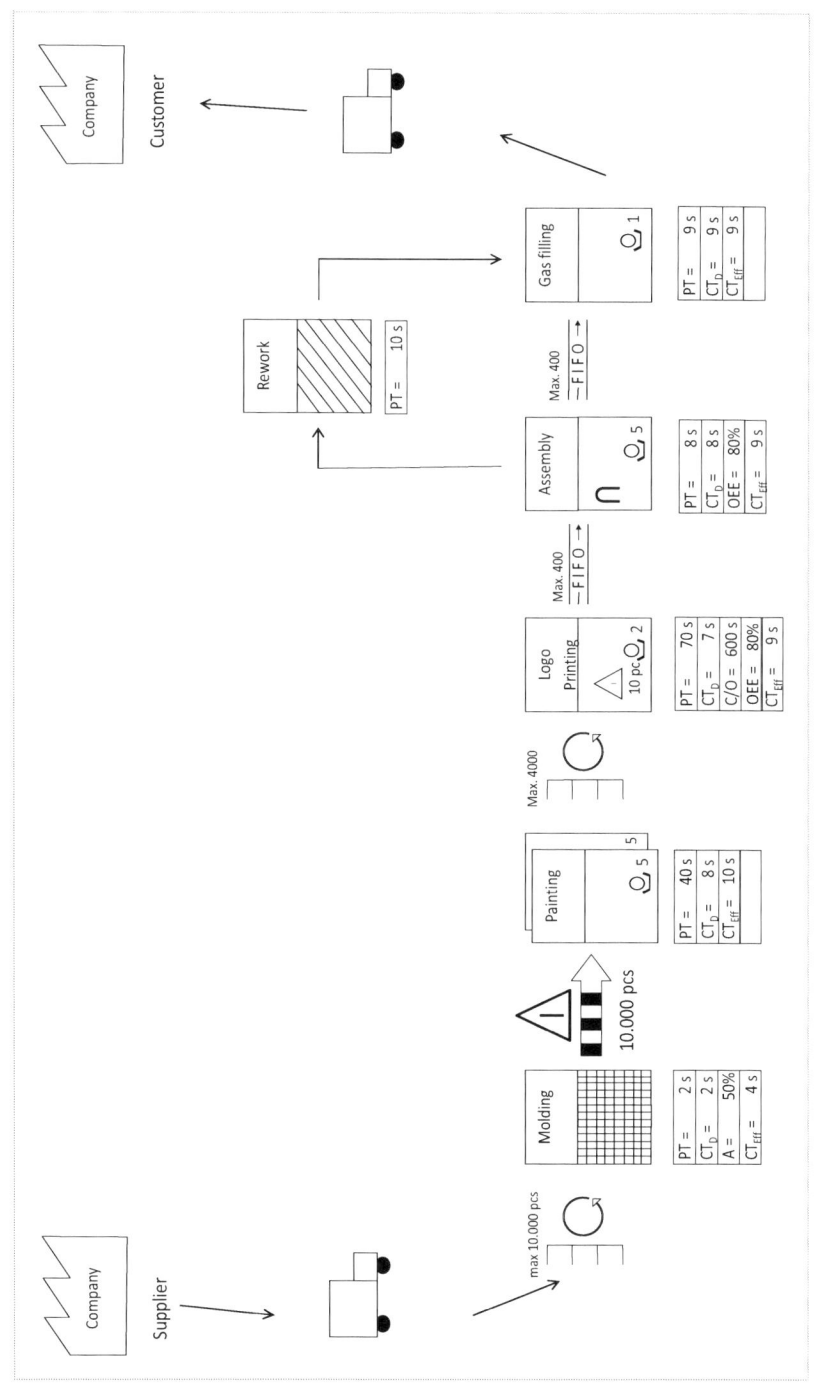

*Figure 38: VSM step four—add customers and suppliers*

The number of products that are waiting in the FIFO can be calculated the same way as in the supermarket.

The only difference is that we only have one type of product waiting, since the sequence of production is already fixed. This means that if we would choose to have a buffer of 4 hours again, the size of the buffer would be 1333 items. Instead, in this example, the buffer size was chosen to be 72 minutes, which leads to a calculated max inventory of 400 items within both the FIFO lanes in figure 37.

Step four describes linking **CUSTOMERS AND SUPPLIERS** to the process.
**The company can link customers** in two ways, depending on the finished-good strategy it has. The lighter case here has a direct-shipping strategy because the lighters are printed customer specific; there is no extra symbol of inventory after the last process box. When a made-to-stock strategy is used, there could be a supermarket there.

**Suppliers** can be regulated in multiple ways, including unstructured inventory (not desirable), a supermarket, or even a manually controlled inventory. Figure 38 shows a supermarket system that automatically controls the suppliers in the lighter example.

The fifth step in creating a current state value stream map is adding the **LEAD TIME LADDER** at the bottom of the VSM, which shows different aspects of time in the value stream. The lead time ladder is added to the VSM in figure 39, and in this example, all times are in seconds.
Beneath each process box, the **process time** is written because it tells us how much time a product spends on that workstation (the measure time using the red-dot principle).
Beneath each inventory level, the **waiting time** is estimated to show how long the product must wait between workstations. This can be calculated by the number of products counted at the moment of drawing multiplied by takt time. For example, when you count ten thousand products in the inventory before painting and the customer demands one lighter every ten seconds, the time the average lighter waits in the inventory is multiplied by ten thousand, which equals one hundred thousand seconds, which is more than one full day of waiting time.

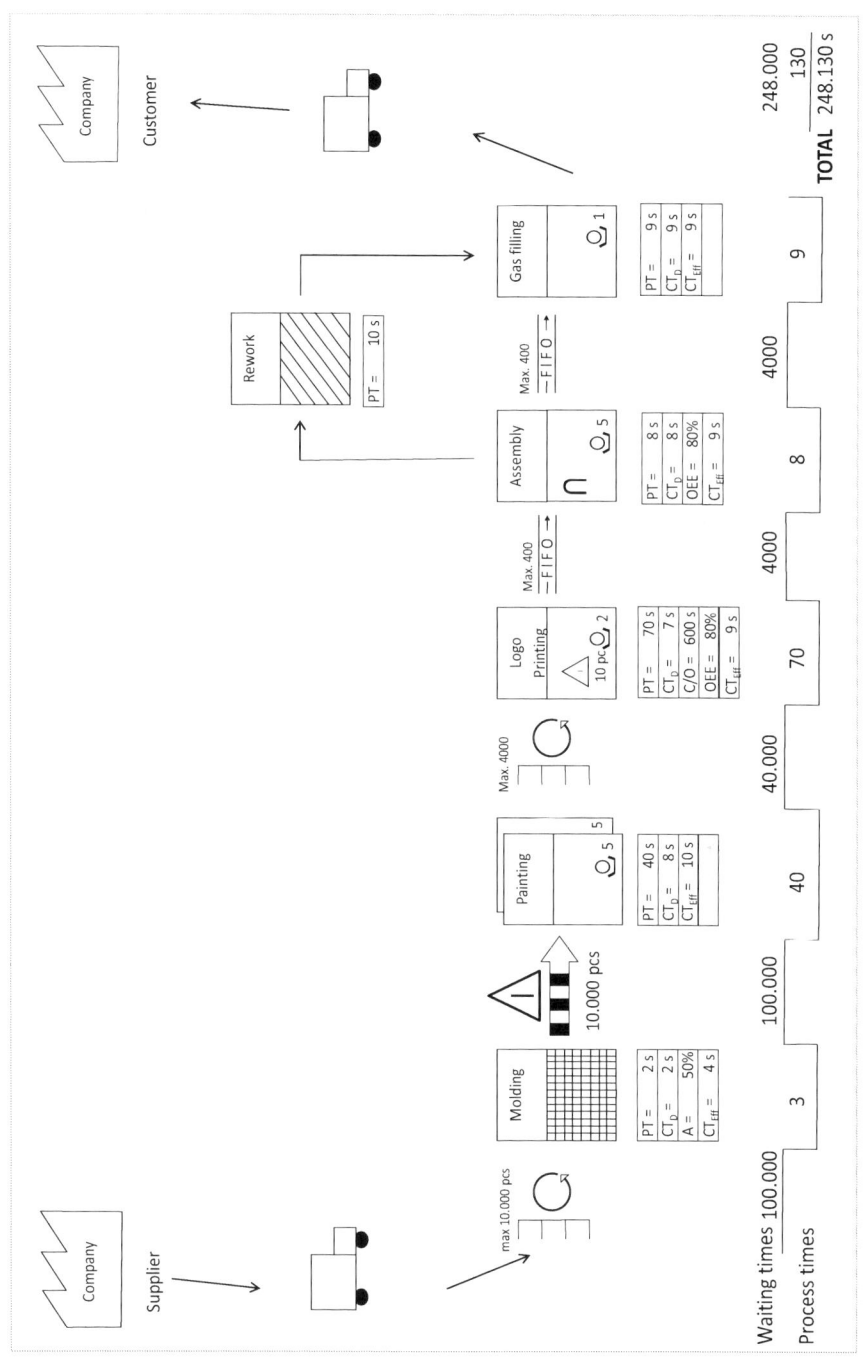

*Figure 39: VSM step five—add the lead time ladder*

For the numbers to be 100% accurate, there is a difference in the waiting times in the FIFO lanes and the waiting times in a supermarket. One big difference is that a supermarket will always be full, because it sends a replenishment signal every time that something is taken out of it, independent of customer demand.
A supermarket *wants to be full*.

A FIFO lane however, can only be replenished if there is a customer order send to the workstations upstream. When there is none, the FIFO lane will run empty. The FIFO lane *wants to be empty*.

This means that there is a difference in the average waiting times of the two types of connection method. In the supermarket, we can simply take the max number of products and multiply it by takt time to calculate the waiting time. in the FIFO lane, it should be less than the total, since the FIFO lane is not always full. How much less, depends on the replenishment time and the size of the FIFO.

Another aspect to consider when you are calculating how much inventory is kept on average in both the supermarket and FIFO lanes, is the ratio between replenishment quantities and total quantities. If I have a supermarket with 4000 products, and they are replenished one by one, the average size of the supermarket will always be close to 4000. If the supermarket is replenished by batches of 500 of each color however, the average number of items in the supermarket will be closer to 2900. This is because there could be a situation in which there is only an inventory of 900 of each of the three colors in the supermarket (so 1800 in total).

For the lighter case example, I chose to use simple calculations and rounded numbers. To quote my own VSM trainer Dirk van Goubergen: you can either hire a six-sigma black belt to measure the exact size of the supermarket and wait six months for him or her to give you the accurate numbers, or you can just make a quick assumption and continue with the exercise on this higher level.

Finally, we can calculate the **production lead time,** which is all the process times plus all the waiting times together. In this example, the total is 248,130 seconds, or 2.87 days. Interesting to note is that only 0.5 percent of the total lead time is process time. The other 99.5 percent is the time the product spends waiting in inventories, and that is considered non-value-adding time.

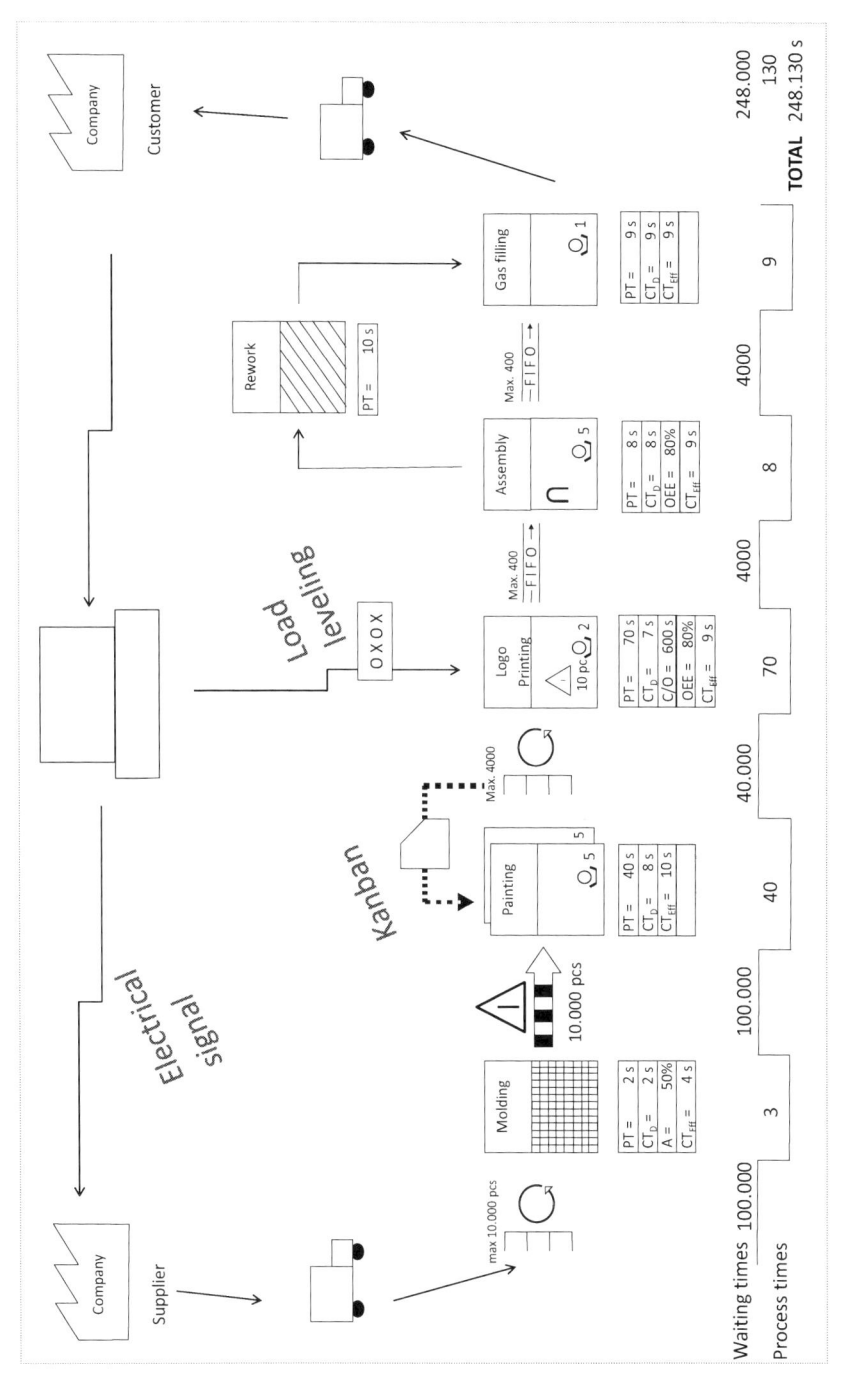

*Figure 40: VSM step six—add the information flow*

After the material flow is drawn, the sixth step of creating a current state value stream map is drawing the **INFORMATION FLOW**. The information flow shows how each workstation knows what to produce. Figure 40 shows the most commonly used symbols for the information flow and includes drawing the following:

The **control signal or signals from planning** to each machine that receives a signal. That multiple machines are sent separate signals is not unusual. Ideally, the production plan is only sent to one workstation, which is then called the pacemaker. In the lighter case, one electric signal is sent to the painting station so that it knows what logo it needs to paint and what color should be used on the lighters. Workstations behind a FIFO lane or before a supermarket do not need their own schedule because they will simply take the next product from the FIFO in front of them or replenish what was taken from the supermarket behind them.

When you use **production leveling**, the signal to a workstation includes a box with "XOXO" in it. This means the customer demand for that workstation is not made in FIFO sequence; it is balanced in time. The tool used for product balancing is called heijunka, and chapter 14.2 will discuss it.

The third added symbol in figure 40 is a **kanban signal**. Kanban is a visual way of managing the replenishments of supermarkets. Physical cards are collected from empty supermarket slots, which tell the upstream machine exactly what should be produced to replenish these. Chapter 19 further discusses kanban.

In general, there are no rules in value stream mapping. If a specific situation cannot be caught on paper using the symbols described above, you can think of icons yourself to visualize that specific situation. The lighter example above covers the most widely used symbols to give an idea of what you can map.

The goal of VSM is to learn about the process and look for possible improvements. You are therefore challenged to add more information to the value stream map to make it more useful for the specific situation you are in.

After the current state of the value stream is mapped, it is time to identify several improvements that directly improve the flow. You can use the eight steps for designing a future-state map; those steps are described next.

**Key Points:**
- *There are six steps of current-state value stream mapping, and each step has several symbols to use.*
- *Process boxes describe the process steps.*
- *Data boxes include data for each process step.*
- *Inventory connections show how inventory is controlled between the steps.*
- *The customer and supplier should be linked to the process.*
- *The lead time ladder adds up all process and waiting times.*
- *The information flow shows how the process is managed.*

# Chapter 13:
# Mapping the Future State

*The mapping process clearly reveals the potential for a major leap in performance if a relatively small number of flow and process kaizens can be conducted and sustained.*
—J. P. Womack and D. T. Jones

There are different methods for designing a future-state value stream map. One of them is randomly putting ideas for improvement on the value stream map, a brain storm approach, and then picking out the ideas that most people think are value adding and define them as projects. The downside of the brainstorm approach is, that you do not know for sure that the projects that you are doing lead to measurable improvements in the entire process. This is where the 8 steps come in. **THE EIGHT STEPS OF FUTURE STATE VALUE STREAM MAPPING** in the example described in this chapter are based on the eight questions by Kevin Duggan (Duggan 2012). Following these will help you identify only those improvements that directly help you achieve your organizational targets. The questions can be split into three categories of improvement:

Putting the need of the customer first:
1. Can all processes keep takt time?
2. What is the finished-goods strategy?

Implement flow in the process:
3. Where can we implement one-piece flow?
4. Where can we implement FIFO?
5. Where can we implement supermarkets?

Improve how production is controlled:
6. Which processes need a production schedule?
7. How is the production plan leveled?
8. In what increments is the production plan released?

Before we go through the eight steps to developing a future-state VSM, we return to the lighter factory example from the last chapter.

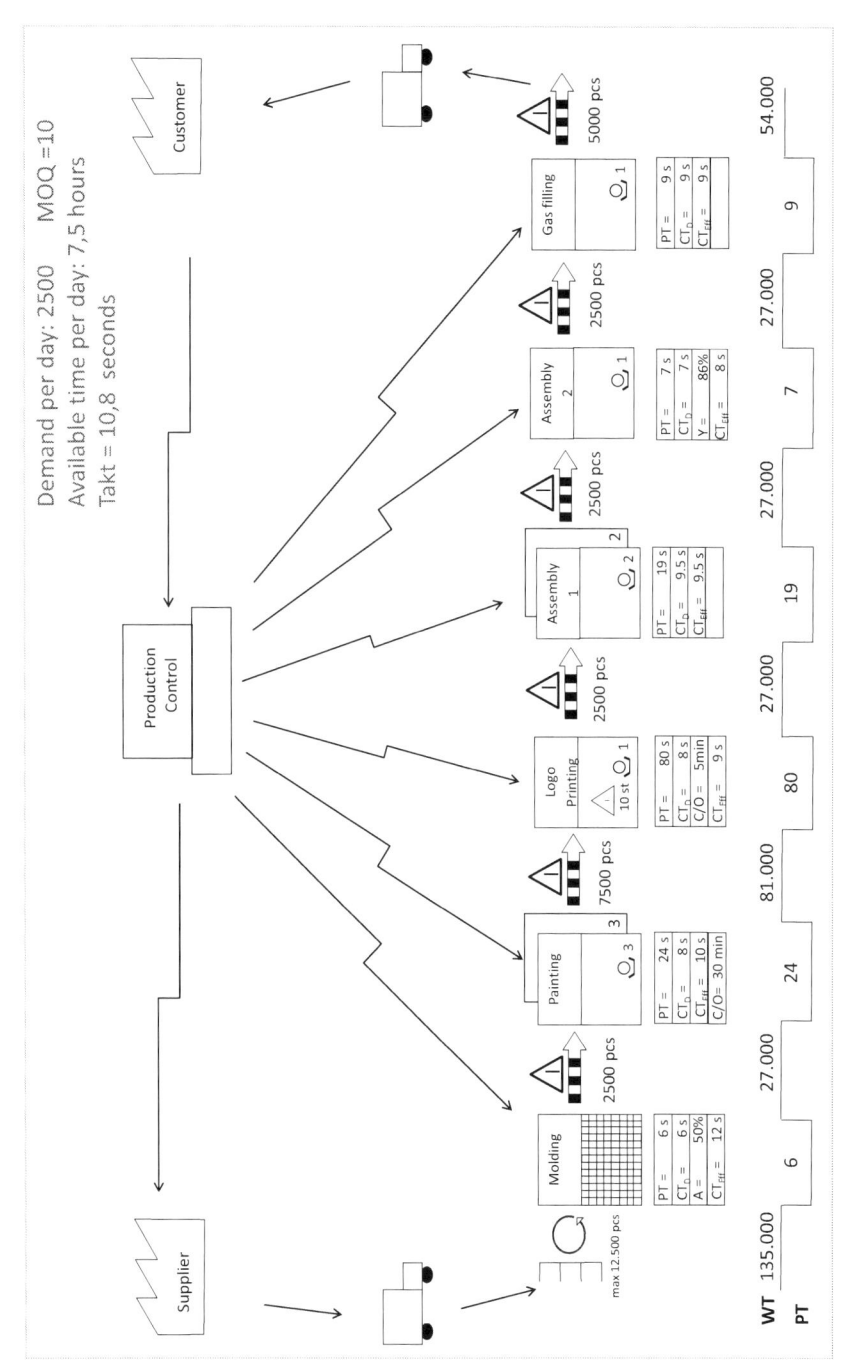

*Figure 41: The real current state of the lighter factory*

The starting point of the journey, the current-state VSM, was not as I described it in the previous section. When I first visited the lighter factory, the production processes used a traditional push system, as Figure 41 shows. These were the Process times:

| | |
|---|---|
| The total waiting time of the process: | 105 hours |
| process Time: | 151 seconds = 0.04 hours |
| Production Lead time: | 105.04 hours |

**THE CURRENT STATE** includes six process steps with uncontrolled inventory between them. Because they are uncontrolled, every process step needs an individual production signal to know what to produce next. This leads to relatively complex information flow from a central planning department to all the individual process steps.

Other information that needs to be gathered before starting the eight steps of future-state value stream mapping is the average daily demand (twenty-five hundred pieces per day in this case) and the available capacity (seven and a half hours) to be able to calculate takt time—10.8 seconds.

An interesting fact is that the order lead time of a lighter is twelve days and forty-two seconds, of which the actual process time is only forty-two seconds. This means we are dealing with a classic process in which **99 percent of the lead time is waiting time**, which means 99% of the total lead time is non-value-adding, or waste.

Each of the eight steps is a question that helps identify an improvement opportunity. There are no wrong answers to any of the questions. Even when a certain kaizen event is specified, it is not certain yet if the required results will be achieved. In that case, you simply go back to the drawing board, your VSM, and find another possible solution to your problem.

In the following illustrations, the starburst icons show the kaizen events, or kaizen blitzes, that need to be implemented to improve flow for the question mentioned in the illustration. The next illustration will show the implications of the change with a gray shadow.

# Step 1: Can all Workstations Keep Takt?

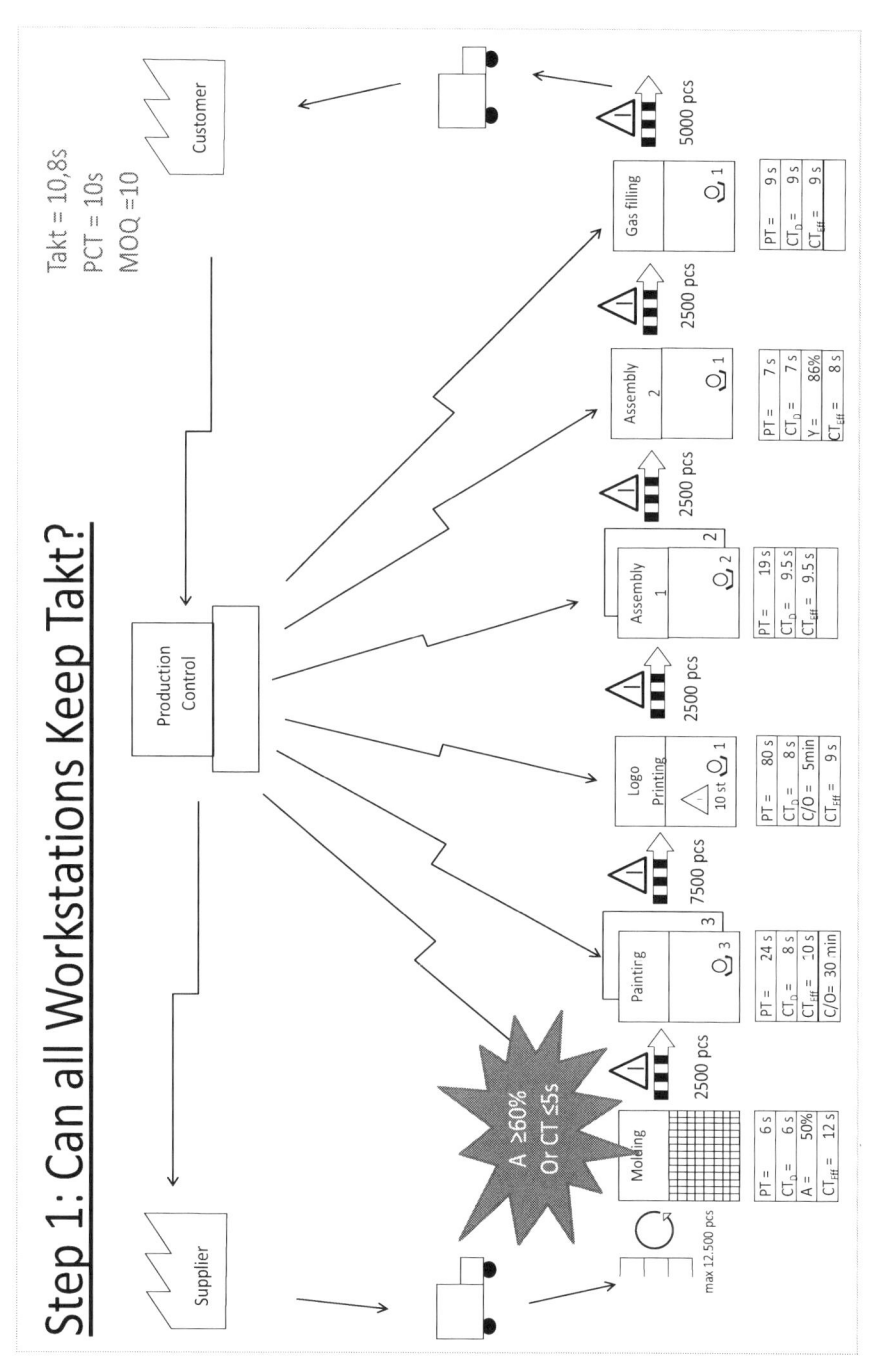

Figure 42: Not all workstations can keep takt

The first step in developing the future-state VSM is to **CHECK TAKT TIME FOR ALL WORKSTATIONS**. Can all workstations meet customer demand? Because value stream mapping should be used at least once a year, using the current sales forecasts to discover your first possible problems is not a bad idea. In the lighter case, the new takt time is calculated to be 10.8 seconds.

So, when we look at all process boxes separately, we find that the most upstream workstation, molding, cannot deliver the new takt time.
With a cycle time of six seconds, but an availability of 50 percent, the effective cycle time of this workstation is twelve seconds, which is too high.

This means that answering the first question leads us logically to the first necessary improvement. There are now at least two possible kaizen events that we can define: either we increase availability for our value stream, or we reduce the process time of the machine. In this case we chose the former and defined the goal for the first kaizen event to increase availability of the molding machine to 60 percent by improving the process times of the other product family. Figure 42 documents the kaizen. Notice that, when a process step already meets the takt time, an improvement of OEE or change over times will not impact the flow of the entire process. It would only be a local improvement and could in theory even create less balance between the process steps in the process.

The second step in designing the future-state value stream is **CHOOSING THE FINISHED-GOODS STRATEGY**. There are (still) two possibilities here: made-to-order, in which products are shipped to the customers after production, or made-to-stock, in which finished goods will be held even though there is no order yet.

In the lighter example, all lighters are customer specific because they have customers' logos printed on them. The obvious choice is a made-to-order strategy, as figure 43 shows.

Steps three, four, and five of future-state VSM are about **IMPLEMENTING THE PULL SYSTEM**. We discussed in chapter 11.2 that there are three possibilities to implement pull: one-piece flow; FIFO lanes or a supermarket.
We also learned from chapter 11.2 that one-piece flow would be the best option, followed by the FIFO, and then the supermarket, which was only our solution of last resort.

# Step 2: Finished Goods Strategy?

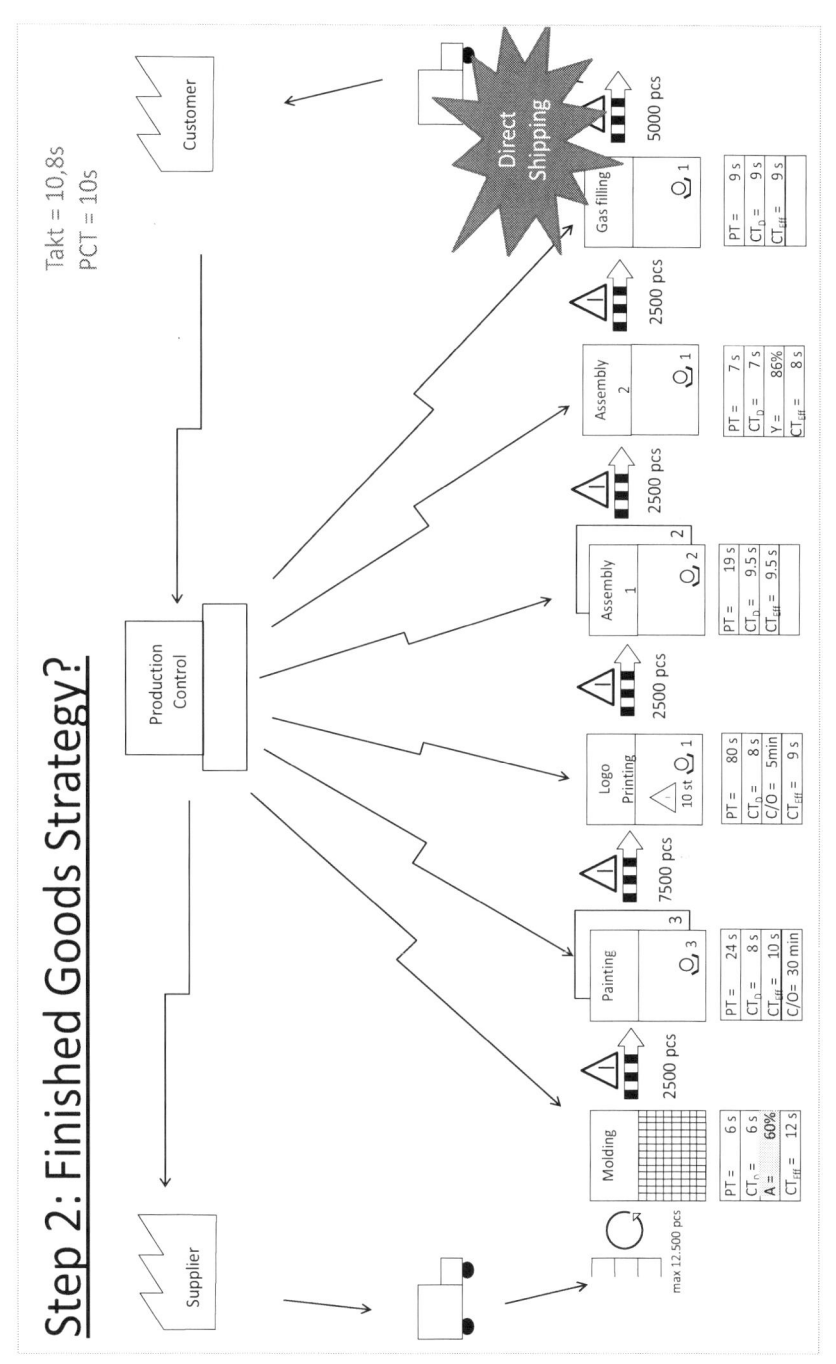

*Figure 43: The finished-goods strategy is chosen to be direct shipping.*

This means that for every triangle, we first check where we can implement **one-piece flow**. As figure 44 shows, in the lighter factory example, the two assembly steps and the assembly steps together could form one new workstation with one-piece flow if we managed to improve the yield of the assembly steps in a kaizen event. In situations in which operator cycles include a high number of steps, we can use the yamazumi to help balance these activities, which reduces the amount of buffer needed between these steps. Chapter 14.1 further explains the yamazumi itself and how in this example the idea of creating one-piece flow line was created.

One-piece flow does not seem to be a viable option for the remaining three triangles at this point. That means we check for the remaining connections to see if we can implement **FIFO lanes** there.
There is one location suitable for a **FIFO**: before assembly. Since the lighters have customer-specific logos printed on them before these two steps, a fixed sequence can be kept within those pull connections.

One important aspect of creating a FIFO lane is to determine the size of it. The maximum stock that a FIFO lane can hold is a choice that you can make. The goal is, that the size of the FIFO is big enough to prevent downstream workstation from slowing down, but small enough to minimize waiting time in the overall production lead time. So, this depends on the situation of the FIFO and whether the bottleneck is in front of it, behind it, or not at all next to it.
Here are two situations that can help you think about determining the size of a FIFO lane.

When you are in a situation in which you have a FIFO lane between machine A and machine B, of which machine A is the bottleneck, and Machine B has a C/O time of one hour; you will probably want your FIFO lane to contain inventory of at least one hour, so that machine A -the bottleneck- never has to idle.

Whenever you are in a situation in which you have a FIFO lane between machine A and machine B, where machine B is the bottleneck and machine A has a delivery time of 24 hours for raw materials; you could decide the FIFO lane to contain at least 24 hours of buffer to make sure the machine does not starve when the delivery is late/cancelled.

The two remaining triangles will have to be **supermarkets**. The triangle between

# Step 3: Where can we implement flow?

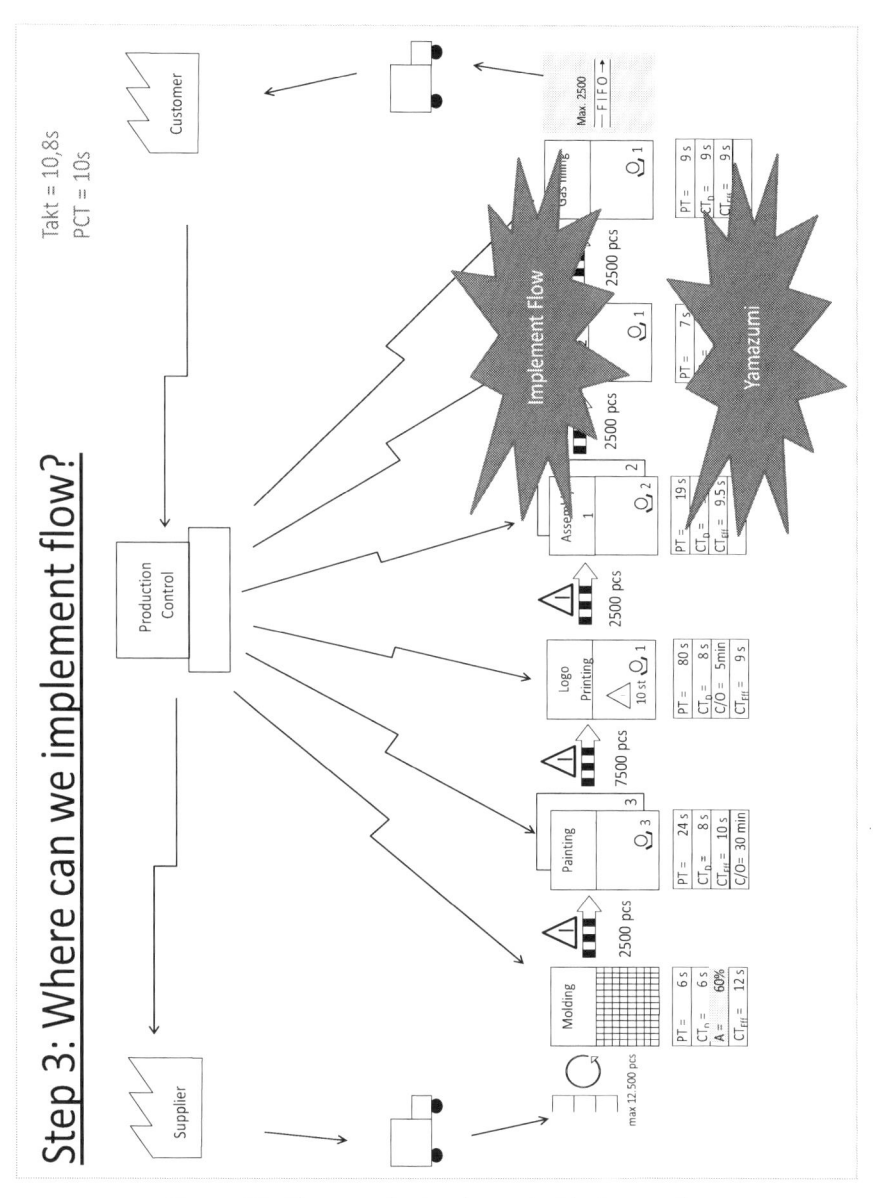

*Figure 44: Flow can be implemented between the three process steps.*

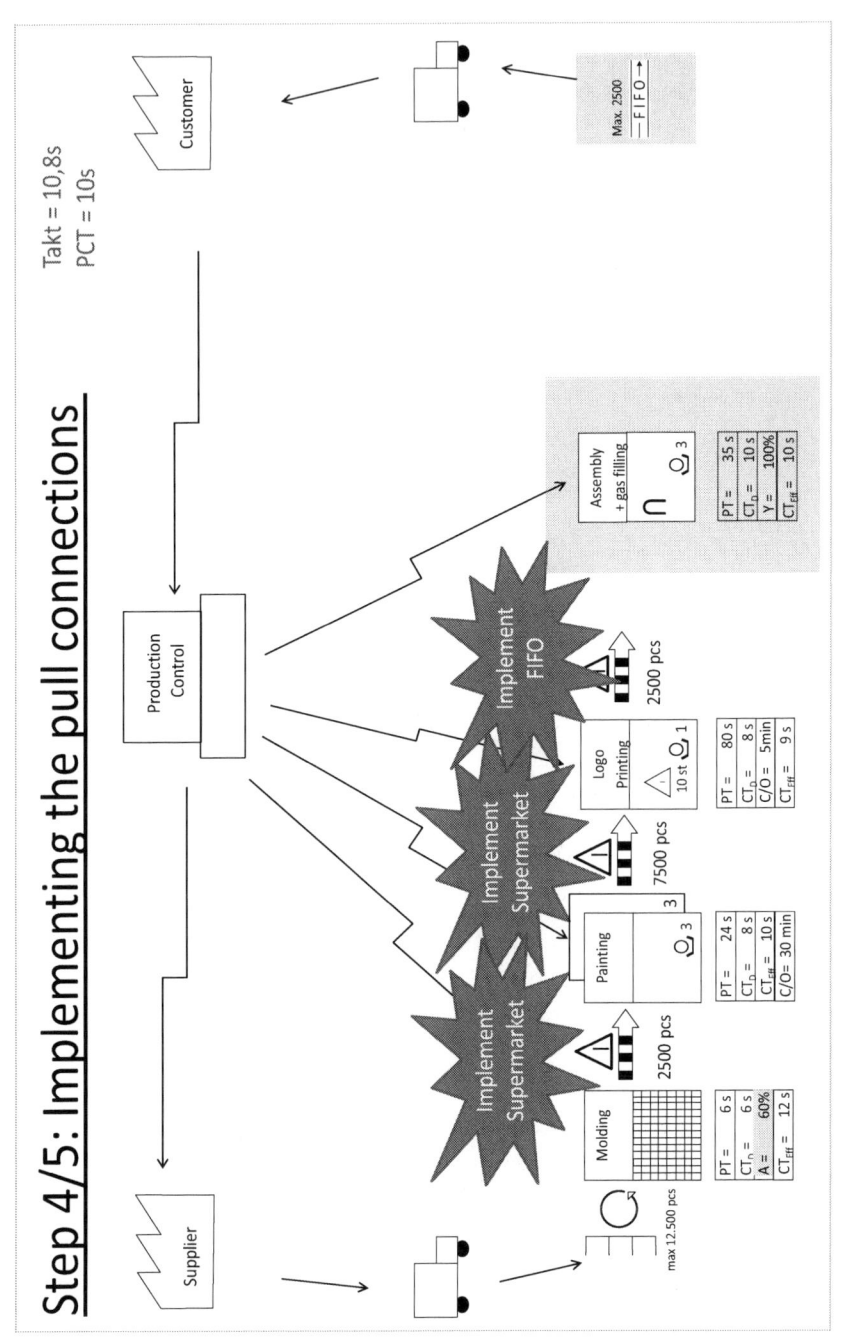

*Figure 45: The remaining triangles are transformed into FIFO lanes or supermarkets.*

the painting station and the logo printing station can become a supermarket, so that the painting station replenish any color of lighter that is taken out of the supermarket by the logo printing station. The supermarket before the painting station is used to buffer for basic molds, which can be taken by the painting station as needed (also shown in figure 45).

Just like with the FIFO lanes, you can make some calculations to determine the ideal size of each supermarket for that specific location. Small enough to reduce waiting times, but big enough to prevent bottlenecks from idling.

Steps six, seven, and eight are about production control. Step six starts with making decisions about **THE PACEMAKER SIGNAL**. The fewer the signals that there are needed in production, the easier it is to manage the process. The goal should therefore be to have only one signal, the pacemaker (Rother and Shook 1999).

Because we changed most of the process into a pull process in the previous steps, only the logo-printing station needs to have a production schedule. The two workstations downstream from logo printing just keep the sequence and take the next order from the FIFO lanes, while the two stations before printing simply replenish the supermarkets.

In step seven, the **PRODUCTION SCHEDULE IS LEVELED**. The speed with which a process can respond to changes in customer demand is dependent on the interval in which all products in a product family can be produced, the **EPEI (every product every interval)**. When the factory produces all colors of lighters once a week, a customer might have to wait four days longer for an order than when it produces every color every day.

In this step, the shortest possible interval is determined in which takt can still be kept. The lean tool used to achieve this is heijunka, which is the topic of chapter 14.2. The lighter factory can produce every color every day without having to define an extra kaizen event. Figure 46 shows a kaizen burst to visualize that we need to talk about the schedule.

The final step is **DETERMINING THE PITCH** of the value stream. The pitch is the word that describes the interval in which production orders are both send to the process and checked for completion. In practice, a *pitch runner* visits the

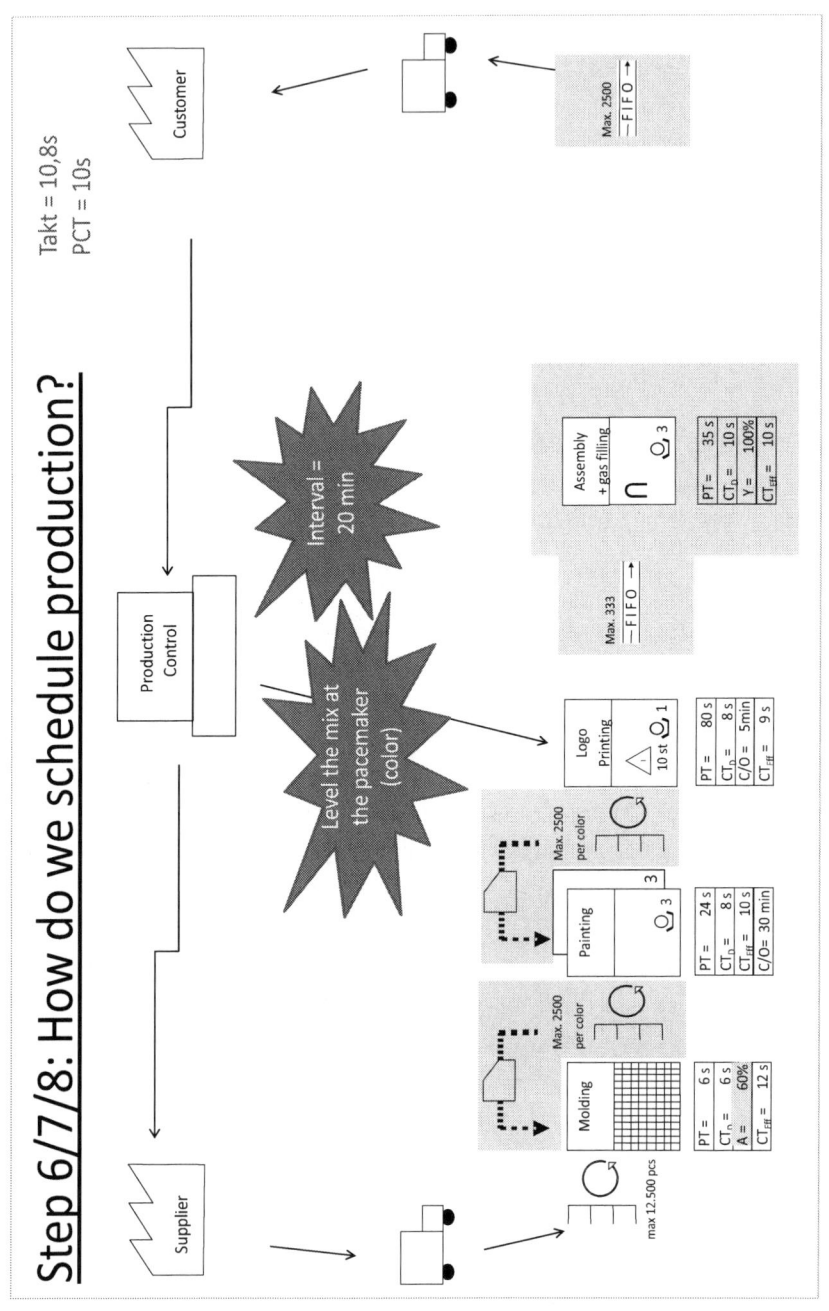

*Figure 46: Production will be controlled using a single signal, which will be released into the process in intervals of twenty minutes.*

workstations and checks the orders for the past interval before he or she releases the orders for the next interval. The shorter the interval, the more flexible is the order that management can plan for the orders for production.

For instance, in our lighter factory example, the interval is set at twenty minutes (as shown in figure 46). This means that, every twenty minutes, the orders for the next twenty minutes are released into the process. The scheduling department can change the order book for the entire production line after the current pitch of twenty minutes without anyone in production noticing.

To conclude the series of illustrations, figure 47 shows **THE FUTURE-STATE VSM** as a result of the eight steps described above, with an updated lead-time ladder. By implementing pull, we have reduced the order lead time from twelve days to five and a half days, an improvement of more than 50 percent.

|  | Current State | Future State |
| --- | --- | --- |
| Waiting time: | 378.000 sec = 105 h | 144.000 sec = 40 h |
| Process Time: | 151 sec | 151 sec |
| Production Lead time | 378.151 sec = 105,04 h | 144.151 sec = 40,04 h |

We also reduced the number of control signals from six to one, which reduces management complexity. And because of heijunka and pitch, every type of lighter can be produced every day, and the daily plan can be changed every twenty minutes without disturbing production.

The most important thing in designing the future-state VSM is using a structural approach to generate the kaizen events to make sure the kaizen events directly improve the performance of the value stream. The kaizen event on yield improvement at the assembly is a good example of that. We could have randomly decided to implement SMED on the logo-printing machine because the changeover times are there. From the structural approach, we learned, however, that the changeover times were not preventing us from delivering to the customer. Maybe it will come up in the next future-state VSM.

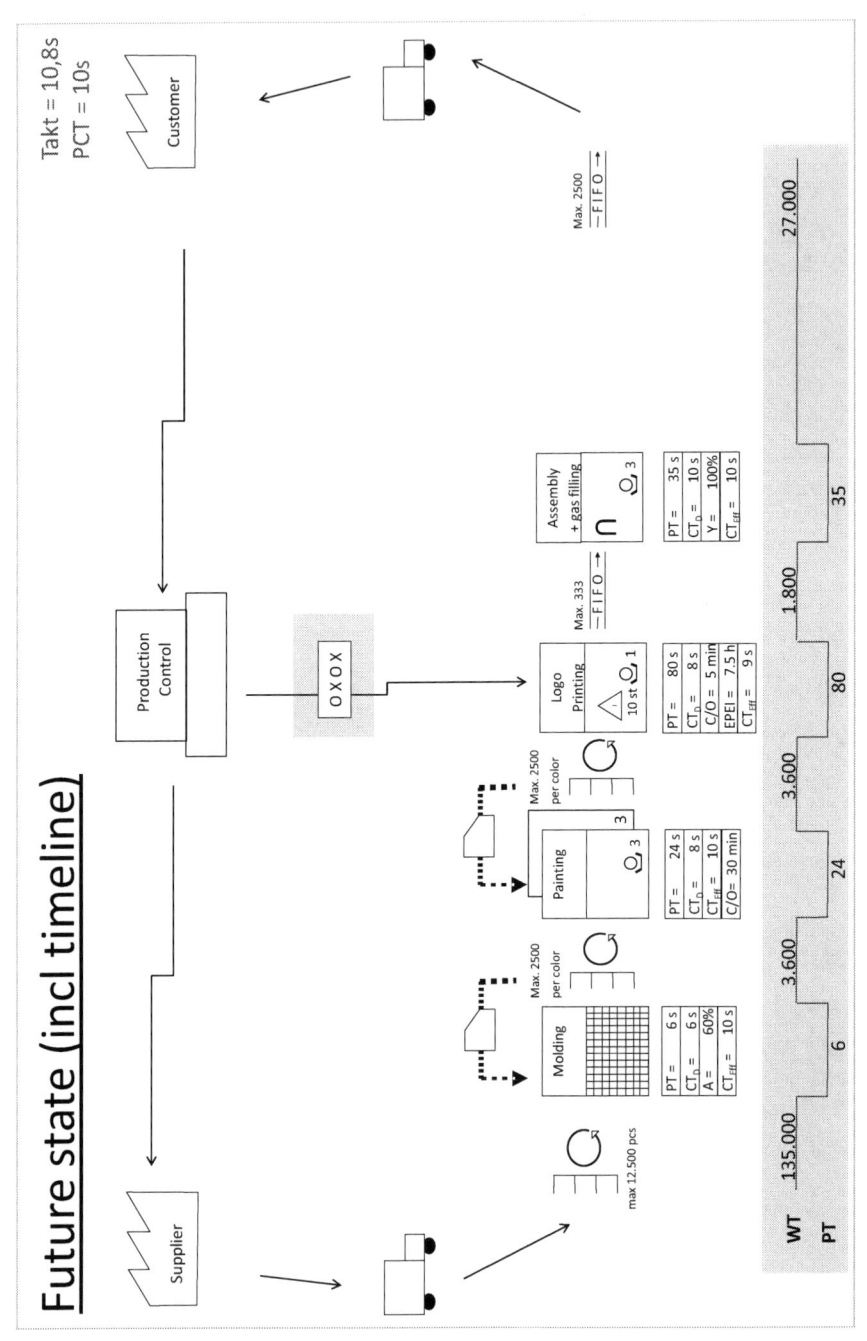

Figure 47: This is the future-state VSM for the lighter factory after going through the eight steps.

**Key Points:**
- *The eight steps of future-state value stream design form a structured approach to redesigning your processes based on your organizational goals.*
- *The first two steps involve a takt time analysis to make sure all customers can get delivery on time and deciding on how the interface with the customers are organized.*
- *Steps three through five are about implementing pull in the process (with one-piece flow as the best option).*
- *Steps six through eight are about production control, which includes discussions about the number of production schedules, how these schedules are determined, and how they are released into the process.*

# Chapter 14:
# Tools useful While Creating the Future State VSM

In the previous chapters we have looked at value stream mapping in general and the 8 steps of designing a future state value stream map. When you design your future state value stream map, there are a variety of tools that can be used to make different design choices.

Two lean tools that are commonly used within Future State Value Stream Mapping are the Yamazumi chart for line balancing, and Heijunka for load leveling. These will both be discussed in more detail.

## 14.1 Line balancing with a Yamazumi chart

> *Balance is not better time management, but better boundary management.*
> *—Betsy Jacobson*

Yamazumi is a tool whose name you could translate literally as "stacking mountain." You use the yamazumi chart to visualize two things: the variation between workstations and operator cycles and whether a workstation can keep takt. After that, you can use the yamazumi to improve the flow of the process.

First, the yamazumi chart can **show the variation** in work cycles for machine cycles or operator cycles. The goal of using the yamazumi chart is to improve flow so that we can reduce inventories between these cycles and therefore lead time. The example in this chapter is based on the lighter factory described in chapter 12 and 13. Figure 48 shows one example of a yamazumi chart, which depicts the current state of the lighter factory, as Figure 41 described. We can see that assembly step two has a lower effective cycle time than does the gas-filling station.

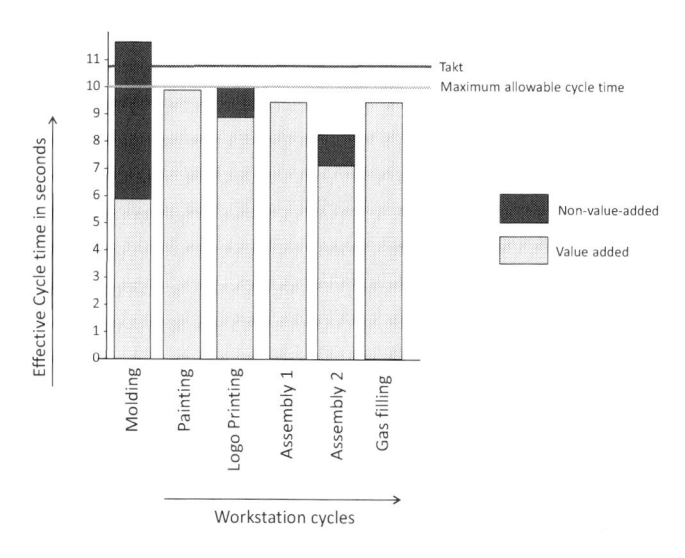

*Figure 48: Yamazumi, a tool to demonstrate machine or operator work cycles*

This means that when inventories between these steps are uncontrolled (using a push system), inventory will build up between these two steps because gas filling cannot keep up with the speed at which assembly two is working unless operator one works slower or takes on extra tasks at another workstation (which increases complexity in the process).

You can also use the yamazumi chart to demonstrate **what workstations can keep the (new) takt time**. Figure 48 already shows that the molding station cannot deliver products in the future-state defined takt time, which is also why we, during the future-state value stream mapping steps, identified the need to improve the cycles at that workstation.

There are at least **THREE SITUATIONS IN WHICH THE YAMAZUMI CAN BE USED** to improve the flow of the product.
The first application is at the level of **process design**. When a new product or product family is introduced, the yamazumi can show the level of flow for the new product(s).

The second application of the yamazumi chart is in **defining product families** (Duggan 2002) as part of process redesign. An important step in mixed model value streams mapping is to reduce the number of shared resources in the value stream. Therefore, product families might be redefined to create more dedicated machines. The yamazumi chart can be built for the sum of work units for the complete family. For every product family, the total cycle time should be kept below takt, and the variance of cycle times between the different products in the family should be kept below 30 percent (Duggan 2002). The bigger the family, the more flexibility the value stream has, because a cycle time for one product that exceeds takt time can be compensated by volume and cycle time for a second product in the same family.

Thirdly, you can use the yamazumi chart to **determine the product interval** for heijunka. For each product family, you can compare the total process times with the planned cycle time for each workstation and visualize how much time is left for changeovers between products within that family. With heijunka, the product sequence is fixed by comparing the total changeover time needed to produce one whole cycle with the time available for all changeovers in total, and the interval can be calculated. The shorter the interval is, the smaller the buffered inventory between workstations must be.

The yamazumi helps reduce all three enemies of lean by directly identifying different forms of **imbalance**. Comparing stack charts depicts the difference in at least four ways: between two products in a product family on one workstation, between workstations in one process, between operator cycles for different products within one family on one workstation, or between operator cycles of multiple sequential cycles.

The yamazumi chart shows whenever a production step (machine or operator) comes close to or even exceeds takt time, which leads to a possible **overburden** of the machine or operators. The yamazumi chart also shows when a person is not challenged at all in keeping the process going, which can lead to waste just the same.

Balancing out the workstations and operators also reduces **waste**. The more balanced the operator and machine cycles are, the less inventory is needed to buffer for this variance. We already learned from chapter 5.1 that inventory increases the chance of other wastes, such as defects, and, of course, the waiting time, which directly increases the lead time of the process.

Yamazumi supports the following Toyota management principles:

**Principle two: Create continuous flow.** Yamazumi is a tool that reduces imbalance between processes with the goal of reducing inventories. This is the *why* of yamazumi. When inventories are reduced to one or fewer, we have implemented continuous flow between the two steps.

**Principle four: Balance the workload**. This is the *what* of yamazumi. When we balance the workload, we create continuous flow.

**Principle seven: Make problems visible**. Yamazumi depicts the variation between process steps or operator cycles and therefore helps identify the problem areas within a process.

**Principle fourteen: Use hansei and kaizen**. Just as with every other lean tool, the goal of yamazumi is to find the next improvement in your process. The following section will elaborate on this.

> **Key Points:**
> - *Yamazumi can help show the imbalance of work cycles.*
> - *You can use yamazumi to improve the balance of the process.*

## 14.1.1 How to Use Yamazumi

*This tool helps us balance flow work content per operator to takt time and, as a result, create continuous flow between operators at the pacemaker.*
—K. Duggan

Figure 49 shows a second example of a yamazumi chart. This time I chose not to show the effective cycle time of each workstation in the lighter example (as I did in figure 48), but to show the **operator work cycle** times of the different steps to demonstrate the variation in the amount of work between process steps for one product.

You can use different blocks to represent different tasks or **job elements**. A job element is the smallest combination of steps that must be done by the same person, which cannot be interrupted. One example would be writing an e-mail. When the task is to write an e-mail to a customer, it is most efficient when one person writes the entire e-mail. Splitting it up between three people leads to a lot of extra work because the second and the third person need to check what the previous person has written already before continuing the task. Writing an e-mail should be one job element and therefore one Post-it or magnet on the yamazumi chart.

When process cycles are defined, the goal is to move these blocks of tasks to different operators until you achieve a balanced workload. The smaller the blocks are, the more flexible the division of work can be at a later stage.

Based on the current information we have from the lighter factory, we can only draw the yamazumi with current process times with a known changeover time at the logo-printing station and some yield loss at assembly two. You can use color-coding to show these changeover times and rework due to yield loss. Value-adding work can be shown in green and non-value-adding activities can be shown in red. This depiction helps define possible improvements in the work cycles.

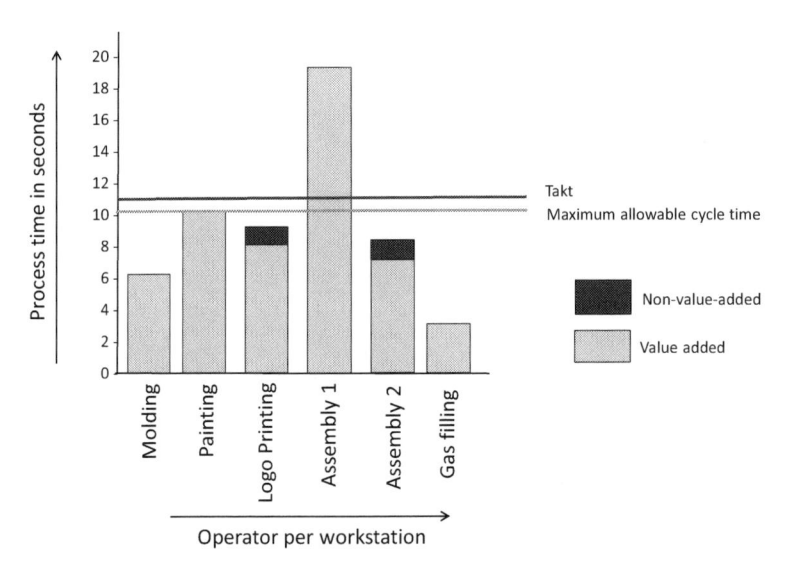

*Figure 49: Yamazumi, a tool to depict operator work cycles*

Finally, we show the **takt time** and the **maximum allowable cycle time** as two single lines across the chart. Since the takt time shows customer demand, all work cycles should be shorter than the takt time to be able to deliver to all customers. If the customer demand changes, the takt time line will move up or down the yamazumi chart, showing both problems as well as opportunities for production.

Like all other lean tools, the **YAMAZUMI IS MEANT TO LEAD YOU TO PROCESS IMPROVEMENTS**. In its simplest form, the yamazumi should be created from **Sticky notes on a flip chart** or magnet strips on a whiteboard. When each unit of work is represented by a Post-it or a magnet, it makes it possible to play around with the chart to improve the flow of work for a certain product and add to your ideas as you go.
You should do two things to improve the balance of the process: move job elements to balance the workload and reduce the process times of elements (preferably non-value-adding blocks).

First, we must create work cycles as close to the planned cycle time as possible. That should, as chapter 11.1 describes, be about 95 percent of takt time at the maximum (Duggan 2002). We do this by **moving job elements** to the left of the chart as much as possible.

Going back to the lighter factory example, figure 49 shows us two interesting things when we compare it with the yamazumi chart in figure 48. First, the operator cycles at the molding station and the gas-filling station are a lot shorter than the other production steps. This shows us that the operator cycle and the cycle times of the workstation are not necessarily the same thing.

Second, assembly step one takes almost twice as long as the takt time, which is probably why the design team created a parallel workstation where, as the observant reader might have noticed from figure 41 in chapter 13, two operators perform the exact same task of nineteen seconds. Two parallel workstations need to be fed by the upstream printing machine, which means a buffer is needed to prevent them from starving.

A better solution would be to see if we could divide the longer work cycle between two people. If we can do this, as figure 50 shows, we might be able to create one-piece flow between the assembly steps,

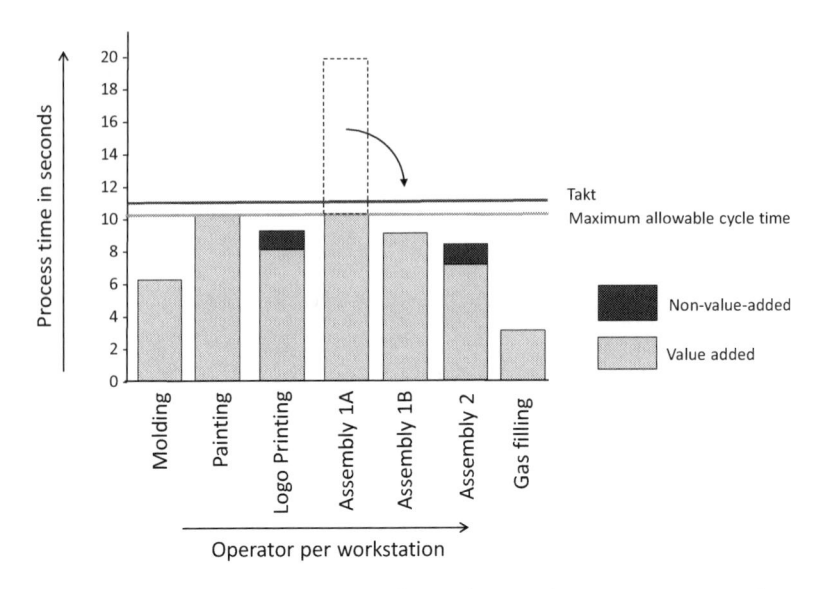

*Figure 50: Lighter example—splitting the process times of assembly 1 in steps A and B*

eliminating the buffers between them as proposed in step three of future-state value stream mapping (chapter 13; figure 44). This also frees up space and tools because we no longer need the second workstation at assembly 1.

While moving the job elements, the goal is to create operator cycles that are as close to the planned cycle time as possible since producing at exactly this speed ensures the customers are served. When we focus on balancing the two (now three) assembly steps, we try to max out all available operator time at station assembly 1A and assembly 1B, collecting all the leftover available time at assembly 2.

Figure 51 shows an example of a possible result after improving the situation shown at figure 49 and figure 50. Fortunately, in this example, the individual job elements within the assembly steps were so small that it was possible to create two work cycles of ten seconds, moving nine seconds from assembly 1 to assembly 1B and moving the first job element from assembly 2 over to assembly 1B.

The second challenge is to find non-value-added job elements and target them for improvements by either **reducing or eliminating those elements.** The number of details that need to be analyzed depends on the situation. When there is a specific improvement target from the future-state value stream event, but there are no non-value-adding job elements in your yamazumi, it may be necessary to dive deeper into the value-adding steps to see if waste can be found within those steps that can be reduced; to find that waste, you might require the help of 5S.

The lighter factory example again shows us an interesting opportunity. Figure 51 shows us that there is known rework in the assembly 2 workstation, leading to extra work. From the same figure, we can see that the actual operator handling of gas filling is only three seconds.

If we were able to combine assembly 2 and gas filling, we would create an even more balanced process and would only need five and a half FTE (full time equivalent, which equals 40 hours in Western Europe) to do the work (half an FTE at molding and five FTE for the rest of the process, as figure 52 shows). Connecting the work of the two machines might lead to some extra work for the operator because he or she must move between the two machines. It might therefore be necessary to increase the yield of the assembly station before it is possible to combine the workstation into one working cycle.

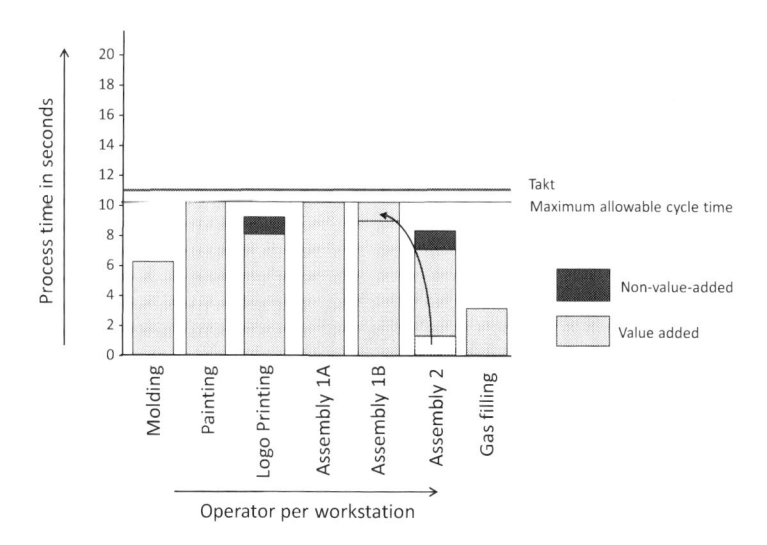

*Figure 51: moving one part of assembly 2 to assembly 1B to balance the workload as close to target cycle time as possible*

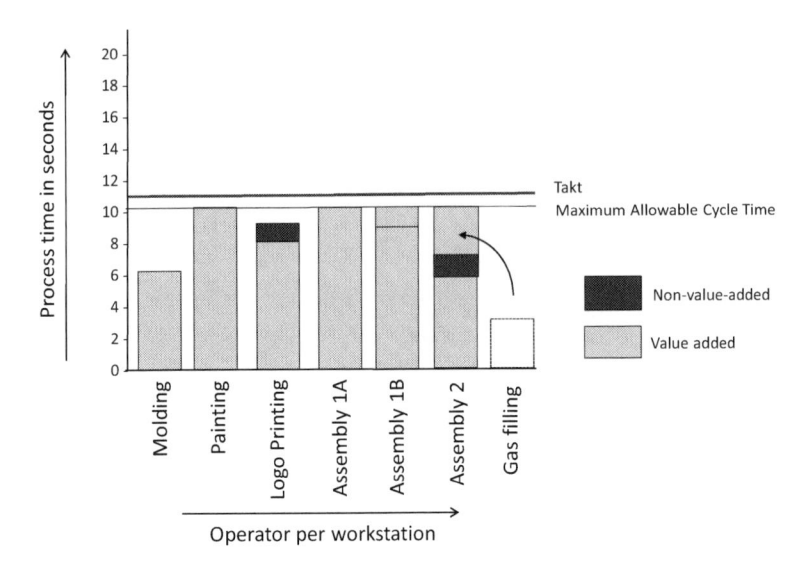

*Figure 52: Possible future state of the yamazumi shown in figure 49*

So, what has changed for the people in the lighter factory? I would assume that the operators took care of tasks outside the production line when their cycles allowed it, which increased the complexity of the working cycles, and that would then produce management challenges. In the new setup, however, all operator work is concentrated in five and a half FTE instead of six and a half, **freeing up** one whole FTE for other activities. Cross-training would make it possible for the team of six and a half FTE to rotate their roles within the team. It would also make it possible for them to take turns using their time outside actual production for other activities.

A final note on the link between the yamazumis from this chapter and the future-state value stream map in chapter 13: the process times mentioned in the value stream map did not change because the operator working cycles were balanced, not the machines. This means that even though the work of the gas-filling station was three seconds and was moved to the assembly 2 workstation, the process time of the lighters within the process of gas filling was still nine seconds.

**Key Points:**
- *You can use yamazumi to show the variation in cycle times.*
- *We can differentiate between machine cycle times and operator cycle times.*
- *We can also differentiate between showing variation between process steps and between multiple products at one workstation.*
- *We can use yamazumi to design a new process, to improve the flow of a process, and to determine the EPEI of a workstation as part of heijunka (see the next chapter).*
- *The work is moved to the front of the process as much as possible. There, operator cycles are designed as close to the planned cycle time as possible.*

## 14.2 Improving the Production Schedule with Load Levelling

> *It is a misconception, perhaps stemming from the pull system idea, that Toyota assembles vehicles in the same order in which customers buy them.*
> —Mike Rother

Heijunka (Japanese for load leveling) is a tool that is used to **balance and sort the order intake** of a process to reduce the need for inventories, which prevents long lead times. When a workstation or production line produces multiple products with different process times, inventories are necessary to buffer for these variances to prevent workstations from idling.

Chapter 5 described the bullwhip effect because of variation in customer demand. Imbalance in customer demand amplifies as the signal moves upstream in the process (Rother 2010). When the signal is filtered, the amplification is prevented to some extent, and Toyota uses heijunka to limit the variation to its suppliers between +5 percent and -5 percent (Lyer, Seshadrei and Vasher 2009).

Sorting the production sequence (step seven of future-state value stream mapping) goes against a lot of traditional ways of thinking because the balancing exercise **usually leads to more changeovers** that on their own are not value-adding. We can see from the lighter factory example that more changeovers lead to less necessary inventory, reducing the lead time of the process, which means that more changeovers can sometimes reduce waste in the overall process.

There are **FIVE ELEMENTS OF LOAD LEVELING**: the interval in which all products will be produced, a fixed sequence of products, a predetermined inventory policy, a variable number of items for each product, and the direction for improvement. Let's look at these one by one.

The first outcome of load leveling is **a fixed interval** in which all different products within the product family can be produced. When comparing total demand and changeover times, you can calculate how many production cycles can be made while delivering to all customers. This is where you can use the yamazumi charts again.

**The fixed sequence** of products in that certain interval manages the time for changeovers that needs to be made in every product cycle (Rother 2010). Combining multiple orders of the same product type might reduce changeovers, while splitting up bigger orders to level the workload for the operators possibly increases the changeover time.

The fixed sequence also reduces the variance of changeovers. When product types one, two, and three are always produced in the same order, a changeover from three to two, or two to one, will not be needed anymore. When changeover times vary between products, try to create a sequence that eliminates the longest changeover times. In that case, the amount of waste necessary to produce each product will be reduced as well.

The fixed sequence also facilitates the defining of the **inventory policies** for raw materials. When the interval in which the workstation will be producing is defined, the size of the inventory buffers can be calculated.

Within the fixed interval and the fixed sequence, the **number of products per type** may still vary, but they should cover customer demand. This means that when an interval is designed to be one day, there should be room to plan each product within the context of the average daily demand each day (Rother 2010). The interval should leave room to react to variations in customer demand. The speed of reacting to the changes fully depends on the length of the interval. The shorter the interval, the faster one can react, and the smaller will be the impact on the work content.

Finally, the heijunka schedule shows the **direction for the next improvement**. The goal of every lean tool is to help you find the next area of improvement (Floyd 2010) (Rother 2010). The exercise of defining a fixed sequence of products or reducing the interval could bring up issues that need resolving. Complexity and variation are both themes that lead to waste and are therefore worth examining. Determining what sequence through which to release the orders in production beforehand not only reduces the necessary size of the buffers, but it also can ensure that all products are delivered in takt time even though part of the product family has effective cycle times that are longer than takt time.

We can conclude that load leveling influences all three enemies of lean, first of all because it prevents **variation** from occurring in the process. By determining the best possible sequence of products beforehand, variation in the workload of the different workstations is prevented, and so are the most difficult types of changeovers. By preventing this variation from occurring in the process, **overburden** on the machines and on operators is prevented, which in turn leads to fewer items in inventory and fewer defects (one of the **wastes**) that result from overburden.

The following management principles can be linked to using heijunka to balance the work flow:

**Principle two: Create flow**. This is the *why* of the load leveling. The shorter the interval of the product portfolio on the line, the fewer the inventory items that are needed in front of that workstation and the faster the product moves through the process.

**Principle four: Balance the workload**. This is the *what* of load leveling. Whereas yamazumi balances the work content between workstations and on workstations, heijunka balances the input of the process.

---

**Key Points:**
- *Heijunka is the tool for balancing the order schedule.*
- *Orders are produced in a fixed sequence and a fixed interval, but the quantities per product may still vary.*

## 14.2.1 How to Use Heijunka

*By using heijunka, Toyota manages to keep the variation in orders they send to their suppliers between -5 and +5 percent*
A.V. Iver, S. Seshadri and R. Vasher

In this chapter there will be two examples of heijunka in practice, the production wheel and the heijunka box.

**THE PRODUCTION WHEEL** is a way to display the production interval and the production sequence within the interval, as Figure 53 depicts.
The production wheel can contain both made-to-order products as well as made-to-stock products (King 2009). The made-to-stock products are planned first because they form the basis of the production portfolio for today and the future. After the standard made-to-stock products are planned, the remainder of the cycle can be planned for made-to-order products. As written above, the sequence of products is fixed, while the number of items per product may vary.

When designing the wheel, the most important decision is the time it takes to go around the wheel once. This represents the interval in which every product can be produced. This is called the: **every product every interval (EPEI) time**. The shorter the interval, the faster supermarkets can be replenished, and thus the smaller the supermarkets need to be (Rother and Shook 1999).

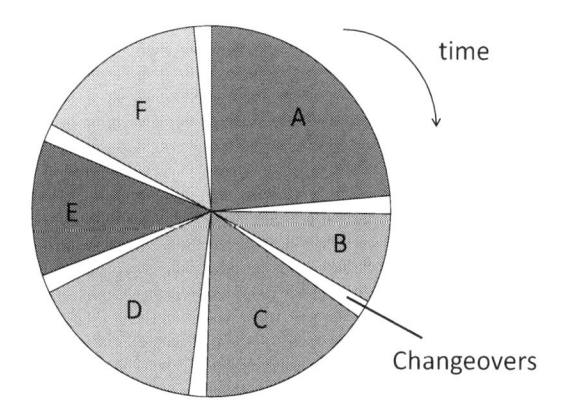

*Figure 53: Example of a production wheel with products A–F*

243

With this, the interval directly influences the total lead time, batch sizes, and number of products, which are possibly affected when an error occurs.

Let us take a closer look at our lighter factory example. Figure 54 shows the future-state value stream map for the lighter factory as chapter 13 described. There is one production schedule delivered to the process—at the logo-printing station. The logo-printing station needs to know what color of lighters to take from the supermarket, and the painting station will then replenish those colors. When there is no defined EPEI time for the production schedule, the supermarket in front of the logo-printing station should contain inventory for each of the three colors to buffer for this uncertainty.

For example, when all products are produced once a week, depending on the replenishing time from the upstream workstation or workstations, the supermarket might need to buffer each product for at least a week of customer demand, which equals one week of lead time. Producing every product once a week also means that batches need to be big enough to fulfill the entire weekly demand in one batch, which increases the waiting time for each individual product. That translates into even more lead time. Finally, when a defect is found at the downstream workstation, the entire batch might be contaminated and could need to be checked.

So, what happens when the interval is one day? The upstream inventories need to keep a maximum of one day of inventory for each part. The lead time will therefore only be increased with one day of those inventories.

The waiting time to batch will be smaller because the demand will be split over more batches, and the possible amount of contaminated product is also one-day, maximum.

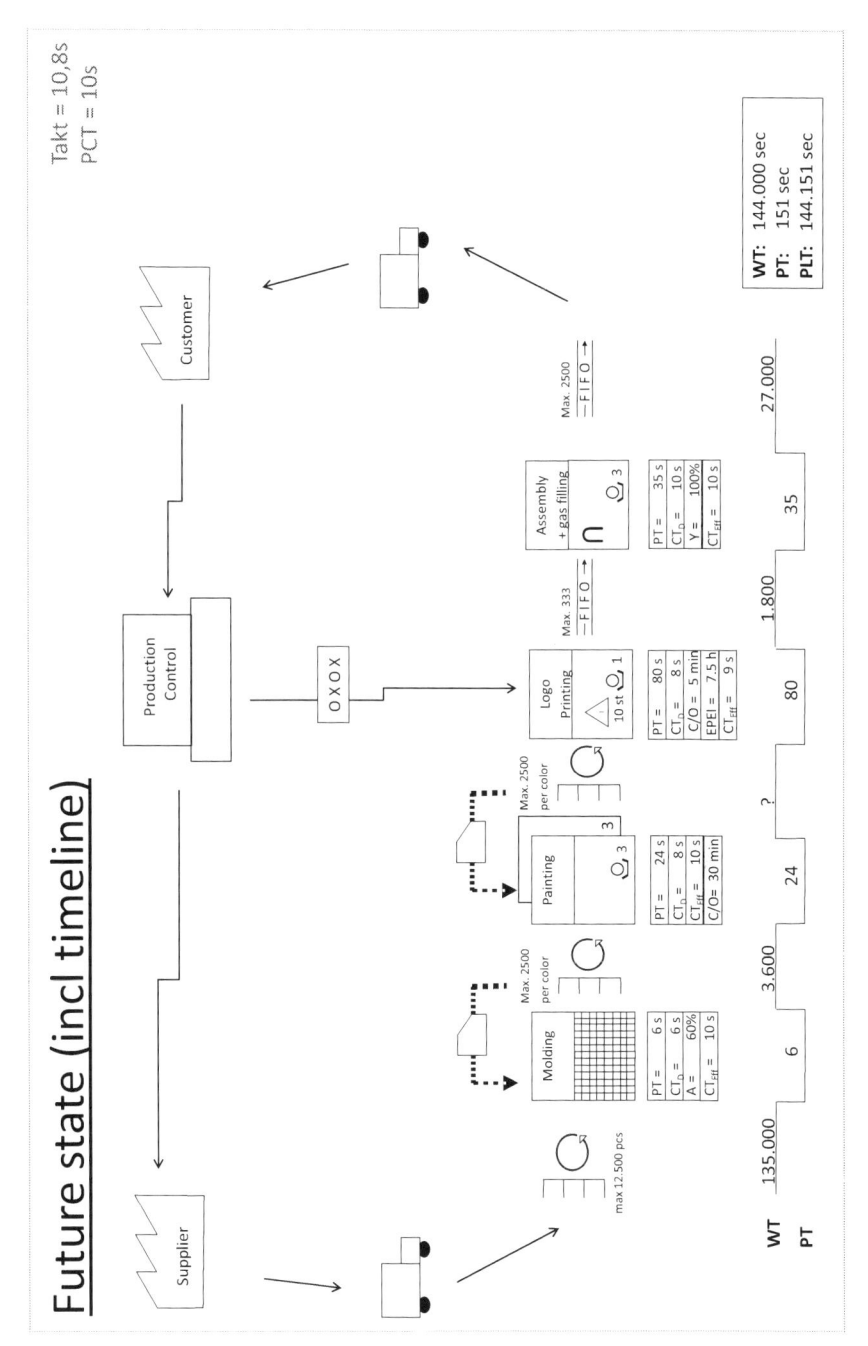

*Figure 54: Future-state lighter factory*

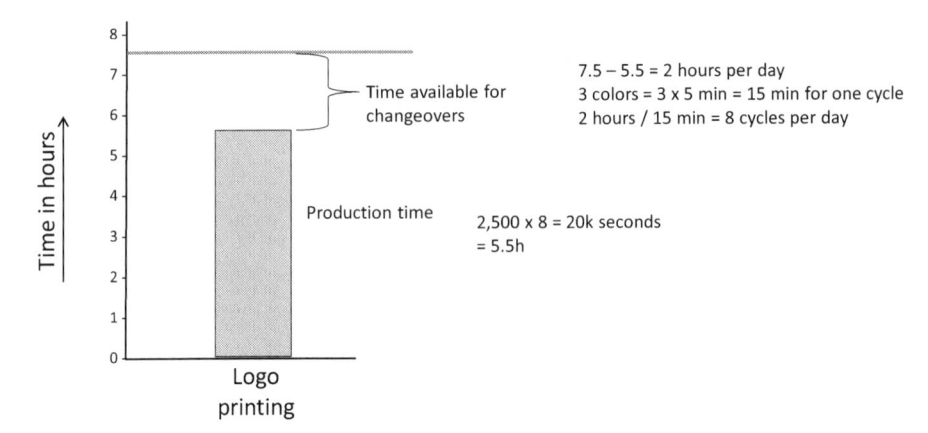

*Figure 55: How to calculate the shortest possible interval in the lighter factory example*

**The shortest possible interval** is the time in which all planned cycle time is planned as close to takt as possible, and therefore it is the time that is as closely planned toward one-piece flow as possible.

You can use the yamazumi chart for this purpose. Let´s go back to the lighter factory example to calculate the interval. Figure 55 shows this interval, and it is calculated as follows:

1. Sum up the process times for all products in the family for the specific workstation for a certain interval—for instance, a day. In the lighter case, this is 2,500 times 8 seconds, which equals 5.5 hours.
2. Take the total production time available in the day and subtract the total process time. The result is the time that is left for changeovers, which in the lighter case is two hours per day.
3. With the fixed sequence, you can also calculate the total time needed for all changeovers for one complete interval. For the lighter case, this means three colors times five minutes per changeover, which is fifteen minutes.
4. The shortest possible interval is the time available for changeovers divided by the total changeover time. In the lighter example, 120 minutes divided by fifteen minutes is eight cycles.

Knowing that we can plan eight cycles a day, a shortest interval of 56.5 minutes does not necessarily mean we should plan at this interval. It does however show what is possible and how flexible this production station is.

For each workstation that has changeovers, we can calculate the shortest possible interval. We can determine the possible interval of the entire process based on the longest of these calculated shortest-possible intervals to make sure the entire process with all its process steps can have the same interval. (We do not want to bring any imbalance to the process, do we?)

For discrete production—for instance assembling cars, paper clips, or mobile phones—you can use **THE HEIJUNKA BOX** as a tool to combine the balancing principle with a visual system for the PITCH. The pitch system depicts whether production is still on track or not (Rother and Shook 1999) and was already addressed in chapter 13 in designing the future-state value stream map. Figure 56 shows an example of a heijunka box. In its simplest form, this box is a wooden or plastic box with different square slots in which work orders can be planned using visual cards. In this example, the pitch is defined to be forty minutes.

The box contains two dimensions: product types (vertically) and time (horizontally). The **different types of products** are planned in their fixed sequence from the top down. This example also shows that the amount of work can vary per product. In this forty-minute interval, products A and B are produced two times each, while C and D are produced once each.

By depicting the production planning in **the time axis**, what needs to be produced on a certain day is not only visible, but the axis also automatically shows when there is a problem at any given time during that day. A problem can delay production, which may result in the operator fetching his or her next order a bit later than planned. This means that the card will still be in the box at the moment it was supposed to be taken out.

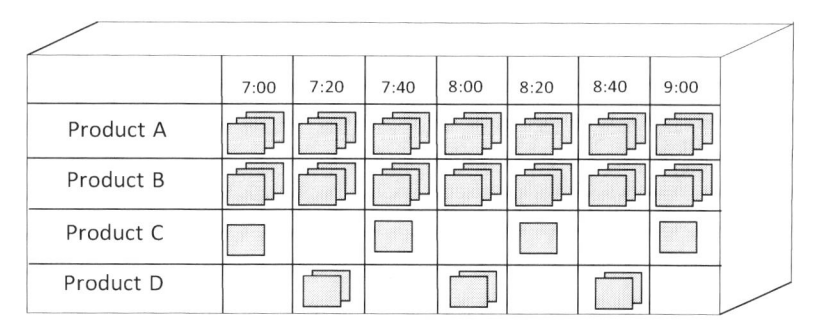

*Figure 56: Example of a heijunka box*

The heijunka box also leaves room for **flexibility**. The operator simply takes the next card from the box when the last order is completed. This means the particular order that is written on each card can be changed up until the last minute without production being impacted.

The fourth principle of *The Toyota Way* (J. K. Liker 2004) states that one should always balance workload to minimize variation. Heijunka is the tool you need to put this principle in practice. We can optimize processes to increase flexibility, stability, and predictability of the processes. Within assembly processes, the heijunka box can combine the balancing principle with a visual management system in which one can see at all times if production is producing to plan or not.

**Key Points:**
- *The heijunka wheel depicts the EPEI time and the time spent on changeovers in a product family.*
- *The faster the wheel turns, the smaller the inventory buffers in front of and behind the process step need to be, so the shorter the lead times are.*
- *When you have a heijunka box, the production schedule can be changed at every pitch interval without anyone in the process noticing.*

# Chapter 15:
# Value Stream Mapping in the Office

*The product that is being created in the office environment is usually packages of knowledge. The faster the complete package of knowledge is created, the sooner a new product can be introduced into the market and therefore create revenue.*
—T. M. Barnhart

So far, we have focused on value stream mapping examples from the production environment. Though the same principles and symbols can be applied for any possible process, there are two types of work that are difficult to capture in the traditional value stream mapping approach described in the previous chapters: project work and office processes. In these kinds of processes, **THE FOLLOWING COMPLEXITIES** usually occur:

**Lead time should be the input of the VSM instead of the output.** In traditional VSM, the lead time is the result of the flow of the process, the final step of value stream mapping that can be calculated when all process steps and connections between those steps are analyzed. In projects, however, the lead time is usually the input for the flow of the process; resources are allocated based on deadlines and not the other way around (Barnhart 2013).
The same problem exists in supportive functions, where, for instance, the planning department should communicate an updated production schedule at a fixed moment of the day (Duggan 2012).

**Most waiting times can be found within process boxes instead of between process boxes.** Traditional VSM is focused on reducing the waiting times between process steps. By implementing flow as much as possible—with the help of U-cells, FIFO lanes, and supermarkets—this type of waiting time is reduced. In project work, however, most waiting times occur within the process boxes. People often need input and feedback from others after they have started, which means this waiting time is part of the process time. If we would create different data boxes for every subtask within this task, the overall VSM would become highly complex, and therefore it would be more difficult to still see the big picture. This is also true for the supportive functions of people who work in the office environment. Every engineering change, planning job, or quality issue needs multiple decision moments and feedback loops that include other people. This communication leads to waiting time.

Third, **most (if not all) people who work in projects can be considered shared resources.** Because of the needs of other people, people work on multiple tasks, possibly in multiple projects (value streams) at the same time. This has further impact on the waiting times within each process box.

Again, the same can be true for our indirect processes, in which the engineer is responsible for different parts that are used in different products within different product families.

Finally, **people can work on one task simultaneously with different capacities and at different times.** One person can work one hour a day on this task, while three others might work for four hours a day on it. How would you depict this in a traditional VSM? You would need enormous data boxes with the availability and capacity required for each of the team members who are needed within that process box.

This chapter offers some ideas on how to tweak the value stream mapping approach in such a way that the above problems are eliminated.

Chapter 15.1 covers the Project VSM that is based on the theory described by Morgan and Liker, which uses milestones and decisions to map the flow of the project (Morgen and Liker 2006).

Chapter 15.2 explains work flow cycles and feedback loops described by Duggan to tweak the value stream mapping approach for indirect processes. For first time projects where process steps cannot be listed yet, the Critical Question Analysis (CQA) can be used to help plan the project. This is further explained in 15.3.

> **Key Points:**
> - *Using the traditional VSM approach, an office value stream map would either be hundreds of meters long or the process boxes would contain 99 percent waiting time hidden in them.*
> - *The roles of people in offices are usually more complex than the roles in production processes.*

## 15.1 Project VSM

*You must have a project system that ensures all tasks begin, not when they are scheduled to begin, but when the required inputs are available.*
—Allan Elder

The **number one problem with projects** is that they are more often than not delivered later than planned. The percentage of late projects ranges between 67 percent and 90 percent, and this is a problem because late delivery leads to overtime, overtime leads to overburden, and we know what happens with people who are overburdened from chapter 5.2.

**FIVE REASONS FOR PROJECT DELAYS** are bad multitasking, Parkinson´s law, the student syndrome, task dependency, and project management math where 2+2=5 (Elder 2006).

Delays result from **bad multitasking** because we must switch between jobs, not finishing a task as soon as it is started, which results in longer lead times for all tasks. Every time we switch between tasks, we take time to remember what we were doing and what the next step is.

**Parkinson´s law** states that the amount of work will fill the time available, which means that, even when we could deliver a task early, we will use up the safety buffer we had and still deliver the task at the deadline (if not later).

Parkinson´s law is linked to the **student syndrome**, where we procrastinate on the task as long as possible before we start working on it. When we estimate a task to take five days and we add three days as a safety buffer, chances are we only start to work on the task at day four, using up the safety buffer before we even start.

**Task dependency** influences the delivery of a project in a way that one early task in the critical path of a project does not influence the project completion date, but one late one probably will.

Finally, there is **the 2+2=5 rule**, which states that when two people perform two sequential tasks that both take two days, the sum of the tasks takes longer than the sum of the durations. The handover of the tasks, short discussion, and preparation of the second person before starting on the task combine to delay the task.

A project value stream that is part of the obeya (as proposed in chapter 8.2.3) will help tackle these problems and will help you keep projects within their planned timeline.

Morgan and Liker (2006) describe a large part of the **solution proposed in this chapter**. They describe an alternative form of value stream mapping, which combines some aspects of traditional value stream mapping, the process map, a swim-lane diagram, and a Gantt chart (Morgen and Liker 2006).

The first difference between the traditional VSM and the project VSM is that the lead time ladder is put on top of the project VSM and that the **project milestones** are depicted on the timeline. The entire project can, for instance, be split into six phases of D2MAIC, each phase contains process steps with feedback loops in which data is exchanged.

Next to the activities done within a project, the **critical decisions** that need to be made to pass the milestones are shown separately. This helps to show the importance of certain tasks within the project plan. Whenever a critical decision is delayed, the project is delayed.

Activities that are done by different teams, sub teams, or individuals can be drawn in different **swim lanes**. The number of parallel activities and different action holders show the complexity of the project task and the workload leveling between these functions.

Just as in a traditional VSM, each process box contains a data box with data that is important to document for making improvement decisions later. For the project VSM, the **process time (PT)** should be documented to know how long it takes to finish the job. I suggest also putting the **needed capacity** in there, which is the process time multiplied by the number of people on the team. This will give us an overview of the number of man-hours (MH) needed to complete each activity of the project.

Figure 57 shows an **EXAMPLE OF A PROJECT VSM** that deals with the implementation of the first set of 5S standards. Because 5S is the foundation for every lean deployment and is therefore implemented in different departments on a regular basis, it is worth demonstrating the process flow.

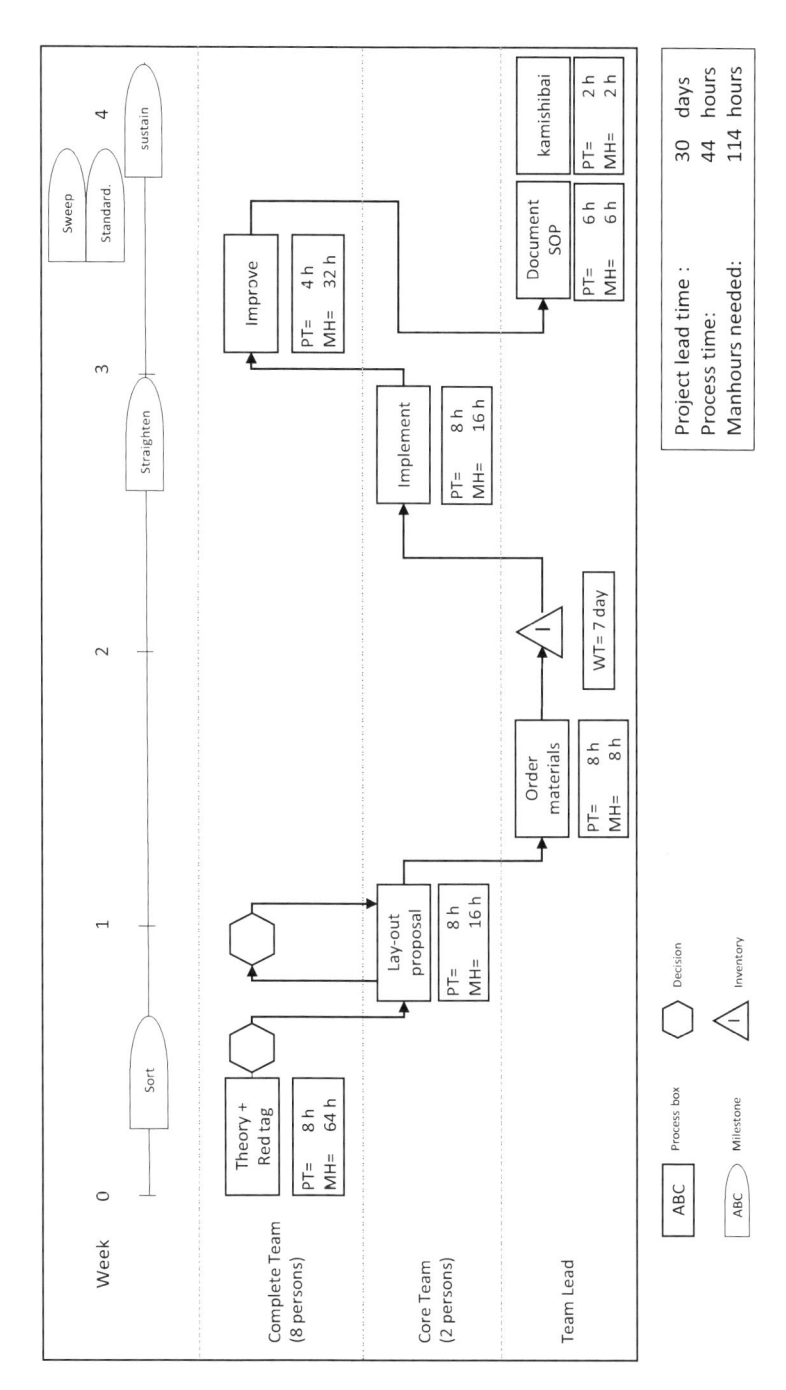

*Figure 57: Example of a value stream map for a 5S project*

The first thing our project VSM shows, thanks to the **lead time ladder** at the top, is that implementing the first complete set of 5S standards in one department takes thirty days when the 114 man-hours are allocated to this project. Of course, this depends largely on the type and size of department. For each of the five steps in 5S (sort, straighten, shine, standardize, and sustain), **a milestone** is defined and shown on the lead time ladder.

Underneath the lead time ladder, the **activities and crucial decisions** that are necessary to pass the milestones are drawn. For instance, to be able to finish the sort phase, the team members need consensus on what tool they need to be able to do their work, which will later be put on a shadow board to prevent a lot of rework at later stages.

In this example, the first version of the layout is worked on by a sub team, but the sub team is in constant interaction with the rest of the team. So, there's a **feedback loop**. In practice, people could gather this feedback in the daily team board meeting or in the obeya meeting.

In terms of **waiting time** between process boxes, the waiting time for material delivery takes up a large part of the total project lead time.

Finally, the necessary capacity in terms of **process time** and **man-hours (MH)** is captured in the VSM. In this example, the total number of man-hours equals 114, and those hours are spread over the thirty-day project lead time. It is, of course, also possible to calculate the number of MH for every swim lane.

Assuming a normal work week of forty hours, the total process time of forty-four hours tells us that when we can deliver all the materials up front, we can also choose to plan a one-week kaizen event in which the entire project is executed.

5S is just one simple example of how to use the project VSM. Complex projects such as new product development or a D2MAIC project could also follow the same principles.

The idea of this representation is that the team focuses on the decisions that need to be made in every project milestone and that actions that need to be executed to make that decision are listed. Whenever an action is finished earlier, it is discussed by the team in the obeya so that the next step of the project can start as soon as possible—and not when it was first planned. This makes it possible to some extent to catch up on lost time and maybe even create the possibility for delivering a project earlier than planned.

**Key Points:**
- *A swim lane setup shows the complexity of the system and the many dependencies between departments that might delay the process.*
- *Decisions and project milestones are added as symbols.*
- *Add the planned number of man-hours needed to execute each task to estimate the duration of tasks.*
- *Discuss the project value stream map in the obeya to be able to start the tasks as soon as the required inputs are available instead of when the tasks' starting points were first planned.*

## 15.2 Office VSM

> *What the work flow cycle is really doing is establishing something called a guaranteed turnaround time for information, so everybody knows when they are going to get that specific information.*

For the supportive functions in the office environment, the following **NINE GUIDELINES FOR OFFICE VALUE STREAM MAPPING** can be used to map the processes (Duggan 2012). These are, by necessity, a little different from the ones that Duggan defined for the production environment.

**One: What is the takt time for the service?** As in the production environment, the first task of the team is to map customer demand. How often is a service asked for? One could already think about the complexity of the mix in this step. For instance, we can deliver five normal orders and one special order per day.

**Two: Where can we implement one-piece flow?** A paper process that needs signatures for approval by a fixed group of people is a process in which one-piece flow can easily be implemented. Create a weekly meeting in which the entire team meets and sign off all paperwork in one go. Or maybe the team that needs to sign off already has a daily management meeting, in which case the signing of the paperwork by the entire team can be put on the agenda of the daily meeting.

**Three: Where can FIFO be used?** In situations in which one-piece flow is not possible, FIFO should be used to determine the sequence in which people work. Files and orders should be sorted by date of completion to be able to keep this sequence, and of course, there is a maximum, which makes it possible for the person providing the support function to signal when he or she is overloaded with work.

**Four: Where can we use work flow cycles?** Work flow cycles are fixed moments in which information flows between departments. In these short, interdisciplinary meetings, people from different departments meet to exchange information. Because everybody knows when the information is shared, there is less of a need to send e-mails or phone calls.

**Five: Where can we implement integration events?** These are similar to work flow cycles, but they only take place once every month or even once every quarter. These are interdisciplinary meetings where projects are handed over between R&D and production and where projects are officially closed, and results are shared.

**Six: How can we define standard work?** The need for standards was already discussed above. The challenge is to document both what needs to be done and when it must be done by. This is a bigger challenge in the office environment because people from supporting roles are used to being able to decide for themselves when to work on what.

**Seven: How can we define the pacemaker?** Just like in the production environment, the goal of an office process is to have only one signal that triggers the process.

**Eight: How can we implement pitch?** Remember that the pitch is the visual management tool to visualize whether the flow is on time. After each work flow cycle, information must flow. Otherwise the flow stops. One example of information that should flow after a work flow cycle is the release for orders for the next interval. Whenever the decision is made, and the orders are released, a signal can be put on the team board to show that everything in the order release process is OK.

**Nine: How do we deal with changes of customer demand?** This is the final question that is related to the self-healing flow described in chapter 4. When the original plan does not work, a process should always have a plan B, a way of dealing with problems to prevent the entire organization from leaving its standards to solve this problem.

There are two topics on which I would like to elaborate a bit further, starting with the **WORK FLOW CYCLES**. In the factory in Hamburg where I worked, we had a **daily** work flow cycle in which we discussed the production plan for the next day and the changes in customer demand as described in question nine above. It was a meeting where, at the start, only representatives from production, logistics, and planning were present.

But because the **information that was shared** in that meeting was so valuable to other departments in the value stream, more and more departments came to the meeting because they knew information would be shared at that time every day. After six months, the meeting sometimes attracted fifteen people. Most people just listened to the latest update to take back to their team board meeting or quickly asked a colleague a short question. The meeting, however, hardly ever took longer than **fifteen minutes**.

The flow that was created in this daily meeting was also **SELF-HEALING**. That means that the result of the work flow meeting was that the people who were present can make almost all decisions necessary to get back into the standard flow. This takes the creation of flow up to the next level because most companies only define the standard flow and forget to put a good plan B in place. In the end, that leads to the deterioration of flow (Duggan 2012).

Not being able to solve your own problems leads to people being dependent on management to heal the flow, which is the worst possible way of doing things. Management attention to heal the flow is like a doctor prescribing medicine to a patient. The flow is sick, you go to a doctor (the manager), and he will tell you what to do. There are two problems with this way of working.

First, there is **the domino effect**. As soon as one department starts to leave the standard, all other departments in the same value stream probably must do the same. E-mails, telephone calls, and even meetings are necessary to discuss this extraordinary situation. All this communication is not only not value adding, it also prevents all people involved from working on their own flow, which means that stopping the flow of one process leads to other processes leaving the standard and thereby stopping the flow there.

The second problem with manager intervention is the **dependency syndrome**. When management pays extra attention to the flow, by means of planning meetings, sending out new priority lists, and production plans, people slowly forget how the process was designed. This leads to chaos as soon as management does not pay attention to the process anymore.

The solution to these problems lies in **training teams** to solve their own problems. This means that there should be standards about how the process works not only under normal conditions but also for when the flow has stopped. When people know how to react to stoppages of flow and solve their own problems, there is no need for extra meetings, production plans, or e-mails, and that reduces the impact of the stoppage to a bare minimum. This is what Duggan describes as self-healing flow.

**Tools that help** demonstrate the stoppage of flow are 5S and team boards. To make it all work, it is not just the production environment that needs standards; the office processes need to depict their flow as well.

> **Key Points:**
> - *The main difference between production value stream maps and office value stream maps is the work flow cycles and integration events, which are fixed moments in which information flows between departments.*
> - *Ideally, these flows are self-healing, which means teams know how to react to changes of customer demand or to problems.*

## 15.3  Critical Question Analysis

*Asking questions doesn't mean you don´t know your job, asking questions means you want to improve the quality of your work.*
R. Allen

Value stream mapping is only useful for **repetitive projects or products**. Only when a part of a project is repeatedly done, or a part of a product is regularly redesigned, does it make sense to create a value stream map. For parts of a project that are only done once, or products that are only designed once, the critical question analysis is more helpful (Barnhart 2013).

The **CRITICAL QUESTION ANALYSIS (CQA) shows all the questions** that need to be answered to finish a project. Two other terms used to describe the CQA are the *knowledge gap map* and the *learning gap map*. There are five steps in the CQA:

1. **Define a strategic goal for the team**. Just as with value stream mapping, it is important that the team has a clear understanding of the goals of the analysis that is about to be made. Creating clarity on the goals beforehand also helps determine who needs to be part of the workshop.
2. **Brainstorm**. In the CQA event, the team starts by listing as many questions as possible that need to be answered to finish the project.
3. **Sort the questions.** In this phase, the questions from step two are sorted in different clusters, including main questions and sub questions. Even better would be to have them already sorted in the sequence in which they need to be answered.
4. **Review the results.** Check whether the sequence is correct, if there are no overlaps in the clusters, and if all questions are really necessary to achieve the goals defined in step one.
5. **Repeat steps two through four** until the team is satisfied with the results. Just as in value stream mapping, the CQA is an iterative process; the results should be improved until there is a robust result.

The goal of value stream mapping is to map possible problems that lead to delays of the project and the obstruction of flow. It is the task of the project team to react to these problems and to define actions to solve them before the delivery of the project results is in danger.

Whether the team decides to use traditional value stream mapping, office value stream mapping, or the critical question analysis, each would be both **an important planning tool and a KPI**. For projects that are longer than a few months, the project VSM should be part of the daily (or weekly) project meetings that are held in the obeya to make sure all the deadlines are met.

**Key Points:**
- *When a process is done for the first time, it is difficult to create the VSM.*
- *You can use a critical question analysis for these processes to still manage time and information flow.*

# PART 5:
# LEAN TOOLS EXPLAINED

We have now reached the fifth and final part of this book in which I describe 3 lean tools that can be used to further support you in your lean transformation and help your organization reach level 4 of lean maturity.

Part 4 covered the importance of flow and described some tools that can help improve flow by showing how we can change the connections between two process boxes in a value stream map. The first step of future-state value stream mapping (chapter 13), however, might lead to a necessary improvement on one of the process steps itself; for those improvements, there are a few more tools to learn, which will be described in this part.

The first possible improvement that might be necessary in a production environment is based on low overall equipment effectiveness (OEE). The tool (or program) **autonomous maintenance** can be used to improve it and will be the topic of 16.

Another improvement that might be necessary and derived from the value stream mapping exercise is an improvement of the long changeover times that lead to a high EPEI. These can be improved using **Single Minute Exchange of Die** (SMED), which will be described in chapter 17.

Third, chapter 18 will describe the tool **kanban**, which is an easy tool that can be used to automatically replenish supermarkets without the need of ordering systems or meetings.

As a final chapter in this book, I would like to share some tips to improve productivity in the number 1 area of waste for every manager in the 21$^{st}$ century: **email**. I personally believe that a lot of lead times are extremely long because we spend way too much time writing, reading, and replying to e-mails. For this reason, chapter 19 provides some tips on how to optimize your personal standard work on dealing with e-mail and your smartphone.

# Chapter 16:
# Autonomous Maintenance

*Autonomous maintenance refers to small group activities calling for total employee involvement...to maximize productivity.*

Autonomous maintenance (AM) is a tool based on the philosophy that people should take care of the maintenance of the machines they work on themselves instead of having the maintenance done by an external team of engineers or technicians. The goal of AM is to improve the productivity of each machine—measured by the overall equipment effectiveness (OEE)—by focusing on reducing the **five essential root causes of breakdowns** (Tajiri and Gotoh 1992): neglecting basic machine conditions, insufficient operator maintenance skills, weaknesses in equipment design, overlooked deterioration, and not observing usage conditions.

Implementing AM has enormous consequences for all the people working in the organization, and therefore it is often implemented as a program on its own, independent of other lean activities.

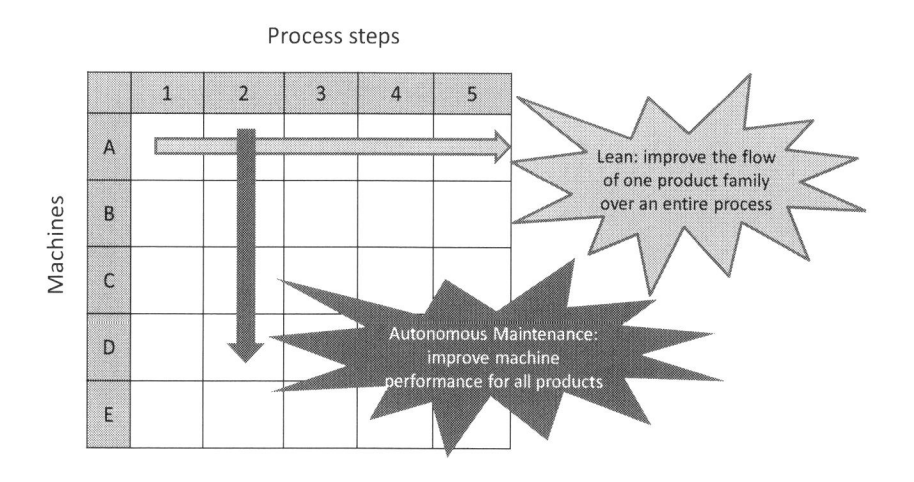

*Figure 58: Lean versus AM*

Implementing AM results in less **waste** and a reduction of **imbalance**, which explains why it can complement or be part of a wider lean program. As we learned from chapter 13, a low OEE can prevent a workstation from being able to produce to takt time or, as we learned in 14.2, can prevent an entire process from producing in a shorter interval. Figure 58 shows how AM and lean complement each other.

The **lean methodology** focuses on improving the product flow through a value stream (between machines) by reducing **the enemies of lean—** imbalance, overburden and waste. **Autonomous maintenance,** on the other hand, focuses on the machines themselves, making sure every machine produces output and that output comes out of each machine as planned.

> **Key Points:**
> - *Autonomous maintenance is about giving people ownership over the machines that they work with.*
> - *While lean focuses on improving the flow of products between process steps, autonomous maintenance is focused on the performance of one process step for all products.*

## 16.1 How to Implement Autonomous Maintenance

*When operators take care of their machines and prevent breakdowns from happening, the technical staff has time available for implementing improvements.*

Autonomous maintenance consists of seven steps that can be divided into **THREE STAGES** (Tajiri and Gotoh 1992). These three stages are defined as standardizing the basic conditions of the machine, maintaining the basic conditions of the machine, and systematically improving the conditions of the machine. Standardizing the basic conditions of the machine reduces waste by 20 percent on average; maintaining that standard by inspections and corrective actions reduces waste by another 70 percent. The final stage deals with the most difficult 10 percent of waste left in the machine, and it includes design and engineering work (Tajiri and Gotoh 1992).

**STAGE ONE: STANDARDIZING THE BASIC MACHINE CONDITIONS** includes the first three steps of implementing autonomous maintenance and are strongly linked with the 5S principles described in chapter 7.1.

Step one is **cleaning the equipment**. This step includes the use of four lists on the team board, where operators keep track of defective parts, a list of questions, a list of sources of contamination, and a list of hard-to-clean areas. In the following steps of implementation, you can use these lists for improvement.

Step two describes the **prevention of contamination of the equipment**. Using list three and four from the previous step, the amount of contamination is reduced—which results in less "stuff" to clean up—and machines are adjusted to make cleaning easier, which means operators can clean the machine faster, just like in 5S.

Step three is **creating cleaning and lubrication standards**. When critical cleaning areas are defined (step one) and improved (step two), cleaning standards can then be created. These standards include a visual representation of the equipment that marks the location of the machine/part, the criteria for "clean," the method to be used for cleaning, and the tools to use while cleaning it.

**STAGE TWO: MAINTAINING THE BASIC CONDITIONS** is done by implementing routine machine inspections (step four) and creating autonomous maintenance standards (step five).

In step four, operators will make **routine inspections** and will perform the inspections in the future. In practice, checklists and process checks often do not work because someone other than the person who needs to use the lists creates them. In those situations, operators are not committed to using the list. To build the needed commitment, operators should first understand the need for clean machinery and then create their own inspection standards.

I would like to point out, that these can be combined with cleaning schedules as part of the 5S standard that was described in chapter 7.1.2. This way, operators would only have one single list with all cleaning and maintaining activities instead of two.

Step five describes the creation of **autonomous maintenance standards** in which operators perform small maintenance tasks on their machines themselves. These standards should include the following: the category of maintenance (for instance "electric" or "moving parts"), the location of the part on the machine, the criteria the part should meet (such as the readability of measuring instruments), the method to check the criteria, and the corrective action to be taken when criteria are not met.

**STAGE THREE: IMPROVING THE STANDARD** consists of the final two steps of implementation: quality assurance (step six) and autonomous supervision (step seven).

In step six, the **basic conditions are improved on quality.** There are five criteria the basic conditions should meet to guarantee high-quality output (Tajiri and Gotoh 1992). Improvements, or kaizen, should focus on these five criteria: It is clear to everyone what the basic conditions of the machine are, the basic conditions are easy to readjust, the conditions are not exposed to variability, deviations from the standard are depicted, and deviations are easy to bring back to standard.

Step seven, the final step, describes the **autonomous supervision** of machines. In this step, operators maintain equipment completely autonomously. They check the equipment for abnormalities, act when certain conditions deviate from the standard, and improve the basic conditions of the equipment. The challenge in this last step is keeping autonomous maintenance at this level, which means continual knowledge-sharing to prevent the general knowledge level from dropping back. That would lead to machine conditions dropping back to their original pre-change state.

Kamishibai checks can support here, to regularly check whether the inspection standards and cleaning schedules are still followed, and whether they are still up to date.

**Key Points:**
- *Autonomous maintenance is a tool that moves machine maintenance from an external team to the people who work with the machines.*
- *AM helps improve the OEE of a workstation and therefore improves the flow of a process.*

# Chapter 17:

# Single Minute Exchange of Die (SMED)

*Quick changeovers are the key to a competitive advantage for any manufacturer that produces, prepares, processes or packages a variety of products on a single machine.*
—S. Shingo

Single Minute Exchange of Die (SMED) is a tool Shigeo Shingo developed to reduce changeover times on machines. Using this technique, you can reduce setup times from four hours to three minutes, which is almost 99 percent (Shingo 1985).

One example in everyday life that illustrates the benefits of this tool is an instance where we need to replace a tire on our car. In our personal lives, it can happen that we get a flat tire while we are on the road. Without preparation or proper training, we start looking for the tools we need to change the tire. When we have a spare tire with us, we might be able to change the tire within an hour (that is, if we do not have to wait for somebody else to help us).

Now, let's think about the Formula One industry and how it has professionalized changeovers in pit stops. With a team of people, the crew manages to change all the tires of a car and perform many more actions on the vehicle within a few seconds!

SMED is all about removing those wasteful steps in the changeover process so that you will be able to convert your production process changeovers from something similar to the roadside tire change to something similar to the Formula One change.

## 17.1 Eight SMED techniques

So how can you analyze and reduce your setup time? Shingo described the following **EIGHT TECHNIQUES** (Shingo 1985):

The first technique is to **differentiate between activities** that are done while the machine is running (these are called the external activities) and those that are done while the machine is switched off (the internal activities) in which precious running time is lost.

Second, you should focus on **transferring internal into external activities** as much as possible so that the machine has less idling time.

Third, you should focus on **standardizing** the different steps of the changeover by creating standard work (as chapter 7.1 describes) to make sure everybody does the step in the same efficient manner. Think about a standard sequence of steps and a standard tool set to use for all changeovers.

A fourth strategy is to **modify machines** in such a way that changeovers can be done faster. Examples are reducing the length of screws, which reduces the time it takes to loosen and fasten them.

Strategy five is to **introduce aids** to prevent having to perform a certain activity in the internal category. In this case external activities are added to reduce internal activities.

Sixth, you can **introduce the use of parallel activities** to reduce the time that the machine is not producing output. Sometimes it is possible that multiple operators perform changeover activities in parallel.

Strategy number seven is to **remove material adjustment tasks** from the changeover process by using measurement tools that remove intuition from the equation.

Finally, strategy number eight is to **automate the changeover** to remove all human activity and delays from the changeover process.

In a production environment, the length of changeovers influences all three enemies of lean, which explains why it is important to reduce them.

Changeovers can lead to **variation** because the workload of people changes when there are setups. This is especially true of when an external team of people do the changeovers and base them on the heijunka schedule in which product quantities vary per interval (see chapter 14.2).

Changeovers also lead to **overburden** when they need a long time to complete and there are more machines that might need changeovers.

Changeovers lead to **waste** when products or people need to wait for the setup of a machine for a different product. Changeovers can lead to defects or a waste of material when actual material is used during the set-up process. Finally, the longer the changeover, the larger the production batches are so that there's economical production. These batches, however, increase the inventory on both sides of the machine.

The next section will describe how the eight strategies of SMED fit into four steps of SMED implementation.

> **Key Points:**
> - *SMED is used to reduce changeover times on machines, which can reduce setup times up to 99 percent.*
> - *The logic behind SMED is about analyzing each step in the changeover process: What can be removed? What can be done while the machine is still running? And how can we improve each step?*

## 17.2 How to Implement SMED

*By simply reflecting on what steps of the changeover process are internal and external, the downtime of the machine can often be reduced by 50 percent, sometimes even 90 per cent*
—J. M. Nicholas

You would usually implement SMED in the form of a kaizen event in which whole teams of people who perform the changeovers map and analyze the changeover process.

To structure the kaizen event, Shingo defined **FOUR STEPS OF IMPLEMENTING SMED** (Nicholas 1998):

The first step is to **identify internal and external steps**. The internal steps are the tasks that can only be done while the operation has stopped. External tasks can be done during production. All preparation activities, such as collecting tools, are external activities and should not be done while the machine is shut down.

The best way to perform such an activity is observing the changeover in real time or filming it when it is not done every day. In this analysis step, you might also encounter activities that are not required anymore and that you can remove from the process immediately.

The second step is to **convert internal steps into external steps.** It is not uncommon that the internal activities can be reduced by 50 percent at this step (Nicholas 1998).

Another strategy is to break up the one big internal task into smaller tasks. Usually part of the small tasks can become external tasks or even removed after improvement (Floyd 2010).

The third step is to **modify machines** to increase the speed at which activities can be performed. The previous steps reduce wastes in the process, but not enough to reduce changeovers to less than ten minutes.

Usually it helps to simplify the machine by changing nuts and bolts so they're shorter (to reduce the time needed to loosen and fasten them) and to standardize them (all tasks are done with the same tool). The goal is to make the changeover simple enough so that operators can do them themselves (Nicholas 1998).

The fourth step is to **reduce the need for the setup overall.** The only thing better than a shorter changeover time is not having to change over at all. You can achieve this by creating dedicated machines for product families or even for specific products, which reduces the number of changeovers for that machine, and by implementing the heijunka schedule in which the sequence is always the same.

To close off this small introduction to SMED, I want to share with you **THREE TIPS** for reducing changeover time: using the yamazumi to show work cycles, improving teamwork, and having proper preparation.

You can use **the yamazumi chart** that chapter 14.1 describes to show the changeover tasks. Put all activities that are done in a big stack chart and use color-coding to show which steps are not adding value, which are external, and which are internal.

Use the benefits of **teamwork** to get the job done faster. Train a team with a clear division of roles (standards) so that the team members can perform their tasks in parallel. Make sure you take personnel needs like coffee and lunch breaks into account when planning a changeover. It is not uncommon for a machine to be shut down for fifteen minutes extra because people are on a coffee break (Floyd 2010).

**Prepare changeovers** well, with a plan and standard work to cover all activities that need to be done. A special tool kit with all the materials and tools needed to perform the setup also helps reduce the preparation time.

> **Key Points:**
> - *The four steps of SMED are identifying internal and external activities, transforming internal activities to external activities, reducing the length of the steps by altering machines, and reducing the number of changeovers.*
> - *You can use the yamazumi to show the work that needs to be done during the changeover.*

# Chapter 18:
# Kanban

*The goal of the kanban is to eliminate the kanban.*
M. Rother

Kanban is a Japanese term that can be translated into "visual signal" and is used to depict production and transport signals in a process. In other words, it helps to manage the replenishments of supermarkets, one of the connection methods described in chapter 11.2 to connect two workstations. Complex computerized systems are no longer necessary when this simple card system can automatically cause the replenishment of standard parts.

This chapter is split into three parts. First, I describe the six golden rules of kanban, then the two most widely used examples of a kanban system, and third, how to calculate the number of necessary kanbans.

Kanban is used **WHEN** a pull-connection between two process steps is chosen to be a supermarket. The upstream processes that **replenish the supermarket** must know what product needs to be produced. The kanban signal provides this information.

As a pull connection, remember from chapter 11.2 that both one-piece flow and first-in-first-out (FIFO) are more desirable than the supermarket because they do not need a separate signal to know what to replenish.

A kanban system is a pull system, and therefore it is a lean system, but **the goal of the kanban** is to eliminate the kanban (Rother 2010), which means the supermarket is transformed into a FIFO lane or a one-piece flow line. Remember from chapter 11.2 that the reason why we prefer one-piece flow lines and FIFO over a supermarket principle is that they have less inventory kept in them, which keeps the waiting time short, and by that the lead time: the number one KPI in lean (chapter 4.1).

**WHAT IS A KANBAN?** The kanban (card) system can be explained best by using the six golden rules:
1. The downstream process only takes products out of the supermarket that are used immediately. In a two-card system (see below), material can only be collected with a kanban card.
2. The upstream process produces the exact number of products listed on the kanban card. Nothing is produced without a card.
3. The kanban signal always stays with the product. As soon as there is material without a kanban, or a kanban without material, a problem has occurred.
4. Defects won't be transported downstream, which means all workstations have their own quality check.
5. Kanban can be used when volumes vary by about 10 percent max.
6. The number of kanban cards represents the amount of inventory, or waste, in a process. The number of cards should therefore continually be reduced.

Kanban cards can be used for production signals and for transport signals. The simplest kanban systems are the so-called **ONE-CARD KANBAN SYSTEMS** in which only production signals are used. The supermarket is usually located right in front of the workstation that claims the most material (which means there is no need for a transport kanban). The signal can be an actual card or a plastic bin in which the product can be moved and kept.

**The kanban card** contains information about what product needs to be produced, in what quantity, for what supermarket, the code number, etc. (see figure 59). This type of kanban can be valuable in processes in which multiple modules can be used for a certain product family. The downstream machine takes whatever module it needs from the supermarket, and the upstream machine will produce accordingly. A card can be used for any number of products, per piece or for batches.

| Part Description | | | Part Number | |
|---|---|---|---|---|
| Smoke-shifter, left handed. | | | 14613 | |
| Qty | 20 | Lead Time | 1 week | Order Date | 9/3 |
| Supplier | Acme Smoke-Shifter, LLC | | Due Date | 9/10 |
| | | | Card 1 of 2 | |
| Planner | John R. | | Location | Rack 183 |

*Figure 59: Example of a kanban card (left) and of a two-bin system (right)*

**The two-bin system** is an example of kanban in which the kanban cards are integrated with the transport material. Instead of a plastic card with the necessary replenishment information, a small container (bin) is used on which the information is printed. Every part has two designated containers, and as soon as one of them is empty, it is put on a cart or on the top of a rack to show that it needs replenishment (see figure 59). This type of system can be used for small materials that are used at multiple workstations, such as bolts and screws.

In a **TWO-CARD SYSTEM**, the kanban signals are split in production and transport signals. This system still 'automatically' sends the quantities that need to be ordered to the upstream party, but provides the opportunity to batch transport quantities together, for instance to fill a box, or even a truck.

Two examples of a situation in which a two-card system can be used are when the **physical distance** between the supermarket and the workstation is relatively large, and when **multiple workstations are fed by the same supermarket**. In these cases, a transport card is used to provide instruction about how many pieces are taken from the supermarket, and another card will represent a production signal to replenish the supermarket with possibly a different number of products (see left part of figure 60).

Another two examples of two-card system situations are when the supermarket is located **in a cross-dock warehouse or at an external supplier**. In these cases, the transport signal will be sent to the external location, after which the third party can start a local signaling standard for replenishment (see right part of figure 60). By managing the transport signals separately, not only is internal inventory shown, but also the inventory that is still in the pipeline.

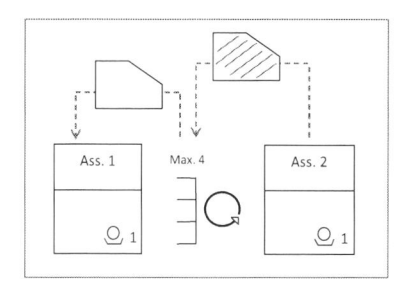

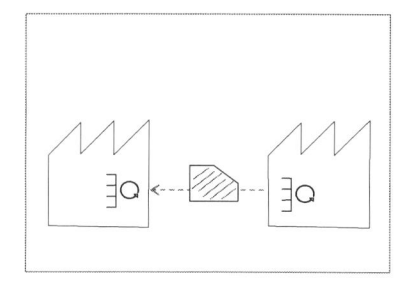

*Figure 60: Transport from workstation to supermarket (left) and from supermarket to supplier (right)*

To **CALCULATE THE NUMBER OF KANBAN**, the replenishment time and the number of items per batch are leading variables:

*(Daily Demand x Lead Time (in days) x Safety Buffer)/# per Kanban*

The more deliveries, the smaller the buffer and thus the fewer kanbans that are necessary.

Kanban is a visual pull system used to replenish supermarkets and to ensure that the maximum amount of inventory is kept in both the supermarket and the supply chain. Since nothing is produced or even moved without a kanban system, overproduction —the mother of all wastes, can be avoided.

Remember, from chapter 11.2, that the supermarket is the last possible option to implement flow, after one-piece flow and FIFO. This means that implementing a kanban system should never be the end state of a production system. The inventory has a maximum, but that only makes it one step better than a system with unstructured inventory.

Whenever you have kanban, you should strive to reduce the number of cards, to create less inventory, or even to eliminate the kanban by creating a FIFO lane or even one-piece flow.

**Key Points:**
- *Kanban provides the visual signal that makes it possible to replenish supermarkets without sending extra information.*
- *The kanban signal can be a card that goes with the product or a box that contains the product.*
- *The number of kanbans represent the inventory levels in the process. Overproduction is prevented, and inventory levels are lowered by taking signals from the process.*
- *The goal of the kanban is to eliminate the kanban.*

# Chapter 19:
# E-mail and Phone Optimization

*Never check your e-mail in the morning. Checking and answering e-mail in the morning gives you a false sense of accomplishment.*
—J. Morgenstern

For most managers, checking e-mails is the most time-consuming activity there is. For some, they arrive in quantities of hundreds per day with the simple result that the owner of the mailbox can no longer keep track of what is important and what is not, let alone know how many actions are requested in the many e-mails.

Microsoft Outlook is a fantastic tool that many organizations use as standard e-mail software. It contains a lot of possibilities, some of which a lot of people are not aware of. This article describes a few personal tips on how to deal with e-mail in an effective and efficient manner. Most of them are derived from what I have learned after reading David Allen´s book getting things done and Stephen Covey´s First Things First.

**READ E-MAILS ONLY TWO TO THREE TIMES PER DAY**
I am convinced that nobody has "read e-mails" on the top of his or her responsibility list, yet the standard notifications in Outlook pull our attention from the task we are currently working on to a newly arrived e-mail. Stephen Covey teaches us that important tasks always come before unimportant or even some urgent tasks (Covey 1994). Since 90 percent of e-mails (if not 99 percent) are not related to the important task the person is working on at the moment to directly help achieve personal and organizational goals, the person should not let e-mails prove a distraction.

Therefore, **switch off the notifications of new e-mails**. Doing this will prevent both the pop-up you will see on the bottom of the screen and the annoying sound. In Outlook (Office 365) you can find these preferences in "File/Options/mail" in the category "message arrival."

The pop-up and the sound that the computer automatically makes causes you to wonder what the new e-mail might be. Even when you can resist the urge to open the e-mail immediately, your brain is still wasting energy on switching topics in your mind. In terms of efficiency, it gets even worse. You believe the e-mail is so important that you drop the task that you are working on to read the new e-mail. Then, without acting on it directly, you switch back to the task you were working on before the e-mail arrived.

**Reading and acting on e-mails only two to three times a day** is now possible. When it suits you, you can read the new e-mails in your mailbox and digest them one by one after you have finished that important task you were working on. The easiest way to increase your sense of accomplishment is to start your day with one or two important tasks before you even open your Outlook (Covey 1994).

**Use the "show as conversation" function** to sort your inbox based on conversations. An e-mail that was replied to by ten colleagues since the last time you checked your e-mail will be shown as one item in your inbox. When you click that one item, you can see the history of all the replies.
You can find the option "show as conversations" in the "view" tab of the Outlook menu.

### THE INBOX AS ACTION LIST
David Allen describes the next step in improving your effectiveness and efficiency in digesting e-mails. The only messages that should be in your inbox are messages that require some sort of action (Allan 2001). All other e-mails should be moved to archive folders. Here are some ground rules:

**E-mails that ask for small actions should be handled immediately**. When you have decided to read e-mails, we want to prevent you from reading the same e-mail twice, which means that you should immediately act on the e-mail when you open it for the first time. When the action takes less than two minutes, you should act on it immediately and move the e-mail to an archive.

**Plan time for execution or delegate the task**. For actions that require significantly more than two minutes, you should block a time frame in your calendar to work on that task as soon as all other important tasks are finished, or, delegated the task to somebody else if you can't. As soon as the task is put in the calendar, the e-mail should be removed from the inbox.

**Archive digested e-mails.** Use as few different archive folders as possible to store your e-mails. As a rule of thumb, you should use a maximum of six. Keeping the options to a minimum makes it easier to find them at a later stage when it turns out you do need it again.

## FILTERING E-MAILS

Now that we have a system in place for dealing with our inbox, we can work on what comes into our inboxes in the first place. A lot of e-mails are so-called "for your information" e-mails and do not contain actions required for you personally or questions asked to you personally. By using the filtering option in Outlook, you can automatically sort your e-mails as they come in, which makes it easier for you to digest them later.

**Move CCs and newsletters to a communications folder.** I did a rough count of my e-mail account over 2016, and 20 percent of all e-mails contained general information about a global or local organization that did not directly impact my actions. Using different rules for headlines containing the title of a particular newsletter or even some e-mail addresses from which relatively unimportant emails are sent, I can have these e-mails automatically put into my communications archive using the rule function. (In the home ribbon, click 'rules' and then 'create rule').

When I am done with all other tasks—or if I am bored—I can scroll down the communications folder to see if I have missed something important. (That has not yet ever happened...) When something really important has been sent, chances are one of my colleagues will start talking about it, and I will be informed after all.

**You can filter out meeting notifications of meetings you initiated** as well. If you plan a lot of meetings with a lot of people, your inbox is overrun by emails with "person X accepted your meeting request." The only things that might require action are the notifications of somebody declining the meeting or the ones requesting another time for the meeting. I therefore have a filter for my e-mails that automatically moves only the "accepted" e-mails to the trash folder using the same rule function.

**You can also send automatic replies to the trash.** For all internal e-mail, you can already see who will be sending an automatic reply when you compose the e-mail. Therefore, automatically send all automatic replies to the trash folder as well (which saves me at least one e-mail per day).

## PREVENTING E-MAILS FROM BEING SENT

One step even further than filtering is preventing the e-mails from arriving in your e-mail box in the first place or minimizing the time anyone needs to digest the e-mails. Here are some tricks to keep the time you and others spend on e-mail even shorter:

**Switch off automatic notifications from social media.** Social media platforms are the easiest ways of working according to the pull system: only go there when you actually want to read something. All social platforms, such as Facebook and LinkedIn, have preferences in which you can simply choose not to receive an e-mail every time something has happened on that platform.

**Keep e-mails short and to the point** to minimize the time others must spend digesting your e-mail. Usually it is not necessary to describe the entire history of a discussion when you want to ask a person a question. If a detailed explanation is necessary, it should probably be done orally.

**Use e-mail only to confirm actions.** Discussions should be done orally, maybe even in a meeting, and not in long texts. Use e-mails only to communicate about agreed-upon actions and other agreements.

With the eleven tips described above, I have drastically reduced the time I spend reading and working on e-mails. Even better, because I use Allen's system of direct execution or planning the execution, I know I have a solid overview of tasks to do. This brings a certain peace of mind, which means I can easily keep on focusing on the tasks that are really important in my job.

The same principles that I described above can also be applied to your **SMARTPHONE**. This minicomputer that we carry around tries to get our attention very time somebody likes our picture on Instagram, sends us a message on WhatsApp or when somebody has sent us a new email. To me, nothing is more distracting than both a sound and visual signal when I am working on something important. Both at work, and at home with family and friends.

Here are some tips to remove the distraction from your smartphone from your life: You can apply a filtering method to see **which notifications you have on your locked screen**. The less the better.

Second, **switch off vibration and sound** please, especially when you are in a public place. These do not only distract you form your work (or conversation) but also the people around you.

Third, when you are in a meeting or in a conversation and your phone is on the table, **put it face down** so that the messages that do come through do not distract you or your colleagues from what you were discussing.

The best conversations happen when people are 100% present in the meeting. The 'laptops closed' rule should therefore be extended to 'switch your phones to silent mode' rules and maybe even to a ban of the use of them in the meeting all together. I promise you that they will not only lead to a more pleasant meeting, but also to a more productive one.

**Key Points:**
- *Limit your e-mail reading to only two or three time a day.*
- *Use your inbox as an action list to prevent reading the same e-mail twice.*
- *Filter e-mail to reduce the number of e-mails arriving in your mailbox.*
- *Prevent e-mails from being sent in the first place*
- *Remove notifications form the locked screen of your smart phone*
- *Keep your phone on silent so that your messages do not distract others too.*

# Conclusions

*Change management is usually preferable to management change.*

Lean transformations are not easy. If you truly want to transform your organization into a lean organization, it is important to understand what it means and what kind of tools can be used to facilitate that transformation.

This book started with a few chapters on the role of the lean transformation leader in part 1. Since lean is not just a project but about leading a cultural change, we need somebody in the organization to be able to teach and coach the behaviors that are part of the lean culture. We also need management support to provide the organization with a vision of where we want to go.
Without proper support from both the management and the lean transformation leader, the lean initiative will not succeed. Plus, if we really would like to have a culture of continuous improvement, these managers must become level 5 leaders themselves.

Part 2 was dedicated to understanding the lean philosophy. The *why* of lean. Why are so many people interested in lean? What does it bring us? We have learned that the goal of all process improvement is to improve flow and that we reduce the three enemies of lean to achieve that goal. Finally, there are the fourteen Toyota management principles; the behaviors that help us focus on what is important in our day-to-day work: improving our processes.
When we do not understand why we are implementing all the different lean tools, we fail to achieve the results that are promised by so many other lean books.

A selection of lean tools that can help you in transforming your organization is described in part 3. The four levels of lean maturity describe the *why, what* and *how* of each tool to help you using them to reduce all three enemies of lean and thereby improving flow. The most important point from this part is that every tool should help you find the next (measurable) improvement. Using the tools described in part 3 will help you mobilize the entire workforce in achieving your organizational goals.

Next to the cultural aspect, there are some tools that can be used to design or redesign all processes in the organization. Part 4 describes the powerful tool of value stream mapping and how to apply that in production processes, office processes, and project work.

Using value stream mapping on a biyearly basis helps you set the targets for teams and departments to improve to, whether they use the daily management boards, the A3 problem-solving, or D2MAIC projects.

So, how do you know where you are as a company? And how do you proceed from there? When visiting a company, you can use the simple checklist in figure 61 for gemba walks, which can help you to ask the right questions. The checklist includes seven topics described in parts three and four, and for each of the topics the checklist has four things to look for when doing the gemba walk.

The 5S row shows the tools that can be used to make sure 5S is a continual way of working and not just a cleaning event. At the gemba, you can see the red tag zone and how the items in it are labeled with dates. You should also be able to see the kamishibai on the team board and when the last 5S audit was done.
For standard work, look for different examples of standards that were discussed in this book, starting with the standard operating procedures for the operators, which explain how the product or service is built.

| | | | | |
|---|---|---|---|---|
| 5S | red tag zone | floor markings | shadow boards | kamishibai |
| Standard work | operator Level | team leader role description | heijunka box | leader standard work |
| Team board (level 1) | people | performance | improvement | regular coaching |
| Suggestion system | IT or ENG ideas | 5S improvements | based on waste observations | based on KPI |
| Projects | Based on P&L | D2MAIC template | root cause analysis | validated results |
| Daily Management | Level 2 team board | Level 3 team board | KPIs cascaded | Bottom up actions |
| VSM | processes mapped | Future state created | Kaizen events implemented | new future state created |

*Figure 61: Gemba checklist*

The team leader role description and leader standard work show whether the organization has thought about how other functions can support continuous improvement. The heijunka box is a standard for managing the processes. Whenever there is a functioning heijunka board, you know that there is one pacemaker process and that all people know what to work on next by using the board.

The team boards on the shop floor, tier 1, should include the three parts described in chapter 8.2: people, performance, and continuous improvement. Even better would be to learn that there is regular coaching present at the meeting. The lean transformation leader, somebody from management, or a team leader from another department are some who could do these coaching sessions as part of their leader standard work.

The four topics to use to evaluate the suggestion system are based on the type of suggestions that are made by the employees. The category IT/ENG means that people write ideas on a piece of paper that somebody else should do. From there, we can move up to improving our own workstations using 5S or improving our own processes based on a waste observation or even on a red KPI.

To see if projects are defined and managed in the best way possible, ask how the projects are initiated. Are they linked to the profit and loss statement? For the projects, the organization should use templates. D2MAIC is the structure that was described in 9.3, but other structures are also possible. More important is the root-cause analysis that is done to improve the processes and the validated results to make sure the project delivered what it was supposed to deliver.

Topic number six is daily management, and for that you would like to see not only different levels of team boards (tier 1, tier 2, and tier 3) but also how they are connected. Is there a proper KPI link between the different levels of team boards? Next to the clearly linked KPIs, see if problems and actions are flowing between the boards. Ideally, management is supporting the solving of problems that the shop flow has (the bottom-up actions), instead of the other way around.

The final topic describes the use of value stream mapping. Since this is a continuous process, we would expect to see not only a current state but also a future state value stream map. When the future state is implemented, and kaizen events are done, expect to see a new future state, with the goals for the coming year.

Don't forget to download your copy of my VSM templates on www.mudamasters.com.

As you go and tick-off the boxes of the above table during the gemba walk, you can take pictures of the topics described above and collect them in photo reporting. Each of the topics could contain two slides: one with the positives and one with the recommendations for improvement. This way you begin every topic with positive reinforcement and provide the team with feedback on what the next steps of the lean journey could be.

And with this final list and quick summary of everything discussed in earlier chapters, we have reached the final pages of this book. I hope it has helped you as a reader to think about the lean initiatives that are ongoing in your company, that you have found inspiration to improve them, and that you are now more equipped to bring your company closer to the fourth step of lean maturity.

If you like what I have written in this book, please write a review in the online store where you have ordered it. If you have other feedback, questions or suggestions for improvement for the next (third) edition, feel free to contact me on LinkedIn and write them to me personally. And to close off this book: keep checking www.mudamasters.com to follow my continuing lean journey.

Stay lean,

Thijs Panneman

# Acknowledgments

I am grateful to many people who made it possible for me to finish my dream project: writing my own book! As you can imagine, it takes a lot of time to put an entire book on paper. That's time that you cannot spend in other ways, which means a lot of people had to pay a little toll for me to be able to finish it.

As with most people, my greatest influencers are my parents, Fons and Helen Panneman, who are always surrounded by books and provided me with my first nonfiction book (*The 7 Habits of Highly Effective People*), which finally got me reading for pleasure. They also provided me with the option to study whatever I liked, even when I decided I wanted something else after my first bachelor's program. Because they motivated me to start a second educational program, I got to learn about lean, and I finally found my passion.

A second person who got me reading more was Gert-Tom Draisma, my friend and role model. He always told me that there is only one way to the top: simply being the best in whatever you choose to do. I figured the more I read about lean, the better I could get at it.

I would like to thank Bojan van der Heide for encouraging and helping me create my blog in 2012 – it was called Panview.nl at the time and had only a Dutch domain. If it wasn't for him, there wouldn't have been a lean blog, and without a blog, I would probably have never started writing, and this book would just have stayed a dream. He also designed this book cover for me.

With respect to my first job at Philips in Winschoten (Netherlands), I would like to thank Nina Huck and Marcel van der Vegt for giving me the opportunity to start putting lean into practice. After two DMAIC projects as project leader, my manager, Marcel van der Vegt, also gave me the opportunity to start teaching, which turned out to be one of my favorite things to do.

Next, I would like to thank Gonny Olthof, my partner in crime in the factory in Winschoten. Our cooperation was so incredibly motivating that we needed only a short chat to define the next (lean) steps to take in our lean journey. I think that because we complemented each other so well, the training sessions we taught together were a huge success, even though we did not have much training experience when we started.

Another colleague from Philips Winschoten who inspired me was Feike Dokter. He is the first one who suggested I create my own model with lean tools to use in our training sessions. Thanks to him, I started taking everything I read to another level: creating my own content. After Feike suggested I build a lean house that would be understandable for all levels of the organization, the lean house for the shop floor was born as the first self-created content on my blog can still be found on www.mudamasters.com, though I have updated a lot of the content over the years.

When I moved to Hamburg, I met my friend and colleague Gunnar Düvel, with whom I did almost all my lean trainings in Germany. I knew a lot of lean content and tools when I moved to Germany, but Gunnar taught me how to interact with the group by asking questions, building in repeating exercises, and improving my storytelling.
Some additional big thanks go out to Gunnar because he is the first one who managed to read every page of this manuscript and he gave me lots of feedback to improve it.

I also would like to thank my friend Martin Rosenkranz. When I met him, he had already written a book himself, and he told me it was a fun experience. That convinced me not to procrastinate any longer, and I started working on this book the next evening.

For this second edition, I am also thankful to my good friend Thomas Hall, who has edited the manuscript to make the second edition even better than the first one, especially in terms of English grammar.

Finally, I would like to thank my partner, Mick Whelan, whose love gives me so much energy that I managed to write the first edition of this book in less than one year, next to my full-time job.

# References

Abramowich, E. *Six Sigma for Growth - Driving Profitable Top-Line Results.* Singapore: John Wiley & Sons, 2005.

Allan, D. *Getting Things Done, the Art of Stress-free Productivity.* London: Penguin Books, 2001.

Asefeso, A. *5S Office Management.* Swindon: AA Global Sourcing Ltd, 2014.

Aslander, M., and E. Witteveen. *Easycratie - De toekomst van werken en organiseren.* Den Haag: Sdu uitgevers, 2010.

Ballé, F., and M. Ballé. *De Goudmijn - een Roman over Lean Transformatie.* Driebergen (NL): Lean Management Instituut, 2005.

—. *De Lean Manager - een roman over een Lean Transformatie.* Driebergen (NL): Lean Management Instituut, 2012.

Barnhart, T.M. *Creating a Lean R&D System - Lean Principles and Approaches for Pharmaceutical and Research-Based Organizations.* Boca Raton: CRC Press, 2013.

Bell, C.R. *Managers as Mentors - Building a Partnership for Learning.* San Francisco: Berrett-Koehler Publishers, 1996.

Brunet, A. P., and S. New. "Kaizen in Japan: an empirical study." *International Journal of Operations and Production Management,* 2009: Vol. 23 Iss: 12, pp.1426-1446.

Buzan, T. *Gebruik je Verstand - Handleiding voor effectiever studeren, gemakkelijker oplossen van problemen en het ontwikkelen van een eigen manier van denken.* Baarn: Uitgeverij Mingus, 1979.

Covey, S. *First Things First.* New York: Fireside, 1994.

Covey, Stephan. *De zeven eigenschappen voor succes in je leven.* Amsterdam: Business Contact, 1989.

Csikszentmihalyi, Mihaly. *Flow: The Psychology of Optimal Experience.* New York: Harper Perennial, 1990.

Daniels, A C. *Bringing Out the Best in People - How to Apply the Astonishing Power of Positive Reinforcement.* New York: McGraw-Hill, 2000.

de Galan, K. *van Deskundige naar Trainer.* FT: Prentice Hall, 2008.

Deutschman, A. *Change or Die.* New York: HarperCollins Publishers, 2007.

Dominick, C., and S.L. Lunney. *The Procurement Game Plan – Winning Strategies and Techniques for Supply Management Professionals.* Fort Lauderdale: J. Ross Publishing, 2012.

Duggan, K.J. *Creating Mixed Model Value Streams - Practical Lean Techniques for Building to Demand.* New York: CRC press, 2002.

—. *Design for Operational Excellence.* New York: McGraw-Hill, 2012.

Elder, A. "The Five Deseases of Project Management." *No Limits Leadership INC.*

2006. http://www.nolimitsleadership.com/images/The%20Five%20Diseases%20of%20Project%20Management.pdf.

Fenkner, A. *Employee Participation in Lean Initiatives: Exploring Drivers and Barriers in Production and Non-Production Environments.* Newcastle: Newcastle University Business School, 2016.

Floyd, R.C. *Liquid Lean: Developing Lean Culture in the Process Industries.* New York: Productivity Press, 2010.

Ford, H. *Today and Tomorrow - Commemorative Edition of Ford's 1926 Classic.* Boca Raton: CRC Press, 1988.

Gallo, C. *Talk Like TED – The 9 Speaking Secrets of the World's Top Minds.* London: Pan McMillan, 2014.

Geiger, G., E. Hering, and R. Kummer. *Kanban.* München: Hanser, 2011.

Gorecki, P., and P. Pautsch. *Lean Management.* München: Hanser, 2010.

Gort, R. *Lean Vertaald naar Projecten - Samen Leren Bouwen Aan Innovatievermogen.* Amsterdam: Lean Vertaald, 2015.

Goubergen, D. van. *Lean Manufacturing Value Stream Design - Master Class.* Lille (BE): van Goubergen, 2014.

Harris, C., R. Harris, and C. Streeter. *Lean Supplier Development - Establishing Partnerships and True Costs Throughout the Supply Chain.* New York: CRC Press, 2011.

Hines, P. *The Principles of the Lean Business System.* Acephaly: SA Partners, 2009.

Hines, P., P. Found, and G. Griffiths. *Staying Lean: Thriving, Not Just Surviving.* Boca Raton: CRC Press, 2011.

Hopp, W. J., and M. L. Spearman. *Factory Physics, sec. edit.* New York: McGraw-Hill, 2000.

Howell, G., G. Ballard, and J. Hall. *Capacity Utilization and Wait Time: A Primer for Construction.* Singapore, 2001.

Imai, M. *Kaizen – The Key to Japan's Competitive Success.* New York: McGraw-Hill, 1986.

Jackson, T. *Hoshin Kanri for the Lean Enterprise – Developing Competitive Capabilities and Managing Profits.* Boca Raton: CRC Press, 2006.

King, P. *Lean for the Process Industries: Dealing with Complexity.* New York: CRC Press, 2009.

Kofman, F. *Conscious Business: How to Build Value through Values.* Colorado: Sounds True, 2006.

Kotter, J. P. *Leading Change.* Boston: Harvard Business Review Press, 1996.

Kouzes, J. M., and B. Z. Posner. *The Leadership Challenge – How to Make Extraordinary Things Happen in Organizations.* San Francisco: Wiley, 2012.

Krafcik, J. F. "Triumph of the Lean Production System." *Sloan Management Review*, 1988: 40-52.

Lareau, W. *Office Kaizen - Transforming Office Operations into Strategic Competitive Advantage.* Milwaukee: ASQ Quality Press, 2003.

Lencioni, P. *Death by Meeting - About solving the most painful problem in Business.* San Francisco: Josey Bass, 2004.

Liker, J. K. *The Toyota Way, 14 management principles from the world greatest manufacturer.* New York: McGraw-Hill, 2004.

Liker, J. K., and G. L. Convis. *The Toyota Way to Lean Leadership.* New York: McGraw Hill, 2102.

Lippitt, M. "The Managing Complex Change Model." *www.enterprisemanagement.com.* 2015 10, 1987. 10.

Lombardo, M. M., and R. W. Eichinger. *The Career Architect Development Planner- An Expert System Offering 103 Research-based and Experience-tested Development Plans and Coaching Tips For: Learners, Managers, Mentors, and Feedback Givers.* Minneapolis: Lominger Limited, Inc., 2006.

Lyer, A. V., S. Seshadrei, and R. Vasher. *Toyota Supply Chain Management - A Strategic Approach to the Principles of Toyota's Renowned System.* New York: McGraw-Hill, 2009.

Mann, D. *Creating a Lean Culture - Tools to Sustain Lean Conversions.* New York: Productivity Press, 2005.

Maxwell, J. C. *The Five Levels of Leadership –Proven Steps to Maximize Your Potential.* New York: Center Street, 2011.

Miedaner, T. *Coach Yourself to Success – 101 Tips from a Personal Coach for Reaching Your Goals at Work and in Life.* Chicago: Contemporary Books, 2000.

Morgen, J. M., and J. K. Liker. *The Toyota Product Development System.* New York: Productivity Press, 2006.

Morieux, Y., and P. Tollman. *Six Simple Rules – How to Manage Complexity Without Getting Complicated.* Boston: Harvard Business Review Press, 2014.

Nicholas, J. M. *Competitive Manufacturing Management.* Boston: McGraw-Hill, 1998.

Niederstadt, J. *Kamishibai Boards, A Visual Management System That Supports Visual Audits.* New York: CRC Press, 2013.

Ohno, T. *Toyota Production System: Beyond Large Scale Production.* Cambridge: Productivity Press, 1988.

Panneman, T., *Sustainable 5S – How to Use the Lean Starting Tool to Improve Flow, Productivity and Employee Satisfaction*, Dublin: MudaMasters, 2019.

Pink, D. H. *Drive - De Verassende Waarheid Over Wat Ons Motiveert.* Amsterdam: Business Contact, 2010.

Rogers, E. *Diffusion of Innovations.* New York: Free Press, 1995.

Rother, M. *Toyota Kata: Managing People for Improvement, Adaptiveness and Superior Results.* New York: McGraw Hill, 2010.

Rother, M., and J. Shook. *Learning to See.* Brookline: The Lean Enterprise Institute, 1999.

Scholtes, P. R. *The Leadership Handbook – Making Things Happen, Getting Things Done.* New York: McGraw-Hill, 1998.

Senge, P. M. *The Fifth Discipline – The Art & Practice of a Learning Organization.* New York: Doubleday, 1990.

Shingo, S. *A Revolution in Manufacturing: The SMED System.* Cambridge: Productivity Press, 1985.

—. *A Study of the Toyota Production System from Engineering Viewpoint.* New York: Productivity Press, 1989.

—. *Zero Quality Control: Source Inspection and the Poke-Yoke System.* New York: Productivity Press, 1986.

Shook, J. *Managing to Learn.* Cambridge: Lean Enterprise Institute, 2008.

Sinek S. *Start with Why – How Great Leaders Inspire Everyone to Take Action.* London: Penguin Group, 2009.

Stamatis, D. H. *The OEE Primer: Understanding Overall Equipment Effectiveness, Reliability, and Maintainability.* Boca Raton: CRC Press, 2011.

Suri, R. *It's about Time - The Competitive Advantage of Quick Response Manufacturing.* Boca Raton: CRC Press, 2010.

Suzaki, K. *The New Shop Floor Management, Empowering People for Continuous Improvement.* New York: Free Press, 1993.

Tajiri, M., and F. Gotoh. *TPM Implementation – A Japanese Approach.* New York: McGraw-Hill, 1992.

Tichy, N. M. *The Cycle of Leadership.* New York: HarperCollins, 2002.

Tisbury, J. *Your 60 Minute Lean Business: 5S.* Raleigh: Lulu Publishing, 2012.

Webers, N. C. *Performance Behaviour – De Lean Methode Voor het Continue Verbeteren van Prestatiegedrag.* Den Haag: SDU Uitgevers, 2010.

Westendorp, R., and D. van Bodegom. *Oud Worden In De Praktijk – Laat De Omgeving Het Werk Doen.* Amsterdam: Atlas Contact, 2015.

Wireman, T. *Inspection and Training for TPM.* New York: Industrial Press, 1992.

Womack, J. P., and D. T. Jones. *Lean Thinking - Banish Waste and Create Wealth in Your Corporation.* New York: Free Press, 1996.

Womack, J. P., D. T. Jones, and D. Roos. *The Machine That Changed the World: The Story of Lean Production – Toyota's Secret Weapon in the Global Car Wars That Is Revolutionizing World Industry.* NY: Free Press, 1990.

Yerkes, R. M., and J. D. Dodson. "The Relation of Strength of Stimulus to Rapidity of Habit-formation." *Journal of Comparative Neurology and Psychology*, no. 18 (1908): 459-482

Made in the USA
Coppell, TX
25 November 2019